The Calling
Tahirih of Persia and Her American Contemporaries

Other Books by the Authors

Nedaye Ellahe (*The Calling* in Persian, forthcoming)

Foreigner, *From an Iranian village to New York City*, *A Memoir* (Persian, forthcoming)

Foreigner, *From an Iranian village to New York City*, *A Memoir* (forthcoming)

Awakening: A History of the Bábi and Bahá'í Faiths in Nayriz (Russian, forthcoming)

Despertar. Historia de la Fe Bábí y de la Fe Bahá í en Nayríz (Spanish, 2017)

L'Eveil: Histoire de la foi bábíe et de la foi bahá'íe à Nayríz (French, 2016)

A Way Out of No Way: Harlem Prep: Transforming Dropouts into Scholars, 1967-1977 (2016)

Awakening: A History of the Bábi and Bahá'í Faiths in Nayriz (Bulgarian, 2015)

'Abdu'l-Bahá in New York (Persian, 2015)

Awakening: A History of the Bábi and Bahá'í Faiths in Nayriz (Traditional Chinese, 2015)

Subhi Bidari (*Awakening* in Persian, 2015)

'Abdu'l Bahá en Nueva York (Spanish, 2014)

Awakening: A History of the Babí and Bahá'í Faiths in Nayriz (Simplified Chinese, 2013)

Awakening: A History of the Babi and Bahai Faiths in Nayriz (2013)

'Abdu'l-Bahá in New York (2012)

THE CALLING
TAHIRIH OF PERSIA AND HER
AMERICAN CONTEMPORARIES

by
Hussein Ahdieh & Hillary Chapman

Ibex Publishers,
Bethesda, Maryland

The Calling
Tahirih of Persia and Her American Contemporaries
by Hussein Ahdieh and Hillary Chapman

Copyright © 2017 Hussein Ahdieh and Hillary Chapman

ISBN: 978-1-58814-145-3

Photograph of Ellen White, Courtesy of the Ellen G. White Estate.

Manufactured in the United States of America

The paper used in this book meets the minimum requirements of the American National Standard for Information Services—Permanence of Paper for Printed Library Materials, ANSI Z39.48–1984

Ibex Publishers strives to create books which are complete and free of error. Please help us with future editions by reporting any errors or suggestions for improvement to the address below or: corrections@ibexpub.com

Ibex Publishers, Inc.
Post Office Box 30087
Bethesda, Maryland 20824
Telephone: 301–718–8188
www.ibexpublishers.com

LIBRARY OF CONGRESS CATALOGING-IN-PUBLICATION DATA

Names: Ahdieh, Hussein, author. | Chapman, Hillary, author.
Title: The calling : Tahirih of Persia and her American contemporaries / by Hussein Ahdieh and Hillary Chapman.
Description: Bethesda, Maryland : Ibex Publishers, 2017. | Includes bibliographical references.
Identifiers: LCCN 2016041282 | ISBN 9781588141453 (alk. paper)
Subjects: LCSH: Qurrat al-'Ayn, 1817 or 1818-1852. | Women mystics—Iran—Biography. | Bahai Faith—Iran—History. | Women—Iran—History—19th century. | Women—United States—History—19th century.
Classification: LCC PK6528.U77 Z54 2017 | DDC 297.9/3092 [B] —dc23

I dedicate this book to three wonderful souls
who are illumined by the spirit of the great Qurat-ul-Ain:
Tahereh, my wife, for her patience;
Tatiana, my friend, for her assistance;
Bahiyyih, my grand-daughter, for her commitment;

May God bless them!

Hussein Ahdieh

CONTENTS

INTRODUCTION

In the mid-1800s, powerful spiritual movements swept across two totally dissimilar countries: the United States and Persia. Faith-filled women helped propel these movements as workers, motivators, instigators, and leaders. This book seeks to introduce one such extraordinary woman of faith who arose in Persia during that period, Tahirih of Qazvin, who may be unknown to an American audience as well as her American female contemporaries, many of whom may have been forgotten.

In the Shi'a Muslim kingdom of Persia,[1] the great spiritual upheaval began with two distinguished clerics who taught that the day had arrived when a great redeemer would arise to purify Islam. Many of their students came to believe that this prophecy was realized in the figure of Siyyid Ali Muhammad, titled 'the Bab', meaning the 'Gate', a Shi'a theological term referring to the chosen intermediary between the promised redeemer who lived in a state of hiding and the body of the faithful. The Bab later went far beyond this initial prophecy by claiming to be both the bringer of a new Divine revelation and the forerunner of a second Divine messenger who was soon to follow. News of his claims and knowledge of his teachings spread rapidly throughout Persia and Iraq, aided greatly by the extraordinarily gifted mystic, teacher, and poet, Tahirih, from the city of Qazvin.

Tahirih's orientation was fundamentally mystical. The mystic's goal is to be re-united with God, the 'Beloved'. To draw closer to Him, the mystic must walk a path on which she engages in specific spiritual practices and disciplines. She will first feel an intense love for her Beloved, then a deep awareness of the Divine ordering of all things, and finally, the ecstasy of reunion with the Divine and becoming something eternal, far beyond the self.[2]

---

[1] In 1935, the official name of the Kingdom of Persia was changed to Iran.
[2] Hatcher, John and Amrollah Hemmat, The Poetry of Tahirih, Oxford: George Ronald, 2002, 28.

Tahirih felt a strong inner calling which gave her the absolute certainty and courage necessary to proclaim the Babi faith in the face of unsparing opposition. Within a short span of time, she emerged as one of the most gifted of the Babi leaders and the sole woman among them. Informed by her spiritual intuition and great learning, she brought a deep understanding of the new teachings to the rapidly growing number of converts.

The Baha'i Faith succeeded the Babi Faith and, with its emergence as a world religion, the figure of Tahirih as a symbol of female leadership and spiritual conviction is recognized across the globe. The Bab had prophesied that his religion would reach its fruition with the appearance of the second Divinely-ordained Manifestation of God, an individual who would be the perfect embodiment of all of the Divine attributes, who would express God's will in words and deeds, and who would move entirely by the Holy Spirit. Baha'u'llah, who had also been one of the principal followers of the Bab and had known Tahirih, fulfilled that prophecy, and most Babis followed him, and now called themselves 'Baha'is' and their religion, the Baha'i Faith.

Worlds away from Persia in central and western New York State, people lived in a state of such spiritual intensity that the whole region came to be known as the 'Burned-Over district' and saw the emergence of the Shakers, the Church of Jesus-Christ of the Latter-Day Saints, the Adventists, the Church of Christ, Scientist, and spiritualism. These were part of a Great Awakening that would energize important reform movements that fought against slavery, alcoholism, and limited education, and for the rights for women. What began in the world of the spirit went on to deeply affect the social realities of the United States.

Through participation in these movements, American women entered the public sphere in large numbers for the very first time. To the dismay of many, women now spoke and taught about religion in public and, in so doing, challenged long-established practices. Among them were Ellen G. White, a theological thinker who shaped the beliefs of the worldwide Adventist movement; Sojourner Truth, who came up from slavery to electrify audiences with her salvation preaching; Susan B. Anthony and Elizabeth Cady Stanton and the women of the women's suffrage movement; hundreds of spiritualist female mediums; and Mary Baker Eddy, the founder of the Church of Christ, Scientist. These female leaders were prefigured in the 18th century by 'Mother' Ann Lee, the founder of the Shakers, and many long forgotten female 'exhorters'.

American and Persian societies both relegated women to a second-class status. Women were not allowed to participate in public life—the world of politics, business, public-speaking, religious teaching—was the exclusive province of men. A woman's proper place was in the private sphere of the home where the mother had the primary responsibility for shaping the moral virtues of the children and, by extension, the society. The privacy of the world of the home in Persian society, though, was absolute; the women of the family should not even be seen. Marriage was a matter in which American and Persian women had little to no choice as these were arranged according to the broader considerations of the family; giving birth to children was expected, and sons were the preferred children. By the 20th-century, though, these two societies had accepted the importance of the education of girls.

In the 19th century, the United States was undergoing an industrial revolution that was creating new economic and social possibilities for women. The young republic codified the idea of human rights in its Constitution which provided a legal basis for the advancement of women and other social change.

19th-century Persia was a culturally, economically, and intellectually stagnant society which had experienced a golden age several centuries earlier but was now corrupted by a largely ignorant clergy and an autocratic government that functioned through nepotism. Lacking a constitution, the Kingdom did not have a legal framework within which to institute social and economic development. The clerics, placated by the nobility, dominated society. The much more powerful empires of Britain and Russia preyed on the weak kingdom's economic wealth.

Since Persian society was entirely dominated by men, women were invisible in the public life. As a result, there are few known facts about Tahirih's life. We have related these in the context of her family, her society, the theological issues of the time, and the Babi movement. So that the reader can hear her authentic, undiluted voice, we have included the fine translations of her poetry by the Persian literary scholar, Prof. Amin Banani, and the poet and master translator, Prof. Jascha Kessler. We have also drawn from the literary analysis of Prof. Banani and Prof. Kessler as well as that of Prof. John S. Hatcher and Dr. Amrollah Hemmat from whose three volumes of translations of her poetry we have also re-printed several pieces.

In our re-telling of the lives of Tahirih and her American contemporaries, we hope to convey a sense of the expectation and exhilaration as well as the suffering and sorrow that these women must have experienced and something of the inner dimension of their lives. As Baha'i authors, we have given preference to the major Baha'i sources which interpret the meaning of her life within the context of her own beliefs and the teachings of the Baha'i Faith; we have also benefitted from other scholarly histories for accurate background information.

This book would not have been possible without the generous gifts of time and knowledge from these individuals to whom we are very grateful:

Dr. Tahereh Ahdieh, Jeff Albert, Naseem Alizadeh, Dr. Iraj Ayman, Sheila Banani, Talat Bassari, Prof. Dominic Brookshaw, Dr. Christopher Buck, Anita Chapman, Deborah Conow, Donna Denize, Tali Ferdowsi, Robert Hanevold, Robert Harris, Kathryn Hogenson, Faruq Izadinia, Tatiana Jordan, Mara Khavari, Dr. Gavin Grant, Prof. Jascha Kessler, Dr. Tony Lee, Prof. Frank Lewis, Gwyneth Magaditsch, Prof. Susan Maneck, Dr. Dorothy Marcic, Della Marcus, Maria Milosheva, Peter Murphy, Bahiyyih Nakhjavani, Judge Dorothy Nelson, Dr. Moojan Momen, Timothy Moore, Pedram Parvini, Prof. Michael

Penn, Dr. Shapour Rasekh, Maliheh Rouhani, Maryam Rouhani, Sana Rouhani, Dr. Nader Saiedi, Julio Savi, Leila Seradj, Velimir Tchatchevsky, Vajiheh Teymoorian, Dr. Duane Troxel, Sheila Vahdati, Prof. Fereydun Vahman, Prof. Christopher White, Prof. Ehsan Yarshater, Farah Zahedi and Abbas Jannat.

— Dr. Hussein Ahdieh,

Hillary Chapman,

2016 CE/173 BE

PROLOGUE

This story—that of Tahirih of Qazvin, and the numberless American women who arose in the great awakenings isn't really one story but many stories—not even many stories—but numberless dreams and letters, speeches and beatings, exiles and homes—which made up the lives of the women—some known, most unknown—who were fired by a powerful faith and a deep sense of calling, whose lives made up a journey that revealed new realities and birthed a new world. So, since this is about a journey, we may as well begin on a boat.

ONE:
PREACHING WOMEN

1.

Because the English mainland had disappeared from the horizon, the shipmates could no longer drop anchor to stabilize their boat in the battering storm; to their surprise, the damn woman who had lectured them regarding the wages of their sins now seemed to be part of their salvation as she and her band of followers helped them to fight the high winds and gigantic waves. Fearless of the anger of nature against them, these religious fanatics were bailing water shoulder to shoulder with the crew after several planks had come loose. The storm subsided, and the sailors' survival gave them a new respect for this curious band and its odd yet courageous leader, Ann Lee (1736-1784). This ocean crossing was as her life would be: a strident voice tossed about in a storm.

She was born one of eight children to a blacksmith and his wife in Manchester, England, in 1736. Her family lived in just a few rooms with little money to spare. Because there was no privacy in the cramped spaces, she was exposed to the physical intimacies of others and, as a result, she developed a deep dislike for the relations of the flesh against which she later preached.

Ann had frequent visions as a child. In 1758, she joined a sect known as the 'Shaking Quakers', or 'Shakers', a breakaway group of Quakers. The name came from the charismatic nature of their services during which the faithful sometimes physically shook and rolled on the floor and spoke in tongues when the spirit came into them. Of her conversion experience, Ann wrote:

> "My soul broke forth to God; which I felt as sensible as ever
> a woman did a child, when she was delivered of it. Then I

felt unspeakable joy in God, and my flesh came upon me, like the flesh of an infant."[3]

Through her visions Ann came to believe that she was the embodiment and return of the Spirit of Christ; her unshakeable sense of calling—"I saw, and knew what I saw"[4]—brought her to the leadership of the Shakers. She based her belief in part on a verse from chapter twelve of the Book of Revelations:

"And there appeared a great wonder in heaven; a woman clothed with the sun, and the moon under her feet, and upon her head a crown of twelve stars."[5]

Mother Ann Lee.

In 1774, she had a vision of the 'new world', and so she and other Shaker leaders decided to move with a band of believers to the great unknown of America.

After the eventful sea crossing, the small band made its way up into the wilderness of New York and settled in a swampy wooded area near the Hudson River and the town of Albany. Even under such arduous circumstances, Ann insisted that the community follow very strict guidelines such as total sexual abstinence—even between married people—and a complete confession of sins.

---

[3] Richard Francis, Ann the Word: The Story of Ann Lee, Female Messiah, Mother of the Shakers (NY, NY: Arcade Publishing, 2000), 44.
[4] Ibid.
[5] Ibid., 48.

In 1780, Ann went on a two-year mission trip up the Hudson River and then to Harvard, Massachusetts, during which she established Shakerism on a strong foundation. The strength of her personal conviction exercised great power over people, even inspiring fear. Followers gave themselves over to her completely and sought salvation from her directly.

The Shakers acquired a large house in Harvard that had been previously owned by a mystical cult, much to the anger of many townspeople who objected to the presence of yet another strange new group.

God was a powerful presence in the everyday lives of the people of New England. According to different memoirs, Shakers saw an active and often terrifying God at work in the New England villages through which they travelled. One Shaker recalls arriving at a home where a two year old boy ran out into her arms. When he looked into her face, he began to shake violently which she took to mean that the spirit had come into him. She brought him back in the house where straightaway the adults became converts and appeared to her to become bathed in a white light.

The presence of the Shakers at the Harvard house brought immediate opposition. Here was a sect led by a woman—one who claimed a Divine station no less—which taught extreme personal practices and broke up families. Ann herself was rumored to be a witch and a spy, made worse by the fact that she was English in the years before the War of Independence when anti-British feelings ran high. Her fearless proclamation didn't help soothe the fears of local people; when asked what she was doing with the Shakers, she responded that "…we are the people who turn the world upside down." The Shakers didn't emphasize the written word of the Bible—Ann was illiterate—but rather Biblical stories, personal spiritual experiences, and living the life of a true Christian. Believers expressed the spirit within them during demonstrative and raucous services which were easily heard from the outside:

"They begin by sitting down, and shaking their heads, in a violent manner, turning their heads half round, so that their face looks over each shoulder, their eyes being shut; while they are thus shaking, one will begin to sing some odd tune, without words or rule;...— Some singing without words, and some with an unknown tongue or mutter, and some with a mixture of English; The mother, so called, minds to strike such notes as make a concord, and so form the charm...in the best part of their worship every one acts for himself, and almost every one different from the other, one will stand with his arms extended, acting over odd postures, which they call signs; another will be dancing, and sometimes hopping on one leg about the floor; another will fall to turning round, so swift that if it be a woman, her cloaths will be so filled with the wind, as they were kept out by a hoop; another will be prostrate on the floor;...some trembling extremely; others acting as though their nerves were convulsed; others swinging their arms, with all vigor, as if they were turning a wheel, etc...."[6]

This full-on worship, as well as Calvinist morality, self-discipline, and hard work were characteristic of the robust Shaker communities that Mother Ann Lee built. After the passing of her powerful presence, Shaker membership declined. The exquisite crafts and furniture they made could not compete with industrially manufactured goods making it difficult for them to support themselves. In addition, Ann Lee's emphasis on sexual abstinence meant that there were no children to carry on the communities.

Mother Ann Lee was the most outstanding female religious figure of the First Great Awakening, the tidal wave of religious emotion that rolled through the colonies in the 1730's and 40's during which Americans rededicated their lives to God and church, including

---

[6] Ibid., 138-9.

African slaves who converted in large numbers for the first time to Christianity.

Church services changed from having formal sermons on theology to fostering the heartfelt experience of personal salvation. People wanted to be caught up in God; a new generation of ministers sought to revive authentic piety. This more heart-centered approach combined with an ecstatic and expressive form of worship may also have resonated with the cultural heritage of African slaves.[7]

To some Americans, the world seemed to have been turned on its head as wives exhorted husbands to piety, children evangelized their parents, and some women even began speaking out in public. As one Reverend put it, "...multitudes were seriously, soberly, and solemnly out of their wits."[8]

The earliest Puritan settlers in the United States had held strong Calvinist beliefs. They valued hard work and community solidarity, and they abhorred sin. Their destinies, they believed, were in the hands of a God that did not tolerate moral transgression. As the colonies emerged, this Puritan consensus began to break apart but the strong and severe Calvinism carried over into the Awakening. The quintessential sermonizer of the First Great Awakening was Jonathan Edwards in Massachusetts who warned the faithful that they were sinners in the hands of an 'angry God'. Hell was very real and awaited those without Christ. God, in His mercy, had given them a respite, but they must 'awaken' to Christ to be saved from Hell. This sermon provided much of the basic theological outlook that shaped the First Great Awakening.

Women had no voice in the traditional Calvinist churches, but with the Awakening, several churches actually allowed women to speak out during services.

---

[7] Susan Hill Lindley, *You Have Stept Out of Your Place* (Louisville, KY: Westminster John Knox Press, 1996), 41.

[8] Catherine A. Brekus, *Strangers and Pilgrims: Female preaching in America, 1740-1845* (Chapel Hill, NC: University of North Carolina Press 1998), 34.

Quakers taught that the spirit dwelt in each human being who could be re-born though experiencing this inner light. Their worship meetings were totally silent until someone was moved by the spirit to rise up and speak. When seized by the Holy Spirit, a man or woman was reborn, and old prohibitions such as the requirement that women be silent in church were washed away. The Quakers had a lay ministry in which women could participate. Women also were a part of the church government; they held their own meetings during which they disciplined female members, judged on the suitability of a woman for membership in the congregation, and approved women for marriage.[9]

The "Strict Congregationalist" or "Separate" churches encouraged testimonials by both men and women who had experienced saving grace. Nevertheless, Separatists maintained that women were subject to their husbands and could not be ministers. Similarly, some Baptist churches—also not a mainstream denomination—permitted female exhortation as long as it did not transgress the boundaries of the Biblically-based social order as they understood it.[10] Among Methodists, there was greater openness towards women leaders because of the strong influence of Wesley's outspoken mother on the founder of Methodism; when she found the curate to be inadequate one day, she had not hesitated to lead her church in prayer.[11]

Ann Lee's preaching voice was the only one to escape the oblivion into which were consigned all women who attempted public preaching and teaching during the First Great Awakening.

But if one rummages around deep enough into the past, a few other voices of 'female exhorters'—individuals who rose up spontaneously to call sinners to repentance—can be heard...

---

[9] Ann Braude, *Sisters and Saints: Women and American Religion* (Oxford, UK: Oxford University Press 2008), 37.
[10] Brekus, 48-51.
[11] Lindley, 43.

Martha Stearns Marshall "melted a whole concourse into tears by her prayers and exhortations."[12]

Margaret Meuse Clay's piety was of such renown that she was asked to lead the public prayer in her church. But female exhorters had to be aware of where the line of social propriety lay: Clay's exhorting had such a powerful effect that she was once sentenced to a flogging on the charge of unlicensed preaching.[13]

Hannah Cave Graves, a woman of great intelligence and piety, saw her role as one of being the moral guardian of her church, but "…her blunt dealings with preachers at times, seemed as if she ran some hazard of violating a saying of God Himself, 'touch not mine anointed and do my prophets no harm.'"[14]

Other times it was the quality of a woman's 'passivity' that made her a vessel for the spirit in the eyes of others. Mary Reed, for example, had visions which she communicated privately to her minister. He, then, related these to his parishioners while Mary sat quietly in the pews. Her meekness gave her words great authority over the congregation.[15]

Female exhorters were an accepted feature of the First Great Awakening. They did not have any institutional standing nor were they permitted to give formal sermons, but their impassioned words electrified congregations.[16]

The main purveyors of the First Great Awakening were the itinerant preachers who evangelized, inspired, and terrified local people into being reborn in Christ to avoid damnation; some of these itinerants were women.

---

[12] Brekus, 62.

[13] Ibid.

[14] Ibid.

[15] Thomas S. Kidd. "Daniel Rogers' Egalitarian Great Awakening." *Medieval Christianity.* Accessed November 2, 2013. https://medievalchristianityd.wikispaces.com/file/view/DANIEL+ROGERS+EGALITARIAN+GREAT+AWAKENING.pdf

[16] Brekus, 48.

Bathsheba Kingsley, known as the "brawling woman," climbed onto her husband's horse and rode from town to town, evangelizing in homes, public squares, and churches. She rebuked townspeople for their sinfulness and warned ministers of a wrath to come.[17]

Jamima Wilkinson claimed to have died of typhus in October, 1776, and then to have been literally resurrected. But in this second life, she was genderless and referred to herself in the third person as the 'Public Universal Friend'. She dressed in a robe that covered her entire body. Her preaching was intensely powerful and dramatic, but her theology was traditional, so she elicited both excitement and revulsion. People derided her for her 'manliness'—she was a woman who had truly stepped out of her proper place and who emasculated men by making them kneel before her. It was not her theological claims but her subversion of femininity that caused the most anger and mockery. This mix of influence and infamy followed her as she travelled the countryside attracting passionate followers. In an effort to get away from the constant criticism, she moved with her group to rural western New York. But as the years went by, the movement waned, and her followers gradually left her.[18]

These preaching women lived, moved, and thought entirely in a world shaped by personal faith. Their Calvinist-bound teachings were too conservative for future generations concerned with the women's suffrage movement but much too radical for their own time.[19]

And, so, the early women preachers and exhorters of the First Great Awakening were forgotten.

2.

The United States underwent important changes in the decades after the First Great Awakening. The colonies became an independent republic, and, having cast off British rule, Americans now saw them-

---

[17] Ibid., 23-5, 52.
[18] Ibid., 80-97.
[19] Ibid, 7-8.

selves as a people who could enact change through their own efforts. This way of thinking led to a deism which had confidence in the individual, a markedly different view from the Calvinism of the Puritans in which humans were helpless in the hands of a powerful deity. With the establishment of the Constitution as the country's legal framework, the government of the United States could no longer be connected with a specific church. This 'disestablishment' of churches made church membership voluntary, so new churches and forms of belief and worship appeared in the American religious landscape.[20]

Change created tensions within American society. Some Americans brimmed over with a self-confident individualism which rendered God remote. They were influenced by the European Enlightenment's view that man was intrinsically good and had free will. Others worried that the changes in society were signs of God's coming wrath; they held to the Puritan forefathers' traditional Calvinist view which stressed man's sinfulness and God's wrath.[21] History in the United States was on the side of the first view: Americans came to see man as having free will and, with God's Grace, being able to effect change. Neither adults nor infants were predestined to damnation; one could choose right or wrong by a conscious act of free will and, in so doing, determine one's personal and spiritual destiny.[22] Man could choose salvation by having a personal relationship with Christ; Christ, in fact, increasingly came before 'God'.[23] One new group calling themselves the Unitarians, put particular emphasis on man's reason and rejected all traditional doctrines of the past such as the Trinity which it deemed unreasonable. The appearance of such a completely non-doctrinal church showed just how much Americans were moving away theologically

---

[20] Lindley, 59.
[21] William G, McLoughlin, *Revivals, Awakenings, and Reform* (Chicago, IL: U. of Chicago Press, 1978), 99.
[22] Ibid., 114, 116.
[23] Ibid., 120.

from the country's Puritan Calvinist roots.[24] This Enlightenment view of free will, reason, and God's Grace, fused with the rapidly growing nation's sense of destiny, so much so that, in a real sense, this 'reasonable' Protestantism became a national religion.[25]

By the late 1700s, a second Great Awakening (c.1790-c.1840) was underway.[26] It was begotten by great preachers such as Charles Finney, who developed the use of passionate revival meetings to set fire to the inner lives of people in Western and Central New York—later called the "Burned Over District"—, and Lyman Beecher, a fervid social reformer and father to several extraordinary daughters.

In this Awakening, women worked, organized, taught, and preached. They outnumbered men in both activity and church membership.[27] They were the backbone of the churches serving as Sunday school teachers, organizers of fundraising bake sales and sewing circles, organ players, preparers of feasts, and educators of children in morals and faith.[28]

Women's societies helped finance and organize the great revivals[29] which powered the Second Great Awakening. These large gatherings could go on for days with men and women having potent personal experiences of the Holy Spirit.

In the emotionally intense atmosphere of the revival, women were more likely to overcome their inhibitions and fears, and stand up and preach.[30] To give themselves strength, such women may well have

---

[24] Ibid., 100.

[25] Ibid., 106.

[26] The exact dates of the Great Awakenings are relative. The usual decade given for the end of the Second Great Awakening is the 1840s. There was also a Third Great Awakening usually dated as the second half of the 19th century though these dates are not firm; so the authors have conflated these two as a 'Great Awakening'.

[27] Lindley, 60.

[28] Ann Braude, *Women and American Religion* (Oxford UK: Oxford U. Press 2000), 11.

[29] Braude, *Sisters and Saints,* 35.

[30] Brekus, 142.

clung to the Apostle Paul's admonition that there is no male or female in Christ.[31] One woman feared the scorn of her parents, ministers, and society, but was so uplifted by the revival that she rose up to preach:

> "Here my peace became as the river and my consolation like the waves of the sea. The cause of the Lord prospered, sinners obtained pardon of their past sins, converts crowded the gates of Zion, and I derived indescribable pleasure in persuading my fellow beings to become reconciled to God."[32]

Women personally exhorted individuals to salvation in front of the whole gathering.[33] Their raw emotional outpourings about self-doubt and salvation told in colorful and plain language moved listeners deeply.[34] They warned of sin and held out the hope of salvation, and they spoke of a God who saved the sincere repentant through His compassion and punished the unrepentant sinner in His wrath.[35] The most humble of people could preach out in such an environment. One woman who rose to preach heard, "Some will laugh at thee, some will scoff at thee, and the dogs will bark at thee, but while thou doest my will, I will be with thee to the ends of the earth."[36] Black women, especially, identified themselves closely with Old Testament prophets and attributed their preaching to a direct link with the Holy Spirit.[37]

During the first decades of the 1800s, about one hundred American women dared to preach—not just exhort—in public.[38] Numerous religious journals, newspapers, and memoirs of these years, testify to

---

[31] Ibid., 119.
[32] Ibid.,142.
[33] Ibid., 206.
[34] Ibid., 200.
[35] Ibid., 215.
[36] Ibid., 145.
[37] Ibid., 183-5.
[38] Ibid., 119

the existence and contributions of preaching by women. The effectiveness of these women to inspire audiences just could not be denied...[39]

Elleanor Knight had married a violent alcoholic and lost two children and then was rebuked by her pastor who told her to "Please your husband, and keep still." After she had fled her abusive husband and began to preach during the assembly, she was thrown out by her church which condemned her as "deceived" and described her as a "worthless character" and a "common prostitute"....[40]

Jarena Lee, a free black woman in Philadelphia, had a vision of a pulpit with a Bible laying on it. She belonged to Philadelphia's Bethel African Methodist Church, founded in 1793 by African-Americans seeking to assert themselves above their second class status in the Methodist Church. Her Bishop had told her that the rule of Methodism "did not call for women preachers." He went on to found the country's first 'African-American' denomination, the African Methodist Episcopal Church, but he did not support this 'woman preaching'. So Jarena settled down, had two children, and forgot about preaching.[41] But then, her husband died, and God seemed to call her again. One day in church, seized by the spirit, she burst out in a torrent of preaching: "God made manifest his power in a manner sufficient to show the world that I was called to labour according to my ability."[42] Her stunned audience and even her Bishop this time supported her, acknowledging that she must have been called to preach. Her spiritual power was undeniable. She knew she heard God's command, and she no longer accepted that any restrictions be placed on her. She began teaching in her home and then left to be an itinerant preacher to both black and white audiences. Few had this courage, and ministers knew that few could preach like Jarena Lee...[43]

---

[39] Lindley, 62.
[40] Brekus, 162-6.
[41] Braude, *Sisters and Saints,* 28-9.
[42] Ibid, 30.
[43] Ibid., 28-30.

Harriett Livermore, a devout evangelist, had convinced the Speaker of the House to allow her to preach to the Congress. In January of 1827, she appeared before the whole gathering of representatives clothed in a simple robe and bonnet. She opened her Bible, looked out over the packed chamber—listeners cramming the doorways—and began to preach on the topic: "He that ruleth over men must be just, ruling in the fear of God." President John Quincy Adams, who had to stand on the steps leading up to her lectern because of the crowd, referred to her as a religious fanatic: "There is permanency in this woman's monomania which seems accountable only from the impulse of vanity and love of fame." Other male clerics derided her as someone who sought public glory instead of remembering her female 'modesty'. In her many years of travelling, this preaching woman wrote sixteen books...[44]

Zilpha Elaw, a free black woman born outside of Philadelphia, had a vision of Jesus Christ which caused her to leave the Quakers for the more charismatic Methodist Church. After the death of her husband, she opened a school for black children in New Jersey. Two years later, she was preaching throughout Maryland and Virginia and evangelizing enslaved and free black Americans as well as whites, gathering followers from both races. In 1840, she left for England where she preached over a thousand times before the Anglican Church put a stop to this on the basis of her being female. The location of her grave is unknown, but she left behind an autobiography, Memoirs of the Life, Religious Experience, Ministerial Travels, and Labours of Mrs. Zilpha Elaw, an American Female of Colour...[45]

Julia Foote was born to former slaves, joined the AME Church, and later became its first deacon. She felt called to preach but was not supported by her husband, parents, or her minister. Still she set off as an itinerant preacher throughout New England, the Mid-Atlantic

---

[44] Brekus, 1-4.
[45] Derek Dureka, *"Elaw, Zilpha."*
pabook.libraries.psu.edu/palitmap/bios/Elaw_Zilpha.html.

states, Michigan, Ohio, and Canada. She, too, left behind an autobiography, *A Brand Plucked From the Fire*.[46]

A slave woman known as "Old Elizabeth" traveled the South preaching against slavery...[47]

There were many other women whose names have disappeared ...

In the South, white women preached out in radical new churches.
One woman "would pour forth an exhortation lasting from five to
fifteen minutes, which neither father nor brother could equal, and
which brought tears from every feeling eye." Some white planter
women such as "Miss Mag" even preached in the slave homes. She
would "come in eb'ry house and hol' prayer meetin'," and "go to one
house on Sunday and another house de nex' Sunday 'till she go all
roun' de quarters. And she could pray, too, lemme tell you. Sometime
she git so happy she git to shoutin'."[48]

Illiterate slave women preached in Sunday services or out in the fields
and prayed aloud and shouted out their stories of salvation. One
woman could "send up the most powerful prayer of anybody on the
plantation," another "looked as if she knowed everything just from her
mother wit. She was the only preacher we knowed anything about."
One slave woman believed that, like unto Jeremiah the prophet, God
was speaking through her as in the verse, "Open your mouth and I will
speak through you."[49]

The very appearance of women preaching was, for many, a sign of
the coming End and the return of Christ. When women stepped into a
pulpit, they were stepping out of their proper place and into a position
that had been forbidden to them by Scripture. When they spoke with
intelligence and power, they were being too 'masculine', and when
they stood up in front of men, they were accused of arousing men's

---

[46] Tonya Bolden, *Biographies*,
digital.nypl.org/schomburg/writers_aa19/biographies.html.
[47] Brekus, 4.
[48] Ibid., 129.
[49] Ibid.

lusts.[50] Even a preacher as radical as Lyman Beecher did not want "bold women" preaching and being the moral guides of the faithful.[51]

Much of this woman-preaching happened in new, dissenting Calvinist sects—the Free Will Baptists, Christian Connection, Methodists, and the African Methodists. Among the Millerites, there were at least twenty-two women who preached between 1841-5. These religious groups were more radical and rejected the world as it existed.[52] In the Bible, the Jewish prophet Joel had spoken about 'daughters' prophesying:[53]

> "And afterward, I will pour out my Spirit on all people. Your sons and daughters will prophesy, your old men will dream dreams, your young men will see visions....And everyone who calls on the name of the LORD will be saved; for on Mount Zion and in Jerusalem there will be deliverance, as the LORD has said, even among the survivors whom the LORD calls."[54]

Despite the great enthusiasm generated by the revival meetings, and the opportunity they afforded women to stand up and testify in public, not all women approved of this; in fact, some were downright opposed.

Mrs. Frances Trollope,[55] an English woman, saw the emotionalism of the revival as having a very negative effect on young women who gave themselves over to it. She observed that the minister preached a sermon that "...had considerable eloquence, but of a frightful kind." He described "...the last feeble fainting moments of human life, and then the gradual progress of decay after death...." then changed into "...the shrill voice of horror..." as he looked down into hell while

---

[50] Ibid., 202-204.

[51] Ibid., 153.

[52] Ibid., 119-121.

[53] Ibid., 159-160.

[54] Joel 2: 28-32 (New International Version).

[55] The mother of the famous English writer Anthony Trollope.

"…perspiration ran in streams…his eyes rolled, his lips were covered with foam…." Then he changed into a "…coaxing affectionate tone…" and asked "…Whether they would avoid the hell he had made them see?" He proffered an invitation for the frightened listeners to accept Jesus and "…Young girls arose…every limb trembling…They seated themselves on the anxious benches…Violent hysterics and convulsions seized many of them…." Mrs. Trollope concluded: "Did the men of America value their women as men ought to value their wives and daughters, would such scenes be permitted among them?"[56]

The preaching women of the Second Great Awakening, though, were not trying to change the traditional roles of men and women. They believed it was *God* who was making them behave this way by *ordering* them to stand up and preach. *They* were victims of God's *Wrath* which aimed at saving sinners and warning the faithful. *He* pushed them into preaching. They were *pens* in *His* Hands. They were sacrifices just as Jesus had been a sacrifice.[57] These preaching women were not trying to upset the established role of women in the family. They held very closely to the literal Biblical teaching and did not seek to change the traditional roles of mothers and daughters in the family.[58]

By the 1830-40s, conservative ministers as well as lay women pushed back against women who tried to preach.[59] The tide was turning and preaching women were booed, jeered, and locked out of churches. Ministers from traditional churches asserted that women could not teach men according to the literal interpretation of the Bible; all congregants had to be taught by trained male ministers, and women must remain silent and learn.

---

[56] Mrs. Frances Trollope, "from Chapter VIII of Domestic Manners of the Americans," *American Studies at the University of* Virginia, accessed October 2, 2013,
http://xroads.virginia.edu/~HYPER/DETOC/religion/trollrev.html.
[57] Brekus, 191.
[58] Ibid., 222.
[59] Ibid, 271.

In addition, since the growing country's dynamic economy was challenging established values, women should be the ones to protect the nation's homes from unhealthy change: "Women are the bonds of society. The habits of men are too commercial and restrained, too bustling and noisy, too ambitious and repellent."[60]

The role of women was clear to most Americans: they were the 'mothers of the Republic' the keepers of the virtues of the nation. The sphere of a woman was the home in which she trained the citizens of tomorrow.

4.

In the 19th century, American women's lives followed a trajectory of marriage followed by motherhood. Their sphere of activity was the home. The reform movements stimulated by the Second Great Awakening drew many women out of this private sphere and into a more public service.

The typical life of a woman began in the arms of a hearth-loving mother who taught her to pray. She grew up obeying the rules pronounced by her father, playing with her siblings around the family farm, completing writing exercises with other children in the one-room schoolhouse, listening to the minister sermonizing fearsomely on Sundays from the pulpit of the church, and accompanying her mother into town to barter and hear the news.

The Calvinist tradition of the church taught that her will had to be broken, and its evil tendencies curbed so that she did not grow up wild. A teacher could strike her if she misbehaved; if she didn't do her work, she might be made to wear a cap with the word 'dunce' written on it.[61] Fear could be induced by locking her in a closet, tying her to a bed post, or warning her of death. Her parents, her minister, and her

---

[60] Ibid., 272-5.
[61] Tim Lambert, *Children in the 19th Century*, www.localhistories.org/19thcenturychildren.html.

teacher, though, much preferred to use loving and wise counsel—as long as she did not get too out of line.

Her mother trained her in the home-making skills that were vital to the family's survival. By the age of six, she was doing real chores;[62] her brothers could be contracted out as labor as early as eleven years old.[63] She was taught amiability, chastity, refinement, and modesty, along with qualities which boys were also expected to acquire—kindliness and usefulness. She enjoyed going to school when she was not needed at home. Her whole town supported her education which prepared her to carry out her domestic responsibilities and be a good wife. Managing a home was a complex job that required many skills such as knitting, soap and candle making, food preparation and preservation, and the very time consuming task of spinning.[64] Being 'at home' for a woman did not mean being 'at leisure'. A daughter was also the pride of her father because he could look to her for support in his old age. From her trips into town, the girl knew of 'spinsters'—women who had never married and, instead, stayed at home, took care of their parents, and spun for a living.[65]

Having avoided the fatal deadly childhood diseases, the girl grew into a ruddy, healthy teenager and was ready for marriage. Her father and mother hoped to have enough land or money to help their daughter find a good match.[66] Her wedding was a simple but joyous affair and a source of fun for their neighbors and relatives, limited only by the

---

[62] K. Keniston and the Carnegie Council on Children, *All our children: the American family under pressure* (NY, NY: Harcourt, Brace, Jovanovich 1977).

[63] Ted Johnston, "Trends in American Child Rearing Practices to 1950," *Generation Ministries.* accessed October 1, 2013, http://www.generationsministries.org/uploads/2/5/2/7/25278738/child_rearing_practices_history. pdf.

[64] Nancy F. Cott, *The Bonds of Womanhood* (New Haven, CT: Yale University Press 1977), 26.

[65] Cott, 27.

[66] James M. Volo and Dorothy Denneen Volo, *Family Life in Nineteenth-century America* (Greenwich, CT: Greenwood Press 2007), 131.

financial constraints of the family and the space available in a family home. The bride wore her very best dress—she usually had only one or two. The custom of wearing white developed after the grand wedding of Queen Victoria to Prince Albert of England in 1840, for which the Queen wore a resplendent white satin wedding gown.[67]

In her new husband's home, the young wife immediately began a demanding schedule of housework which might include laundry on Monday, ironing and mending on Tuesday, constant cleaning up of the kitchen, preparing meals, giving hospitality to visitors, and making clothes, soap, candles, and other necessary household items. She also had a good deal of work related to the daily maintenance of the farm, such as growing the family garden and feeding animals. If she and her husband had to hire an extra hand, she had to look after him as well. All of these jobs were ongoing when she began the next major stage in her life: raising children.[68]

The young wife was expected to bear children, one after the other. She did not have the luxury of waiting because many childhood dangers lurked. She knew of women in the farms farther out who had seven children or more. Young mothers were often sick, and they might not go for medical attention out of personal modesty or lack of available doctors.[69]

She was a concerned young mother and read magazine articles such as one by Eliza C. Allen, the editor of *The Mothers' Journal*, which stated that it was the responsibility of both parents to model good behavior for their children:

"To do right, and to do good, should be the grand aim

---

[67] Carol Wallace, All Dressed in White: The Irresistible Rise of the American Wedding (NY, NY: Penguin Books 2004).
[68] Dorothy W. Hartman, "Women's Roles in the Late 19th Century," *Conner Prairie*, Accessed September 24, 2013, http://www.connerprairie.org/Learn-And-Do/Indiana-History/America-1860-1900/Lives-Of-Women.aspx.
[69] Ibid.

placed before children; –but then they should have continual proof in their parents' practice that it is their aim also."[70]

Fortunately for her and her husband, there were different institutionalized educational offerings by mid-century such as Sunday schools in factories and monitorial schools in which older students taught younger ones, allowing education to be more inclusive and broad.[71] So the young mother could reasonably look forward to having a loving home environment in which children developed their characters and life skills.[72]

5.

The family itself was affected by the rapid changes in the United States. Change brought uncertainty, challenging established roles, but it also brought opportunity. Women found new avenues opening to them in the areas of education and in the great reform movements of the times, especially abolition.

In the early 1800s, the United States was still overwhelmingly a rural, agrarian society. A wife and husband had an interdependent relationship. While the husband was the one to harvest the wheat, she was the one who turned it into bread.[73] Their family functioned as an economically productive unit. Work—such as spinning or making shoes—was done in the home, and homemade goods were either sold or brought to the general store to barter for other items such as eggs or milk while the husband worked in the field. Everyone depended on

---

[70] "Eliza C. Allen (1803-1848)," *Portraits of American Women in Religion,* accessed September 24, 2013,
http://www.librarycompany.org/women/portraits_religion/allen.htm.

[71] J. Hawes and N. Hiner, editors, *American childhood, a research guide and historical handbook,* Westport CT: Greenwood Press, 1985.

[72] T. Hareven, "Review essay: origins of the "modern family" in the United States," Journal of Social History 17 (1983-4): 339-344.

[73] K. Keniston and the Carnegie Council on Children, *All our children: the American family under pressure* (NY, NY: Harcourt, Brace Jovanovich 1977).

each other and worked closely together.[74] This was a very useful system for a rural and small town population where little cash was circulating. A family was embedded in a community of churches, neighbors, farmers, store owners, merchants, and artisans.[75]

Prosperous families had their daily items made outside the house, so a woman could devote herself to 'female accomplishments'—playing the piano, embroidery, and religious work.[76] For such families, the house changed from being an economic unit to being thought of as a 'home', a place of protection from the rough outside world, a place of some leisure and nurturing. The word 'home', as a result, came to mean a place of retreat and protection from the rough outside world. Home was managed by the mother and protected by her from the decadence of alcohol, the corrosive effects of materialism, the destructiveness of poverty, and all other vices.

American society was changing rapidly, and these vices seemed to multiply. By 1840, the population had tripled to seventeen million, and the country's tremendous natural resources were fueling a vibrant market economy. This drew people into a more materialistic way of life in which God seemed less necessary. Ministers bemoaned this turning away from God, as well as the social ills brought on by so much change.

At the same time, the ideas of salvation through Grace and one's free will spread by the Awakening meant that the Christian believer should demonstrate his or her faith by working to alleviate the suffering of his fellow human beings. As Finney explained:

> "…a change from selfishness to benevolence, from having a supreme regard to one's own interest to an absorbing and

---

[74] Braude, *Sisters and Saints*, 51.
[75] Cott, *The Bonds of Womanhood*, 23.
[76] Braude, *Sisters and Saints*, 52.

controlling choice of the happiness and glory of God's King-dom."[77]

The Second Great Awakening brought millions of Americans into a much more engaged, committed, and passionate religious life that expressed itself in working for the betterment of society.[78] Though their accepted sphere of activity was in the home, women became very active in reform movements aimed at addressing the huge challenges brought on by rapid change—alcoholism, prostitution, slavery, poverty, the abandonment of children, spiritual deprivation, lack of education, the treatment of the mentally ill, and working conditions in factories, among others. This reform work changed the American consciousness by championing social justice, religious devotion, and community-mindedness to an increasingly individualistic and materi-alistic society, and women served alongside men in the movements and, even, spoke and preached publicly in advocating for them.

Activism for women could be close to home. Such was the case with the rise in the early 1800s of maternal associations, groups of mothers who got together for mutual support and purposive prayer. These associations began in Maine in 1815 with one founded by Ann Louisa Payton, the wife of a Congregational minister. Soon, others sprang up throughout New England and New York and on the frontier. These associations were much more organized than those of the past. By the 1830s they were publishing magazines focusing on the formal Chris-tian upbringing of children. Sunday schools became another vehicle through which women could develop teaching, organizational, and administrative skills.[79]

A more public form of activism for women was the church-based benevolent association to serve the less fortunate. For example, the Female Charitable Society of Rochester, NY, was founded in 1822 to aid the poor who were sick, and a Female Orphan Asylum was begun

---

[77] McLoughlin, 129.
[78] Volo and Volo, 124.
[79] Lindley, 63-4.

by the women of Petersburg, VA, in 1812. These were highly organized, pro-active efforts by women to apply principles of Christian charity for the betterment of society. Women came to view the poor as those who could be both brought to Christ and aided such that they could eventually lift themselves out of poverty.[80] The enthusiasm generated by the Second Great Awakening gave great impetus to these types of efforts which proliferated over the decades.

One of the most important reform efforts was in education. The Second Great Awakening resulted in the founding of important colleges for the training of ministers: Wesleyan in Connecticut, founded by the Methodists,[81] Amherst College founded for the "education of indigent young men of piety and talents for the Christian ministry."[82] Oberlin College, the first college to admit and to graduate black Americans,[83] and Gettysburg College, founded by a Lutheran abolitionist, among others.[84]

Educational reform and progress very much included women. By the 1800s, educating girls was a widely accepted idea because women were thought of as the mothers of the Republic who imparted religious morals and national ideals to the future sons of the nation. Education itself, though, came to challenge this very role.

The primary promoter of education for girls was Catherine Beecher, the daughter of famed preacher and abolitionist Lyman Beecher. She

---

[80] Ibid., 65.

[81] "Wesleyan University: A Brief History," *Wesleyan University,* accessed October 3, 2013,
http://www.wesleyan.edu/about/history.html.

[82] "Amherst's History," *Amherst College,* accessed September 9, 2013,
https://www.amherst.edu/amherst-story/history.

[83] Roland M. Baumann, "Constructing Black Education at Oberlin College," *Ohio University Press,* accessed September 10, 2013,
ohioswallow.com/book/Constructing+Black+Education+at+Oberlin+College.

[84] "Witness to American History," *Gettysburg College,* accessed September 9, 2013,
http://www.gettysburg.edu/about/college_history/.

had received a standard education for girls, and because she longed for more, she taught herself other subjects. After working as a teacher, she opened the Hartford Female Seminary in May, 1823, which continued to operate for sixty years.[85] Mostly, she advocated for the education of girls in writing. While she did not seek to destroy or challenge women's traditional roles, she insisted that 'woman's work' such as teaching and homemaking, be respected as professions:

> "Most of the details which are continually discovered and lamented in present systems of education may be traced, either directly or indirectly to the fact, that the formation of the minds of children has not been made a profession securing wealth, influence, or honor, to those who enter it...[Other professions are honored; they have a long period of training and stiff requirements.] But to *form the mind of man* is deemed so simple and easy an affair, that no such preparation or precautions are required."[86]

Abigail Adams wrote:

> "much depends...upon the early education of youth, and the first principles which are instilled take the deepest root...if we mean to have heroes, statesmen, and philosophers, we should have learned women."[87]

Catherine Beecher was an ardent proponent of this view:

---

[85] "Catherine Beecher," *An American Family: The Beecher Tradition*, accessed November 4, 2013.
http://www.baruch.cuny.edu/library/alumni/online_exhibits/digital/2001/beecher/catherine.htm.
[86] Lindley, 66.
[87] Abigail Adams quoted in Cott, 106.

"The proper education of a man decides the welfare of an individual; but educate a woman, and the interests of a whole family are secured."[88]

While this very practical, utilitarian view of the education of girls was widely held, the idea of a woman pursuing learning for its own sake was condemned as undermining the useful activity associated with traditional female roles. In reaction to a proposal to include philosophy in a girls' school curriculum, one father wrote:

"I had rather my daughters would go to school and sit down and do nothing, than to study philosophy, etc. These branches fill young Misses with *vanity* to the degree that they are above attending to the more useful parts of an education."[89]

Learning for its own sake might also hurt a woman's chances for marriage. In a play written by a woman on this topic, one female character tells another:

"How will the young fellows take it if we shine away and don't like their humdrum ways—won't they be as mad as vengeance—and associate with the girls that don't go to school?"[90]

In fact, many people thought that too much school learning—especially of the wrong kind—took away from the qualities most suitable to marriage and domestic life. One publication wrote that intellectual acumen might:

---

[88] Dorothy W. Hartman, "Women's Roles in the Late 19th Century," *Conner Prairie*, accessed September 24, 2013.
http://www.connerprairie.org/Learn-And-Do/Indiana-History/America-1860-1900/Lives-Of-Women.aspx.
[89] Cott, 111.
[90] Ibid., 110.

"…make them regret the station which Providence has assigned them, or have recourse to unjustifiable ways to get from it. The best taste for science only contributes to make them particular. It takes them away from the simplicity of their domestic duties, and from general society, of which they are the loveliest ornament."[91]

Nevertheless, the efforts towards the education of girls had a significant impact on the lives of women. Emma Willard founded the Troy seminary in 1821, Troy, NY, with the goal of bringing:

"…its subjects to the perfection of their moral, intellectual and physical nature: in order that they may be of the greatest possible use to themselves and others."[92]

This school was the first institution in the country created to provide women with a quality of education similar to that of a college for men. Most schools for girls at this time instructed students in areas which were considered useful for them such as conversational French and embroidery.[93]

The curriculum at Willard's all-female academy consisted of religious and moral instruction, literature, human psychology, philosophy, and a scientific approach to running a household. Another academy balanced more intellectual learning with physical exercise and, yet another included botany, Latin, chemistry, geometry and composition.[94]

The Mount Holyoke Seminary, a famous girls' academy, was founded by Mary Lyon in 1837. Lyon had been left on her own at the age of thirteen and was working as a professional teacher by the age of seventeen earning 75 cents a week, a job at which she excelled and for

---

[91] Ibid., 110.

[92] Ibid., 119.

[93] "Troy Female Seminar," *Encyclopaedia Britannica,* accessed October 10, 2013, http://www.britannica.com/EBchecked/topic/606900/Troy-Female-Seminary.

[94] Cott, 122.

which she gained an excellent reputation. She became a master teacher and sought to continue her education—though she could not afford to be a full-time student—by travelling, sometimes for several days, to hear lectures. Her decades of teaching in Massachusetts and New Hampshire turned her into a leading expert in women's education. In 1834, she left her job at a seminary to found her own school which required several years of ceaseless travel and fundraising. Mt. Holyoke had very innovative guidelines: its curriculum was to be equal in content to those of the men's colleges, tuition would be low, the requirements of the entrance would be high, everyone had to work on campus to keep costs down and a permanent endowment was built up to prevent the school from going bankrupt as many others had.[95]

Another woman who made a very important contribution to the education of girls and young women and who was at the inception of the Catholic school system in the United States was Elizabeth Ann Seton. Unlike most female spiritual leaders in the United States up until that time, she came from a privileged background; her family heritage traced back to the earliest colonists of New York. She married William Seton, a wealthy New York merchant with international business concerns, whose family worshipped at the Trinity Episcopal Church on Broadway. But like many of the other women of the awakenings, Elizabeth was driven by a powerful sense of calling and an impulse to serve. She and her beloved friend and sister-in-law spent their time helping those in need in their close circle of family, friends, and neighbors. Elizabeth helped to found the Society for the Relief of Poor Widows with Small Children in 1797.

Catastrophe struck her family when her husband's business went bankrupt because of a monetary crisis and international piracy, and the family lost their home and possessions. Soon after her husband showed signs of tuberculosis. Elizabeth took him to Italy hoping that the dry

---

[95] "History," *MountHolyoke,* accessed October 28, 2013, www.mtholyoke.edu/about/history.

warm air there might save him, but he died leaving her alone and broke at age twenty-nine with young children.

In Italy, she was drawn to and instructed in Roman Catholicism and returned to the United States in June, 1804, a Catholic at heart. This posed a great personal challenge to her as the mostly Protestant people of the United States were very prejudiced towards Catholics. Her friends and family were completely opposed to her new faith, but she remained steadfast, guided by a strong feeling of connection to the Virgin Mary, which is why she chose 'Mary' as her confirmation name. After running a school in Baltimore, MD, she was recruited by an order of the Church to found and direct a new sisterhood, the first such institution in the United States. Elizabeth was now 'Mother Seton'.

A wealthy convert donated a large tract of land in Maryland to be the home for her new order, the Sisters of Charity of Saint Joseph's, founded officially on July 31st, 1809. The following year the order opened a free school for girls in need and a regular school for boarding students who paid tuition; these two schools began what became the widespread system of Catholic education which, by the 20th century, was the best alternative school system to the public schools. Her name was also given to the first diocesan university in the country—Seton Hall University. Mother Seton struggled on through years of deprivation to bring education to children. She buried eighteen of the sisters including two of her own daughters. During the Catholic holy year of 1975, Pope Paul VI presided over her canonization, making Mother Seton the first American Saint. On this occasion, he spoke of her: "Elizabeth Ann Seton is a Saint! She is the first daughter of the United States of America to be glorified with this incomparable attribute. Rejoice for your glorious daughter."[96]

---

[96] "Sr. Elizabeth Ann Seton." *The Archdiocese of Baltimore.* Accessed January 10, 2014
http://www.archbalt.org/about-us/the-archdiocese/our-history/people/seton.cfm.

All-female academies provided the most substantive education available for girls, but there were also many other valuable—though less academic—opportunities for education such as church run schools, tutoring, schools that taught the more 'ornamental' skills for being a good wife, and the all-important coeducational, public schools. The rise and multiplication of public schools over the course of the century was phenomenal. By mid-century it was as common for a girl as it was for a boy to be in school.

There were 160 public schools in 1870; by the turn of the century, there were 6,000. According to the 1880 census, literacy among girls was higher than among boys.[97] In the days of the Revolutionary War in New England only half of all women could even sign their names but, by 1840, literacy among the women of New England was nearly universal.[98] Out west, higher education opened to women on farms. Land grant colleges were founded and taught the science of managing a household, thus validating 'women's work' and bringing a formal training to it. At these colleges, farm women learned:

> "...liberal and practical education, which should fit them for their great duties and trusts, making them the equals of their educated husbands and associates, and enabling them to bring the aids of science and culture to the all-important labors and vocations of womanhood."[99]

6.

The westward movement of the country brought the issue of slavery to a head. The application of frontier territories for membership as new states in the union upset the balance of power in the Congress between the slave and non-slave states. This balance had held the country together without resolving the deep regional differences

---

[97] Hartman.

[98] Kenneth A. Lockridge, *Literacy in Colonial New England*, (New York: Norton, 1974), 38-42, 57-8.

[99] Hartman.

between the North and South. The disagreement over slavery was a moral one for abolitionism, a cause in which women played a crucial role and which was the most important reform movement of the pre-war era.

Though abolitionists were a small minority in both the North and South, they nevertheless began to sway public opinion. William Lloyd Garrison, the most fervent of the white abolitionists, made an impassioned appeal to end slavery in the first issue of his influential paper, *The Liberator*, published in 1831. Two Unitarian women responded. One, Maria Weston Chapman, helped to organize the Boston Female Anti-Slavery Society in 1832. The other, Lydia Maria Child, wrote, in 1833, the first anti-slavery book to be published, *An Appeal on behalf of That Class of Americans called Africans*. A Quaker woman in Philadelphia, Lucretia Mott, who later became instrumental in the fight for women's suffrage, founded the Philadelphia Female Anti-Slavery Society in 1833. In these abolitionist efforts, women wrote, spoke, organized, and administered, honing important skills despite not being allowed to be full public figures.

Few white women showed more courage and were more reviled in the struggle for abolition than the Grimke sisters, Angelika (1805-1879) and Sarah (1792-1873). Raised in a wealthy South Carolina family, the sisters' abolitionist views drove them North where they became Quakers and agents of the American Anti-Slavery Society in New York. They published tracts addressing the women and the clergy of the South, calling on them to abandon slavery. In 1837, they began a groundbreaking tour of New England in which they spoke to women first and then to much larger audiences which included men as well. This tour raised so much alarm that the Congregational Ministers of Massachusetts put out a pastoral letter warning parishioners against the sisters. The ministers cautioned women not to transgress the limits of propriety and enter the man's sphere by speaking out publicly. In response to the letter, the sisters wrote a series of letters of their own.

Sarah Grimke published *Letters on the Equality of the Sexes*, in which she asserted that Jesus made no distinction between the sexes:

> "Men and women were CREATED EQUAL; they are both moral and accountable beings, and whatever is *right* for man to do, is *right* for women."[100]

As the Grimke sisters crusaded for abolition, they became increasingly aware of their own lack of rights as women. While women were very involved in the abolitionist cause, most men did not support the cause of women's rights. This issue divided the American Anti-Slavery Society with many members being uncomfortable with the larger role being played by women and not wanting to take any focus away from the slavery issue. Abolitionist and poet John Greenleaf Whittier asked, "Is it not forgetting the great and dreadful wrongs of the slave in a selfish crusade against some paltry grievance of [your] own?"[101]

The person who swayed the general public's opinion more than anyone else towards the abolitionist view was a woman, Harriett Beecher Stowe. She was the sixth of eleven children of preacher Lyman Beecher, one of the catalysts of the Second Great Awakening and a leading abolitionist. All of her brothers entered the ministry; her younger sister, Isabella, founded the National Women's Suffrage Association; and her other sister, Catherine, promoted the education of girls and women. Stowe wrote thirty books on a variety of subjects but one had a huge impact on the history of the nation: *Uncle Tom's Cabin*.[102] This book depicted the struggles of slavery through the nobility of the long-suffering slave Uncle Tom who accepted punishment for others.

Harriett Beecher Stowe had never seen slavery in person but two factors may have deeply moved her: her minister's railing in church

---

[100] Lindley, 109.
[101] Ibid., 110.
[102] "Harriet Beecher Stowe's Life Introduction," *Harriet Beecher Stowe Center*, accessed October 2, 2013, www.harrietbeecherstowecenter.org/hbs/.

against the Fugitive Slave Act of 1850, which allowed posses of Southerners to ride into a neighboring free state and recapture escaped slaves, and her own private pain from the death of her young son to cholera:

> "It was at his dying bed and at his grave that I learned what a poor slave mother may feel when her child is torn away from her. In those depths of sorrow which seemed to me immeasurable, it was my only prayer to God that such anguish might not be suffered in vain."[103]

Her depiction of slaves—though fanciful—struck a loud chord with the American public. For the first time, many white people—who themselves had never seen a slave or the brutal reality of slavery first hand—began to empathize with the plight of slaves and to conceive of them as full human beings. This and the fact that *Uncle Tom's Cabin* was the biggest selling book of the 19th-century—second only to the Bible[104]—meant that it significantly influenced general public opinion against slavery in the years prior to the outbreak of the Civil War. Stowe did not hesitate to speak courageously as well to her Northern countrymen regarding their role:

> "A day of grace isn't yet held out to us. Both North and South have been guilty before God, and the *Christian Church* has a heavy account to answer."[105]

This book also conveyed something which was immediately understood by a broad spectrum of Americans in the wake of the Second Great Awakening: 'Christian love'. Stowe's underlying message was that through this Christian love shown by Uncle Tom's sacrifice, the

---

[103] Lindley, 111.
[104] Gail K. Smith, "*The Sentimental Novel: The Example of Harriet Beecher Stowe.*" *The Cambridge Companion to Nineteenth-Century American Women's Writing*, Dale M. Bauer and Philip Gould, Eds. (Cambridge, UK: Cambridge University Press 2001), 221.
[105] Lindley, 112.

hearts of men could be changed even in the wickedest of circumstances.

7.

Few women demonstrated more passionate Christian feeling and personal courage than did the extraordinary preaching woman born Isabella Baumfree (c. 1797-1883). Out of the violent and oppressive world of real slavery she arose to preach Jesus, Christian love, and witness to the horror of slavery and, in this way, embodied much of the Second Great Awakening and its reforming spirit.

For her, slavery was not a fiction —she had risen from it.

Born into bondage in Ulster County, New York, in the last years of the 18[th]century, Isabella's earliest memory was sleeping with all the other slaves in a cellar under the owner's large house. A few rays of light shone into the darkness through small windows. Men, women, and children spent the nights on loose floorboards covered with straw and blankets. Her father was tall and called 'Bomefree', meaning 'tree' in Low Dutch, the language spoken in that area of New York. Low Dutch was her first language; she did not speak English during the early part of her life. Her mother was called "Mau-mau Bett" and gave birth to possibly as many as twelve children, of whom Isabella knew six as a child. Their owner died when she was nine. Often, she found her mother in tears, and when Isabella asked her why she was crying, her mother told her she was thinking about her children who had been sold from her. Isabella feared that this might be her fate as well.[106]

When their owner died, Isabella and her whole family were included in the auction of his belongings. The elderly Baumfree couple was allowed to live on in the dark cellar, but their children were sent to work on nearby farms. Neighbors looked out for the elderly couple, and Isabella was desperate to help them but could only visit occasionally. One evening her elderly father came down into the cellar for

---

[106] Nell Irvin Painter, ed., *The Narrative of Sojourner Truth* (Penguin Books: NY, NY 1998), 10-12.

dinner and found the body of his wife of many years lying lifeless on the floor. His new masters—who had not owned slaves before—continued to look after him, shuttling him from house to house until they freed an elderly slave couple on the condition that they took the old Baumfree man with them. He lived the last period of his life isolated and helpless in a shanty in the woods until an old woman came upon him, and helped bathe him and clean off the lice that covered him, and soon thereafter, he passed away. His former owner, in recognition of his loyal service paid for a coffin and a jug of spirits.[107]

Now the property of the Dumonts, Isabella prided herself on working hard for her new owner who praised her often. This attracted the jealousy of other slaves who referred to her as the, "white folks nigger." To her, though, obedience and service to her owner was akin to service to God.

Isabella fell in love with Robert, a slave from a neighboring estate. When his owners discovered him on the Dumont property, they beat him so severely—despite Mr. Dumont's efforts to protect him—that he was never seen again. After a time Isabella married Thomas, an older slave, who had already had two wives, both of whom had been sold away from him. With Thomas, Isabella had five children. When she had to work in the field, she hung her infants in a cloth hammock from a tree limb to protect them from snakes.[108]

Isabella came upon her first religious meeting in 1817. Black people were not allowed inside houses of worship unless there was a specific pew set aside for them, so she had no experience whatsoever with organized religion. Jesus Christ was a very vague figure to her about whom she knew next to nothing, and the Bible, a largely unknown world about which she had only heard. She remained illiterate all of her life so all that she knew of the Scripture, she had memorized aurally, mostly through song. This first religious meeting was held in a

---

[107] Painter, 13-17.
[108] Ibid., 23-25.

private home; fearing to enter, Isabella stood outside and peered inside and listened. A circuit rider—preachers, often Methodist, who rode around a certain region—named Ferriss was preaching on the text: "Behold, I come quickly, and my reward is with me/To give to every man according as his work shall be." Then he taught the listeners a hymn which began "There is a holy city...." which Isabella was able to commit to memory.[109]

Isabella expected she would be freed on July 4th following her agreement with her owner; New York State had abolished slavery in 1827. Mr. Dumont demanded, though, that she stay longer because she had previously injured her hand and had not had a productive year. She agreed to stay and spin the remaining wool. Once done, she picked up her infant and walked away in the predawn hours.

Isabella's elderly husband chose not to follow her into uncharted waters; anyway, he had not shown himself to be especially inclined to helping her. Several of her children had to stay back, because she could not support them, but she was able to take her youngest with her.

She realized that she had no idea where to go, so she stopped to pray. She found a home with the Van Wageners who took her in as an employee. When Mr. Dumont arrived at their home and asked her why she had run away, she told him that she had not: she had walked away in the full daylight![110]

Once with the Van Wageners, she found out that her little boy, Peter, had been sold by Mr. Dumont; Peter was supposed to have been taken to New York City and then freed after a period of service. Instead, Peter was sold to a man in Alabama—an illegal action. Horrified that her boy was now in bondage in the South, Isabella set out on foot to get him back, going to her former master's house and confronting his wife who attempted to discourage her search. Isabella retorted that with God's help she would find her son. Eventually she was brought to the Quakers, who were early advocates for the rights of

---

[109] Ibid., 27.
[110] Ibid., 28-9.

slaves. They helped her in bringing a lawsuit to retrieve him. Her son's current owner was made to travel to Alabama and bring the boy back. This was the first time in the history of the United States that a black person had brought—and won—a suit against a white person. When the boy was brought back, he was too traumatized to go to his mother. Later, Isabella examined his body and found bruising and cuts everywhere as a result of beatings he had received in Alabama.[111]

Now living with the Van Wageners, she experienced relative comfort: she was safe. Gradually, she began to forget about God. Then, one day, as she prepared to go to a local festival, she saw in one wrenching moment how far removed she had become from God and was filled with a great fear which opened her spiritual eyes and proved to be a turning point of her life:

> "She became instantly conscious of her great sin in forgetting her almighty Friend and 'ever-present help in time of trouble'. All her unfulfilled promises arose before her, like a vexed sea whose waves run mountains high; and her soul, which seemed but one mass of lies, shrunk back aghast from the 'awful look' of Him whom she had formerly talked to, as if he had been a being like herself; and she would now fain have rid herself in the bowels of the earth, to have escaped his dread presence. But she plainly saw there was no place, not even in hell, where he was not; and where could she flee? Another such 'a look,' as she expressed it, and she felt that she must be extinguished forever, even as one, with the breath of his mouth, 'blows out a lamp,' so that no spark remains. A dire dread of annihilation now seized her...."[112]

Isabella's most basic belief was that God was real, and that His power was imminent. God was not an abstraction or an intellectual idol. He was everywhere, all the time, and His power could be called on

---

[111] Ibid., 30-37.
[112] Ibid., 44.

through faith to fight the battles of each and every day. These battles might be personal—loneliness, poverty, illness, or social, such as abolition. God's power was awesome and before it, people were helpless. The believer was an empty vessel through which God's power could flow by His own will. For many preaching women, this power could inspire terror, and sin was a futile rebellion against it.

Isabella was seized with fear at the awareness of her own sinfulness, and then she sensed the presence of a being that she could not recognize but who seemed to stand between her and the Divine wrath, like a parasol protecting someone from the sun:

> "'Who are you?' was the cry of her heart, and her whole soul was in one deep prayer that this heavenly personage might be revealed to her, and remain with her. At length, after bending both soul and body with the intensity of this desire, till breath and strength seemed failing, and she could maintain her position no longer, an answer came to her, saying distinctly, 'It is Jesus.' 'Yes,' she responded, 'it is Jesus.'"[113]

For the first time in her life, the Jesus of faith had entered into Isabella's consciousness. Before that moment Jesus had been a figure like a "Washington or a La Fayette."[114] Now the Jesus of faith became a deeply heartfelt reality, one who journeyed by her side and helped her to escape God's wrath.

She experienced a new found depth in her prayers. She would need it. Her elderly husband was emancipated on July 4th, 1828, and died a few years later in utter poverty. Their hope of one day owning a small house had been evaporated by the long delay in being freed. Her children were growing up, but Isabella didn't know how to steer them right. She moved with her son Peter to New York City where she worked in various homes. Much to her chagrin, her son turned out to be untrustworthy. Isabella found a benefactor who hired Peter as a

---

[113] Ibid., 45.
[114] Ibid., 55.

sailor on his ship. She received a few letters from him, but he later disappeared from her life completely.[115]

In New York City, she was reunited with her sister, Sophia after seventeen years, and discovered a brother she had not known. Isabella joined a religious sect headed by a man who titled himself the 'Prophet'. She put her funds in common with others in the sect but lost everything when criminal allegations closed the group down.

The unfulfilled promises of her life lay before her. Now, in anticipation of old age and after having lost her meager savings, she redoubled her efforts to work and save but found that the money she could save was insufficient. At this difficult point she had a second spiritual awakening in which she saw herself as someone who was grasping for material things instead of giving herself over wholly to the spirit: what she truly needed was to be free of this material world.[116]

She placed a few necessities in a pillow case, put two coins in her pocket, and headed across the river to Brooklyn. She told her landlady that her name was no longer 'Isabella'. She would now be a 'Sojourner' who lived only for God's truth—both a truth seeker and a truth teller. This was her true calling. By this new name, she would become one of the most powerful voices in American history: Sojourner Truth.

In later years, she explained to Lyman Beecher how she came to be 'Sojourner Truth':

> "My name was Isabella; but when I left the house of bondage, I left everything behind. I wa'n't goin' to keep nothin' of Egypt on me, an' so I went to the Lord an' asked him to give me a new name. And the Lord gave me Sojourner, because I was to travel up an' down the land, showin' the people their sins, an' bein' a sign unto them. Afterward I told the Lord I wanted another name, 'cause everybody else had two names;

---

[115] Ibid., 50-52.
[116] Ibid., 54-68.

and the Lord gave me Truth, because I was to declare the truth to the people."[117]

She wandered now, led by the Spirit, to testify to "the hope that was in her."[118] and to exhort people "to embrace Jesus, and refrain from sin."[119] She slept sometimes in empty corners of small houses, sometimes in a lean-to owned by a poor person, sometimes in the house of a rich family—if they let her in—sometimes she went to over twenty different places before finding a place to stay. She attended religious meetings when she heard of one or organized one of her own. When she needed rest, a home just seemed to open up to her.[120]

Sojourner Truth knew very little about the Bible because she could not read and had heard very few sermons, so her understanding of her faith was personal and idiosyncratic. She took any opportunity to listen to the words of the Bible but always preferred having children read to her because she disliked when adults offered their own commentaries. She also took many opportunities to learn from conversations with ministers. This was the case when she met the Millerites, the followers of William Miller. She remembered having heard him once but had understood nothing about the charts he had put up on the stage regarding the end times. Soon, though, she was preaching among them.

In her meeting with the great preacher Lyman Beecher, she expressed an authentic conviction:

> "Sojourner, this is Dr. Beecher. He is a very celebrated preacher."
> "*Is he?*" she said, offering her hand in a condescending manner and looking down on his white head, "Ye dear lamb, I'm

---

[117] Ibid., 111.

[118] Ibid., 68.

[119] Ibid.

[120] Ibid.

glad to see ye! De Lord bless ye! I loves preachers. I'm kind o'
preacher myself."

"You are?" said Dr. Beecher. "Do you preach from the Bible?"

"No, honey, can't preach from de Bible—can't read a letter."

"Why, Sojourner what do you preach from, then?"

Her answer was given with a solemn power of voice, peculiar
to herself, that hushed everyone in the room.

"When I preaches, I has jest one text to preach from, an' I
always preaches from this one. My text is, 'WHEN I
FOUND JESUS!'"

"Well, you couldn't have a better one," said one of the ministers...

..."Well, now, I'll jest have to go back an' tell ye all about it.
Ye see we was all brought over from Africa, father, mother,
an' I, an' a lot more of us..."[121]

The content of Sojourner's preaching was peculiar to her, untutored
as she was in any formal theology. Nevertheless, she made a great
impression on her audiences. She stood over six-feet tall, wide-eyed
with a very dark complexion, and conveyed her absolute conviction in
a sonorous voice interspersed with heart felt singing. She made an
especially strong impact when she spoke of being a slave.

Harriett Beecher Stowe, author of *Uncle Tom's* Cabin, described
meeting her:

> "I do not recollect ever to have been conversant with anyone
> who had more of that silent and subtle power which we call
> personal presence than this woman...Her tall form, as she
> rose up before me, is still vivid to my mind. She was dressed
> in some stout, grayish stuff, neat and clean, though dusty
> from travel...She seemed perfectly self-possessed and at her
> ease; in fact, there was almost an unconscious superiority,

---

[121] Ibid.,105.

not unmixed with a solemn twinkle of humor, in the odd, composed manner in which she looked down on me. Her whole air had at times a gloomy sort of drollery which impressed one strangely.

"So this is *you*," she said.

Sojourner Truth.

"Yes," I answered.

"Well, honey, de Lord bless ye! I jes' thought I'd like to come an' have a look at ye. You's heerd o' me, I reckon?" she added."[122]

Her powerful presence and authentic voice impressed all kinds of audiences. At a camp meeting, a large number of white louts were disrupting the services. Sojourner stood on a small hill and began to sing a hymn aloud. The young men rushed over to her because they wanted to hear her and, soon, they were subdued. When she spoke before a colored regiment at Camp Ward in advance of the civil war, the colonel made the soldiers stand at attention for her, and afterward, she met the soldiers individually and engaged them in "motherly conversations."[123] The next day, when she came to the camp to speak, a very large crowd of white people were there specifically to hear her.[124]

---

[122] Ibid., 103.
[123] Ibid., 117.
[124] Ibid.

Her words and presence pierced the hearts of white people. A white man wrote to her from Missouri:

> "Dear Grandmother:—
>
> "As the present is your first visit to Missouri, I want to it on record in your 'Book of Life,' (i.e. Sojourner's scrapbook) that there is at least one native Missourian who entertains no prejudice against colored people, but, on the contrary, values all alike according to their worthiness. Your noble labors for the freedom of the colored race are among my earliest re-membrances, and your beautiful ideas of life, death, and God, will be among the last things I shall forget.
>
> "W.H. Miller, Journal of Commerce,
> "*KansasCity, Mo., June 15, 1872.*"[125]

She could also show real grit and toughness. In 1858, she found herself giving a series of lectures in a church in Indiana, when some pro-slavery Democrats shouted out that they doubted she was a woman and that she should have to prove it by showing her breasts to the women. The women were shocked by this suggestion, and Sojourner's friends outraged. She told them that her breasts had suckled many a white child—much to the neglect of her own children—and that she was ready to suckle them if they wanted. To prove her truthfulness she began to disrobe in front of all of them, at which point two men jumped up to cover her.[126]

She joined the progressive, utopian community named the North-ampton Association for Education and Industry and settled for many years in Florence, MA. After that she lived out her days in Michigan. She spent the better part of thirty years travelling across the northern states fulfilling her life's mission. These circuits took her throughout the northern United States and even all the way to the United States Senate chambers where she, an old former bondswoman, appeared

---

[125] Ibid., 81.
[126] Ibid., 95.

before the cream of the American political class and received its honor and respect.[127]

Though portrayed later as an activist reformer for abolition and women's rights, which she was, Sojourner Truth may even more accurately be thought of as a prophet stepped out from the pages of the Old Testament and nurtured by the Second Great Awakening.

She was a reformer but her drive to reform was born out of her deep spiritual convictions. Mostly, she preached Jesus and the imminent presence of God. God was all-around her in her life. She felt Him everywhere and all the time.

Half a world away and in another religious universe, a woman lived contemporaneously to Sojourner Truth who also sensed the real presence of God in her life and who arose to preach a new Jesus.

---

[127] Ibid., 89.

Two:
Tahirih of Persia

1.

Her legal name was Fatimah, the same as her grandmother, so family members used the name Umm Salmah out of respect for their older relative.[128]

She became a deep thinker in a mass of ignorance, an outspoken voice in a muzzled gender, a poet calling to God, and a mystic who would stun and galvanize her Muslim country-folk.

As a little girl, she was affectionately nicknamed Zarrin-Taj, 'crown of gold'.

And it was this little girl who caused her learned family to be remembered around the world as the family of the mystic, apostle, and poet Tahirih of Qazvin (c.1817-1852).[129]

Tahirih grew up in a world bounded by the lattice work on the walls of the spacious family home, dominated by the presence of powerful clerics and learned women, and suffused with education and learning. The women's wing in which she was born and the quaint second floor library where she studied,[130] the traditional theology of the men in her family, and the learning and customs current in her day eventually became a prison to her.

In time, she transcended them all.

The eldest of the seven daughters of a prominent cleric, Mullah Salih, who also counted eight sons among his children from several wives, Tahirih most likely had one full brother and sister. Her mother

---

[128] H. M. Balyuzi, *The Bab*, (Oxford, UK: George Ronald, 1973), 27; Mírzá Asadu'lláh Fádil-i Mázandarání, *Zuhúr al-Haqq, Volumes 1–4* (Tihrán, Iran: Bahá'í Publishing Trust, 1973), 311; Hoseini, 309; Momen, "Usuli, Akhbari, Shaykhi, Babi." 327.

[129] Mázandarání, 331; Shoghi Effendi, (*God Passes By* (Wilmette, Il: Bahá'í Publishing Trust, 1979), 73), gives the birth date as 1233 AH/1817 CE.

[130] Martha Root, *Táhirih the pure* (LA, CA: Kalimat Press, 1981), 49.

was from a prestigious family who came from a long line of clerics even more prominent than those in her husband's family, though she was not Mullah Salih's first wife.[131] Tahirih had the good fortune to be able to attend the girls' section of the large school founded by her father, which numbered hundreds of students including some from other parts of the kingdom and as far away as India. She studied Persian literature and poetry with her mother, religious jurisprudence and its principles, Islamic traditions, and Qur'anic commentary with her father, uncle, and brothers, and different branches of philosophy with two clerics who were her cousins. Because of her ability, she taught all of her sisters in the woman's section of the school. Later on she also educated her sons there as well. Not only did she demonstrate real intellectual capacity, she also memorized the entire Qur'an and may well have learned to speak Turkish along with Persian and Arabic. Her family lived in a Turkic-speaking neighborhood of Qazvin, an important trading center in northern Persia, and, later in her life, she may have written some poetry in that language. Given the talent she exhibited, her father wished she had been born a boy to enhance the public prestige of the family and to be his successor.[132]

Several of her male contemporaries attest to her extraordinary intellect and eloquence.[133] Her brother confessed that she was by far the superior sibling:

---

[131] Hoseini, 141. Tahirih's mother, Amina, was much younger than Mullah Salih, Tahirih's father, and was not his first or only wife (Momen, "Usuli, Akhbari, Shaykhi, Babi: The Tribulations of a Qazvin family." *Iranian Studies,* volume 36, number 3, (September 2003): 327). She was awarded licenses from her father, brother, and Shaykh Ahmad, by demonstrating her proficiency in certain Islamic texts and her good moral character (Nosratollah Mohammad Hoseini, *Hadrat-i-Tahirih* (Dundas, Ontario, Canada: Association for Bahá'í Studies in Persian 2000), 143; Momen, "Usuli, Akhbari, Shaykhi, Babi." 327).

[132] Tahirih's father's school was called the Salihiyyah (Momen, "Usuli, Akhbari, Shaykhi, Babi." *321, 328*).

[133] Momen, "Usuli, Akhbari, Shaykhi, Babi." 326-8 f. 66.

"We were all, her brothers and cousins, fearful to speak in her presence, so much did her knowledge intimidate us, and if we hazarded to put forward an opinion on a point of doctrine that was in dispute, she would prove to us where we were going wrong in a manner so clear, precise and magisterial that we were thrown into confusion and withdrew."[134]

Tahirih's home in Qazvin, Persia.

Nevertheless, her natural ability and her education separated Tahirih from the mass of Persian women whose early lives were very different. An ordinary woman would have been expected to follow a carefully arranged course because her life was completely scripted, her role having been assigned to her by the chance of her birth. The arc of her life followed a trajectory determined by tradition.

---

[134] Ibid, 328 f. 66; A. L. M Nicolas, *Seyyed Ali Mohammed dit le Bab* (Paris: Dujarric and Cie, editeurs, 1905), 273, accessed September 5, 2013; Nabil-i-Zarandi, *The Dawn-Breakers: Nabil's Narrative of the Early Days of theBahá'í Revelation*, Translated by Shoghi Effendi (Wilmette, IL: Baha'i Publishing Trust,1932), 84 f. 1.

A girl's unfavorable status began before she was even born. Her family-to-be visited shrines and made promises in prayer in the hope of influencing the baby's gender and seeing a boy emerge from the mother. The birth took place in the expectant mother's home. A midwife arrived. The baby was eased out into a large copper tray filled with ash to absorb the blood. Prayers were offered, along with songs and jokes. The baby girl was cleaned and dressed in white cotton. The mother's status among the multiple wives in the family might decline because the baby was a girl.

In honor of the birth of the child, the wife's family would give a collection of small gifts—such as earrings, bracelets, and soap—the value of which depended on the wealth of the families. This kind of gift-giving in Persian society followed very specific rules of reciprocity which were determined by economic and social status and had to be followed for the sake of public honor.

Though most Persians were Shi'a Muslims, they held on to numerous folk beliefs. Some wealthy families, for example, hired astrologers to foretell the future of the child; other families might pin a written talisman to the baby girl's clothing, and invoke the prophets of old, the Imam Ali, and his wife, Fatimah, for protection against the evil eye, illness and malevolent spirits.

On the sixth day after the baby's birth, the midwife returned for a follow-up visit because it was believed that the newborn was in the greatest danger from harm by evil spirits on this day. The midwife performed certain rituals such as the burning of camphor and the recitation of specific verses to provide protection. In the following weeks, ceremonial baths were taken, a practice harkening back to the Iranian goddess of fertility, Anahita, who was associated with water.

The sixth day was also the naming day. The men of the family gathered with the local mullah and decided on a name. Then the cleric went to see the new mother. Before he entered her room, all clothing related to the women had to be removed, and the mother fully covered. The baby was placed in the cleric's arms, and he recited the chosen name several times and prayed. Since a mullah had to be paid for this service, poor people had the family grandfather fulfill this function. In cities, all given names were from important Shi'a Islamic figures, while in rural areas, and especially among nomads, ancient Persian names were still in use. Once the men left, the women relaxed and enjoyed themselves by singing, dancing, and playing games to ward off sleep during which demons could come and take the mother away.

Rear View of Friday Mosque, Qazvin.

A little girl's education was usually minimal. If she was fortunate, she learned basic reading, writing, and religion at an elementary school until the age of eight or nine. A few women were blessed with both talent and the support of their families—like the heroine in our story—and received excellent educations.[135] Most of an average little

---

[135] Afsaneh Najmabadi, "EDUCATION xxv. WOMEN'S EDUCATION IN THE QAJAR PERIOD," in the Encyclopaedia Iranica, edited by Ehsan Yarshater, accessed October 18, 2013,

girl's learning happened in the home by observing and assisting older women who taught them home skills.

Because Tahirih had been born into a family that valued education for both its boys and girls, she was able to acquire the learning current at the highest levels of Persian society which was not the case for most other Persian girls who had neither the means nor the opportunity. But Tahirih did not simply acquire knowledge and then adopt the conventional views held by other men. She possessed an original mind and a deeper capacity for spiritual insight than most others. So as she grew into maturity, she was able to marshal her high-quality education in service to her highly original ideas which led her down a path towards direct conflict with powerful men.

2.

The men in Tahirih's family, her two uncles and her father were all mujtahids, high-ranking clerics who had the authority to render legal decisions, which brought them prestige, power, and influence. Such clerics spent much of their time and effort engaged in theological disputation and writing essays advancing or defending points of theology and law as well as arguing these in person. Because being a mujtahid brought a man wealth from land ownership and fees charged to petitioners, these theological disputes could easily turn into economic and political ones. One such dispute drew in the three Baraghani brothers, Tahirih's uncles—Taqi, Ali, and her father, Salih.

The brothers rose from humble beginnings by studying to become mujtahids in the holy cities of Qum, Isfahan, and Karbila.[136] Clerics received most of their education in these holy cities of Iraq where several of the Holy Imams of Shi'a Islam were buried. Their study included the Qur'an, Arabic literature and grammar, the philosophy of law, and the interpretation of texts. To earn a license to teach could

---

http://www.iranicaonline.org/articles/education-xxv-womens-education-in-the-qajar-period.

[136] Mázandarání, 308.

take years and required the presentation and approval of a written treatise.

Once they had finished their education, the brothers settled in the city of Qazvin and became deeply involved in the ongoing theological disputes between the different Islamic schools of thought. Over the centuries, many schools of philosophical, legal, and mystical thought and practice had proliferated making the Islamic world rich in intellectual inquiry and speculation. Large fissures, though, had divided the original sacred community founded by Muhammad in Medina.

The religion begun by the life of Muhammad and the revelation of the Qur'an had split into two branches early in its history; the vast majority of Muslims were Sunni and accepted the authority of the early rulers of Islam and of the caliph who was both a political and religious figure. The minority were Shi'a who looked for guidance to a line of Imams, holy men who were believed to be the living presence of Muhammad's authority[137] and to have access to divine knowledge. The Shi'a looked to Ali, Muhammad's son-in-law, as their first Iman. They also mourned and honored with great emotion the life of the third Imam, Husayn. The killing of Husayn and his companions at Karbila at the hands of an unjust ruler was the central drama of their history, so the idea of rebellion against unjust rule became embedded in Shi'a consciousness. This 'rebel consciousness' was reinforced by the reality that the Shi'a were a minority in most Muslim Kingdoms.

The line of Imams was believed to have ended with the twelfth Imam who had gone into a mystical form of hiding, or 'occultation', in the 9th century CE. From this hidden place, he guided the Shi'a world through a series of holy men or 'gates'. There had been a succession of four gates, and now all was silent until the return of that hidden Imam. The Shi'a world lived in a permanent state of expectancy.[138]

---

[137] Hamid Dabashi, *Shi'ism, A religion of Protest* (Cambridge, MA: Harvard University Press 2011), 44.
[138] Dabashi, 86.

Persia had become Shi'a during the great Safavid period (1501-1722). In the centuries since the last of the 'gates', many schools of mysticism, law, and philosophy, had flourished and contributed to the culture of great civilizations, but the Turkish 'Qajar' dynasty was not one of these. The Qajars came to power in an intra-familial bloodbath in the late 18th century. This line of kings proved mediocre and incompetent, and England, Russia, and France wasted no time in restarting their colonial intrusions into Persia.[139]

By the time of the Qajar dynasty, Persia was a land in decline. Lack of competent administrators, undeveloped roads and transportation systems, unused and abandoned lands and irrigation systems due to a large nomadic population that did not farm, profoundly superstitious and corrupt clerics, and incompetence at all levels of government with no stable cadre of trained individuals to effect change kept Persia from developing into a functioning, modern nation. The stability brought by the Qajar rulers in the early decades of the 19th century, though, strengthened the economy. Industrious craftsmen produced goods which were greatly valued abroad in the Ottoman Empire and Russia to the north, Afghanistan to the east, India to the south, and Britain, which was most interested in using Persia for its trade with India. Though this trade and the Kingdom's infrastructure continued to develop during the19[th] century, foreign involvement in Persia's economy was often not to the advantage of its people and, by the middle of the 19th century, the Kingdom remained weak.[140]

An ongoing struggle for power between the ruling class and the clergy also stymied the development of Persia. To help legitimize their claim to the throne, the Qajar rulers gave over a great deal of power to the clergy to arbitrate in public matters which, in turn, reinforced the clergy's hold over the Persian people. The mass of the Persian popula-

---

[139] Ibid., 165.
[140] Hassan Hakimian, "ECONOMY viii. IN THE QAJAR PERIOD." In the *Encyclopaedia Iranica*, edited by Ehsan Yarshater. Accessed September21, 2013. http://www.iranicaonline.org/articles/economy-viii-in-the-qajar-period.

tion was illiterate and received all of its understanding of Shi'a Islam from its clerics who filled many functions for this illiterate population as judges, arbiters in disputes, intermediaries between common people

Sheikh Ahmad Ahsai.

and the ruling class, instructors of students and dispensers of various licenses and agreements, for which they received fees that amounted to substantial amounts of money. The clerics took advantage of their enhanced position to fuel the people's animosity towards religious minorities, foreigners, and Sufis.[141]

By the 19th century, the dominant school of religious interpretation in Persia was the Usuli school which stressed the use of reason in shaping Islamic law. The Baraghani brothers had returned to Qazvin as Usuli adherents. A much more mystical understanding of Shi'a Islam, was also emerging that challenged the Usuli school—Shaykhism.

Shaykhism was founded by Shaykh Ahmad al-Ahsa'i, an Islamic philosopher born in Bahrain. He taught an allegorical reading of certain parts of the Qur'an, an approach that went against the accepted

---

[141] Dabashi, 171-2.

literal method prevalent at this time.[142] Shaykh Ahmad came to believe that Islam's time of fulfillment had arrived which created a great deal of excitement among his theological students and resulted in a dynamic new movement.

He had earned multiple teaching licenses in the holy cities of Iraq. In addition to the course of study pursued by all high-ranking clerics, he also took an interest in astronomy, medicine, mathematics, and music.[143] Dissatisfied with the status quo among his fellow clerics, he began a rigorous practice of meditation. He had powerful dreams of the Prophet Muhammad and the Imams in which he drank of their saliva—meaning he received great insights from them and had a strong connection with them.[144] He travelled, taught, and wrote constantly, attracting many students to him. He took as his source of authority the Qur'an, authenticated stories of the teachings, deeds, and sayings of Muhammad known as hadiths, the traditions of the Imams, Muslim spiritual practice, and his own reasoning.[145] He wrote some one-hundred and thirty-two works, including commentaries and replies to theological questions.

Shaykh Ahmad sought, in part, to synthesize the two great schools of thought at the time—the Usuli and the Akhbari. The question of religious authority in the absence of an Imam was central for the Shi'a clerics. One school, the Akhbari, condemned the corruption of the mujtahids which made them unworthy of interpreting Islamic law; only the Qur'an, the accepted hadith, and the Imams could be held up as having authority. The other major school, the Usuli, upheld the independent judgment of the mujtahids as authoritative when rendering decisions on law and religious teaching. Most clerics of this latter school were Persian, working in Persia and the holy cities of Iraq,

---

[142] Vahid Rafati, *The Development of Shaykhi Thought in Shi'i Islam* (PhD Dissertation, UCLA, 1979, unpublished), 9.

[143] Ibid., 41.

[144] Ibid., 42.

[145] Ibid., 52.

whereas those of the former school, were Arab, working in Arab-speaking areas.[146]

Most of all, Shaykh Ahmad brought an enormously fresh spiritual and intellectual energy to the stagnant Shi'ism of the time; most books and treatises on religious subjects in this period were on minor points of law. Shaykh Ahmad's dynamic work harkened back to the earlier, and culturally richer, Safavid period. His supple and original thinking attracted many students and much controversy as well.

Shaykh Ahmad taught that God was transcendent and unknowable and that man was limited to this world. Man could not know God's Essence because this implied similarity or likeness with God which was impossible because man was a dependent creation, and God was independent; his understanding could not take in God's Essence. According to the Qur'an: "Vision comprehends Him not, and He comprehends (all) vision." (6:104)

Man could know God's 'actional' attributes—His characteristics as they act in this world—but these 'actional' attributes and the attributes that Man wishes God to have—are all limited by Man's station of existence and in no way describe the attributes of God's essence.

Man could not come to know God purely by his own effort as the Sufis taught. Man was part of the finite world while God was infinite. God made Himself known to Man through His attributes. God was one in His being, simple not complex. The intermediaries between God and Man were His prophets who expressed God's Will.[147]

One of Shaykh Ahmad's most controversial views was that reason should be reconciled with revelation. He interpreted the Qur'anic verses on the end times allegorically because the literal meaning conflicted with reason. The resurrection of the dead did not mean that the physical body would be reconstituted because the body disintegrated into its earthly elements. Rather, it was Man's non-material body, his 'subtle' body, which continued.

---

[146] Ibid., 30.
[147] Ibid., chapter III.

He did not interpret the Day of Judgment according to tradition as the day the world would end and all would be judged but, instead, as the day when a 'rightly-guided one'—the 'Qa'im in the Shi'a tradition—would appear to usher in a new time in which old laws and customs would be abrogated and new ones revealed. People would be judged, in this interpretation, by whether they recognized God's manifestation in His new form. The bridge between Hell and Paradise from the Qur'an, which many Muslims believed to be a physical bridge in another realm, was actually the new teaching of this 'rightly guided one' through whom believers could come into the Paradise of the nearness to God. Shaykh Ahmad taught that the time of the appearance of the rightly guided one was at hand, and so he wanted to prepare his students to recognize him.[148]

The rapid growth of Shaykhism challenged the dominant Usuli school of thought, which the Baraghani brothers followed.[149]

The Baraghani brothers had become the most influential family in Qazvin through their status as mujtahids, their involvement in the affairs of the city, and their intermarriages with other prominent families. They settled in the western part of Qazvin and went on to exercise power over the rest of this important city.[150] Once the capital of Persia under the Safavid dynasty, Qazvin was an ancient settlement, going back nine thousand years; the oldest paved street in Persia ran through it. Located on the same high plateau as Tihran over a hundred miles to the southeast, it had a dry, temperate climate. The brown Alborz mountains rose up to the north with patches of green valleys in which had grown small villages. The central mosque—the fifth to be built in Persia—had been constructed over an ancient Zoroastrian fire temple; Islam had largely replaced that ancient faith. Qazvin became a center for mysticism, the study of Islamic philosophy and jurisprudence, and the development of calligraphy. Mosques and religious

---

[148] Ibid., 106-122.
[149] Momen, "Usuli, Akhbari, Shaykhi, Babi." 324.
[150] Ibid., 322-3.

schools multiplied to over fifty; one important mosque and school was built by the middle Baraghani brother, Salih, Tahirih's father. Qazvin's location on a trade route stimulated its economic growth and attracted a diverse population of Persians, Turks, Jews, and Armenians.[151]

This dynamic city was ideal for the talented and energetic Baraghani brothers.

The eldest brother, Mulla Taqi, had married a sister of the king of Persia[152] while in Tihran. He strengthened his relationship with the king by issuing an official decree, a *fatwa*, in support of Persia's war with Russia.[153] Now back in Qazvin, he demonstrated his interest in politics by actively consolidating his power. Taqi took advantage of his high position by charging money to petitioners for providing his legal decisions in writing. While it was possible for a mujtahid to convey his decision verbally, this was not useful to petitioners because they needed a written text to show as proof of the ruling. Taqi took advantage of the latitude the Usuli school gave its clerics by charging a fee to write down his rulings, contrary to standard practice.[154] His other forms of revenue included adjudicating in financial and business disputes from which he got a percentage of the settlement money, collecting alms, pocketing the proceeds from land endowments which no longer had owners, and participating in business ventures, some of a dubious nature.[155] Though he remained highly respected in the city, there may well have been resentment towards his practices which obviously benefitted him financially at the expense of others. In two decades, Taqi had become one of the richest clerics in the whole kingdom.[156]

---

[151] Hoseini, 114.
[152] Fath-'Ali Shah (1772-1834).
[153] Ibid, 124.
[154] Momen, "Usuli, Akhbari, Shaykhi, Babi." 320-321.
[155] Abbas Amanat, *Resurrection and Renewal, the Making of the Babi Movement in Iran, 1844-1850* (Ithaca, NY: Cornell U. Press, 1989), 318.
[156] Ibid.

He was also willing to shift positions if he could benefit from doing so. In one case, he overturned his own ruling against congregational Friday prayers—such prayers should await the return of the Imam of the Age—when an opportunity came up to lead them at the central mosque in the absence of the regular cleric. By leading these prayers, his prestige increased. He certainly coveted the position of head Imam of the Friday Mosque—the most important mosque in a city—because such a position would have given him access to the revenues from the mosque's extensive landholdings.[157]

Tahirih's library in her father's house in Qazvin.

Taqi did not hesitate to enter into disputes with other clerics if doing so could increase his social position. He took a strong stance against Shaykh Ahmad, opposing his allegorical interpretations of passages from the Qur'an.[158] Following a debate with him,[159] Taqi issued a

---

[157] Ibid.
[158] Hoseini, 129.
[159] Momen, "Usuli, Akhbari, Shaykhi, Babi." 325.

decree declaring him an infidel—the first cleric to do so.[160] Such an action was quite shocking because Shaykh Ahmad, though unconventional in his views, was a profoundly learned and respected figure.[161]

Taqi may have taken a clear stand against Shaykhism to ingratiate himself with the king and prominent Usuli clerics who were concerned with the spread of its teachings. Another possible reason may have been personal. During his visit to Qazvin, Shaykh Ahmad had chosen to stay with Taqi's main rival who was the head of a large mosque and his relative by marriage.[162] His area of influence was in the east and south of the city. Having a mujtahid from another town stay in one's home was a sign of great respect, so Taqi must have been insulted by having his home passed over in favor that of his rival. Shaykh Ahmad believed that Taqi was concerned about losing a portion of the revenues from religious activities to his rival because of this favor.[163]

The middle Baraghani brother, Mulla Salih, was not politically oriented like his older brother. His school attracted hundreds of students. One of its female graduates even went on to become a secretary to the king.[164]

The youngest brother, Mullah Ali, taught at this school and was interested in mystical philosophy. He engaged in ascetical spiritual practices[165] to the point where he was rumored to chain himself to a

---

[160] D. M. MacEoin, "Baragānī, Moḥammad-Taqī," In the *Encyclopaedia Iranica*, edited by Ehsan Yarshater, accessed September 24, 2013.
http://www.iranicaonline.org/articles/baragani-molla-mohammad-taqi-qazvini-sahid-e-ale-an-important-shiite-alem-of-qazvin-d.
[161] Momen, "Usuli, Akhbari, Shaykhi, Babi." 323.
[162] The cleric was Mulla 'Abd al-Wahhab; his sister had married Taqi's brother (Moojan Momen, "Usuli, Akhbari, Shaykhi, Babi: The Tribulations of a Qazvin family." *Iranian Studies* volume 36, number 3 (September, 2003): 321).
[163] Ibid, 324.
[164] Ibid., 321.
[165] Ibid.

wall to stay awake and study.[166] During Shaykh Ahmad's stay in Qazvin, Mullah Ali was drawn to his teachings.[167]

In the theological debates, Taqi took an aggressive anti-Shaykhi position, Salih attempted to remain neutral and act as a peacekeeper, and Ali became a Shaykhi.

At the height of his power and influence, Taqi could not have foreseen that the greatest challenge to his dominant theological position and to his religious authority would come from the most unlikely of people—his younger brother's extraordinary daughter, Tahirih.

3.

When she became a teenager, Tahirih was expected to marry. Her family decided that she should marry her paternal first cousin, Mulla Muhammad, the son of Taqi; her sister married her maternal cousin, and had one daughter [168] [169]

A teenage girl was considered ready for marriage. A suitable husband might have already been chosen by her parents when she was younger. Her prospects for marriage were linked to her family's wealth and position. The groom's parents asked her father and mother for her hand in marriage, and then the father negotiated a bride price. By strict Islamic law, this money was meant for the bride's needs, but in practice, it went to her family. The bride and groom spent little if any time together prior to the wedding day; often, the bride's face was revealed to the groom for the first time on that day. The wedding itself was to be announced publicly and celebrated as elaborately as the family could afford. Proper etiquette in gift exchanges and visits had to be followed in all phases of the preparation and performance of the marriage. This union was not just of a man and a woman but of two

---

[166] Mázandarání, 306.

[167] Momen, "Usuli, Akhbari, Shaykhi, Babi." 324.

[168] Mullah Mohammad Ali Qazvini (Nosratollah Mohammad Hoseini, *Hadrat-i-Tahirih* (Dundas, Ontario, Canada: Association for Bahá'í Studies in Persian, 2000), 155).

[169] Mázandarání, 311.

families mainly for the purpose of producing children, especially sons. The men and women celebrated in separate quarters. After the wedding, the young couple spent a few nights together and had to produce evidence of the girl's virginity to the groom's family.[170]

The new bride was then taken into her husband's home. She was expected to work with the other women of the household and, if there were more senior wives, she had to defer to them. The structure of the household was determined by religious law, and its head was the eldest male. He made all the important decisions and had to be obeyed by everyone under his roof. Each person in the household had a prescribed role—the men worked to provide for those in the home, and women took care of all the household duties. The two sexes were segregated throughout the day. Men from outside the family could never see the women of the household nor go into their quarters; poor families without much living space might just use some kind of curtain for the separation of the genders.

Tahirih's marital arrangements may well have followed this traditional pattern. But this union would be a very limiting one for her because her cousin was much more conventional and orthodox in his views than she turned out to be. A wife during this time was expected to conform to her husband's ideas and not take an active public role. Tahirih did just the opposite as she matured.

4.

Tahirih was now a part of her cousin's household. The couple moved to the city of Karbila in Iraq so that her husband could pursue his religious studies.[171] There they welcomed three children into the world.

---

[170] Massoume Price, "Iranian Marriage Ceremony, Its History & Symbolism," *Iran Chamber Society,* accessed September 21, 2013, www.iranchamber.com/culture/articles/iranian_marriage_ceremony.php.
[171] Abbas Amanat, "Qurrat al-'Ayn," in *Tahirih in history: Perspectives on Qurrat al 'Ayn from East and West,* ed. Sabir Afaqi (Los Angeles: Kalimat Press, 2004), 115.

Children stayed around the women and had no designated space of their own. The most decorated space in the house was the public room in which the men welcomed male visitors. The family itself gathered in the main room of the women's section. Most areas in the house were used for multiple purposes, and had carpets and pillows instead of sofas and chairs. A young mother had responsibilities such as organizing the different foods, cleaning, preparing meals, maintaining clothing, and educating children in proper manners. An essential aspect of hospitality was serving tea, so a samovar was always ready to dispense hot water. Servants and slaves did all of these tasks for wealthy families, while the women of the family supervised them.[172]

One of the most enjoyable activities for women was the trip to the bathhouse. In Tihran alone, there were over one hundred and forty bathhouses by the mid-19th century. In a bathhouse, a woman could relax, discuss her life, share ideas, hear news, tell stories, and get groomed. Entrance to the public bathhouse was free, so women of various social classes used them, except for the poorest women who could not afford to tip the bathhouse attendants. Five days of the week were reserved for men and two days—mornings only—were for women; men entered the bathhouse by the main street whereas the entrance for women was at the end of a lane.[173]

Women changed from inside to outside clothes for the trip to the bathhouse. A typical inside outfit consisted of wide trousers, a long transparent shirt open to the navel with a long-sleeved short jacket over it, and a bouffant skirt. There were many variations to this basic combination among urban women in the cities including the use of jewels, the elaborateness of the floral patterns of the materials, and the

---

[172] Shireen Mahdavi, "*THE QAJAR-PERIOD HOUSEHOLD.*" In the *Encyclopaedia Iranica*, edited by Ehsan Yarshater. Accessed November 11, 2013. http://www.iranicaonline.org/articles/qajars-period-household.

[173] W. Floor, W. Kleiss, "BATHHOUSES," in the *Encyclopaedia Iranica*, edited by Ehsan Yarshater, accessed October 1, 2013, http://www.iranicaonline.org/articles/bathhouses#pt1.

quality of the fabrics themselves. All women wore some form of head scarf out of modesty, and, in rural areas, this also kept a woman's hair clean. Rural women did not wear the face veil much for practical reasons—they did almost constant physical work, and a face veil was a real impediment. Over the course of the 19th century, the black body covering known as the *chador* became more common.

The wearing of veils was an ancient practice throughout the near East, possibly originating in ancient Mesopotamia or with the Assyrians and then picked up by the Persians as their empire extended over regions where women were veiled. The veil seems to have been used as a way of distinguishing women of high birth from slave women and prostitutes. When the Arabs conquered the Byzantine territories in the Middle East, they came into contact with the face veil and incorporated it into their own way of life. The veil did not originate with either Persia or Islam but rather in local tribal customs so there was a great deal of variation in its use throughout these regions. Though it became a sign of religious purity, it also served as a means of secluding and owning women.

Shi'a law and Qajar period practices did not allow women to initiate divorce, something which was not universally the case in the Muslim world and for which there was little Qur'anic basis. While some women did leave their husbands in this period, there were considerable obstacles to doing so. Women, for the most part, did not have an independent source of income and could not simply live on their own; they had to be a part of a household headed by a man to whom they were related. While women could get trapped in an unhappy marriage, a man had a religiously-sanctioned way of having relations with someone other than his wife—he could pay a cleric a fee to get permission to have a 'temporary marriage'. This practice was thinly justified by a particular interpretation of one Qur'anic chapter but actually predated Islam. 'Temporary' marriages were a reflection of women's inferior position in Qajar Persian culture and Shi'a law rather than a true expression of Qur'anic teaching on the correct moral behavior of men and women.[174]

In families of the nobility, the wives lived in harems, meaning as a group in a specifically designated set of rooms into which men were not allowed. This institution demonstrated the isolation of women from the outside world but its inner working showed how a woman could exercise influence. Several very capable women in the Qajar royal circles influenced public affairs through their intellectual and emotional dominance of their sons or husbands all while being completely isolated from public life.[175] At the royal level, a harem could consist of over a thousand people and had strict rules of etiquette and honor. The most important woman in the royal harem was the king's mother followed by his first wife. The wives came from a variety of backgrounds; many marriages were arranged to create alliances with powerful tribes and aristocratic families. While the wives could not interact directly with the rest of the palace complex—this was done through eunuchs—they did use outside connections to advance their own interests. In this way, the harem could be a center of political intrigue. This was especially true during the long reign of Nasir al-Din Shah, the monarch in our story, whose harem of over one hundred wives affected his reign at its most crucial moments.[176] His mother, most famously, had a great deal of influence over political affairs with which she sought to protect her son from potential rivals who might hinder his authority or, even worse, attempt to overthrow him. She was the best example of how Qajar aristocratic women could

---

[174] Shahla Haeri, "MOT'A," in the Encyclopaedia Iranica, edited by Ehsan Yarshater, accessed October 26, 2013,
http://www.iranicaonline.org/articles/mota.

[175] Muhammad Hasan Khan I'timad al-Saltanah, "Khayrat-i hisan," *Women's Worlds in Qajar Iran*, accessed November 7, 2103,
http://www.qajarwomen.org/en/items/901D4.html.

[176] Anna Vanzan, "Harem ii. in the Qajar period," in the Encyclopaedia Iranica, edited by Ehsan Yarshater, accessed November 11, 2013,
www.iranicaonline.org/articles/harem-ii.

wield power behind the scenes.[177] In one famous family photo, she is even seated higher than her son, the King.[178]

5.

To get to Karbila from Qazvin, Tahirih and her husband, Mulla Muhammad, crossed under the snowy peaks of the Zagros mountains which separated Persia from the Ottoman Empire—Iraq was a part of the Turkish Ottoman Empire at the time—and then down into the flat and hot Mesopotamian plain where Karbila sat between the Euphrates River to the east and the lake of salt to the west.

The city of Karbila was a place of profound spiritual importance for Muslims because the third Imam, Husayn, was buried there. In the Battle of Karbila, in 680 AD, Husayn and seventy of his companions were massacred by troops sent by the caliph whose authority he publicly rejected. Husayn became the most powerful symbol for Shi'a Muslims of devotion, sacrifice, and defiance against oppression. His martyrdom is commemorated every year by the Shi'a on the Day of Ashura with such great devotion that, in certain places, the faithful flagellate themselves in the street to honor the suffering of the Imam. This is a day of mourning for the Shi'a but, for the Sunni, it is a day to celebrate God's victory over the powers of the world in the form of Husayn's sacrifice. So venerated was the third Imam that the city of Karbila grew up around his golden-domed shrine because of the flocks of pilgrims who came there over the centuries—including many elderly people who wanted to die and be buried near his blessed tomb. Another golden domed shrine rose up in honor of his brother, Abbas, who also perished in the Battle of Karbila. Pilgrimages and the funeral business made Karbila a thriving and wealthy city which grew up all

---

[177] Abbas Amanat, *Pivot of the Universe* (London, UK: I. B. Tauris 2008), 172.
[178] Prof. Manoutchehr M. Eskandari-Qajar, "Mahd-e-Olia," Portraits of Qajar Women, accessed October 24, 2013, http://www.qajarpages.org/mahdeolia.html.

around these sacred sites in a maze of one to three story buildings of about thirty-thousand permanent residents.[179]

The young couple spent the next thirteen years in Karbila except for a stint in the holy city of Najaf to the south.[180] Tahirih gave birth to two sons, Ibrahim and Isma'il, in Karbila and a daughter, Zaynab, in Najaf.[181] But the future with her children was one of conflict and loss. As long as she remained a dutiful wife and did what was expected of her, there were no problems. Eventually, though, she was separated from her sons who remained under the influence of her husband. In time, they turned against their mother, becoming important orthodox mujtahids in their own right.[182] Despite this, when her sons were mentioned in future Shi'a biographies, they were designated by one of her titles 'al-Qurat ul-Ayn' not that of her husband—evidence of the great respect in which her learning had been held.[183]

During this period of her life, Tahirih took her first giant step outside of her role of obedient wife when she began reading the writings of Siyyid Kazim, the leader of the Shaykhis. The founder of the Shaykhi school, Shaykh Ahmad, had stayed in Qazvin for two years[184] back when she was a little girl, but her uncle, Taqi, had opposed him with such vehemence that there was no more discussion of his teachings within the family.[185] She may have first come into direct contact with Shaykhi writings when she happened on these in her cousin's

[179] Juan Cole and Moojan Momen, "Mafia, Mob and Shiism in Iraq: The Rebellion of Ottoman Karbala 1824-1843," *Past & Present* No 112 (1986): 112-143.

[180] Momen, "Usuli, Akhbari, Shaykhi, Babi," 328.

[181] Hoseini, 312; Mázandarání, 311; A few sources state that she gave birth to a fourth child, a son, after the couple returned to Qazvin (Momen, "Usuli, Akhbari, Shaykhi, Babi." 329.)

[182] Amanat, "Qurrat al-'Ayn." 148 f. 13.

[183] Momen, "Usuli, Akhbari, Shaykhi, Babi." 329.

[184] Ibid 326, f. 51.

[185] Ibid., 329.

library.[186] She studied these new ideas with the guidance of her paternal uncle, Mulla Ali, her mother, and relatives of her mothers.[187] In the years after the young family's return to Qazvin from Karbila, Tahirih became a devoted follower of the Shaykhi teaching.

Her marriage now became much more strained. She was willing to follow her beliefs whether her husband approved of them or not. He adhered to the orthodoxy of his father, Taqi, and completely opposed Shaykhism. Finally, Tahirih had to move out of their marital home and back in with her children into her father's house.

She decided to go and seek the Shaykhi master, Siyyid Kazim, in Karbila. She set off for the holy city with her sister, daughter, and others, while her husband kept their two sons with him in Qazvin.[188]

Tahirih had now leapt out into unknown territory following what mattered most to her: the search for truth and the belief that it would soon make itself manifest.

---

[186] Bahá'í sources don't state that she ever met Siyyid Kazim, so she may well not have discovered the Shaykhi writings until after her return from Karbila, otherwise she would have sought out Siyyid Kazim who was actively teaching in Karbila (Momen, *Usuli*, 329).

Several sources ('Abdu'l-Baha, *Memorials of the Faithful* (Wilmette, IL: Baha'i publishing Trust, 1971), 191; Zarandi, 55 f. 1) indicate she first came into contact with Shaykh Ahmad's writings in the library of her cousin, Mulla Javad Viliyani.

[187] According to Momen, "Usuli, Akhbari, Shaykhi, Babi." 329, she may have learned more about Shaykhi teachings from, among others, her maternal uncle, Mulla 'Abd al-Wahhab, and her maternal cousin, Mulla Javad Viliyani.

[188] Ibid.

THREE:
YEAR OF DISAPPOINTMENT, YEAR OF FULFILLMENT

1.

On May 24th, 1844, in the chambers of the Supreme Court in Washington, DC, Samuel F.B. Morse tapped out a question: "What hath God wrought?" Morse chose this quotation from the Bible because a woman with whom he was in love suggested it. Soon a reply was received from forty miles away. The simple, hobbled together machine had sent and received a message across a long distance in just a few seconds. The telegraph worked. The communication age had begun. This was one of those moments in history in which human ingenuity, opportunity, and means, all converged to open up—in the blink of an eye—worlds that had been previously inconceivable.

The industrial revolution of the 19th century overthrew the tyranny of distance with two inventions: the telegraph and the railroad.

The completion of the Transcontinental railroad in 1869 joined Iowa to California. Now a person could go from Nebraska to California in a matter of days for $65 in a sleeper car which led to the rapid settlement of the interior of the country.[189]

The struggling American rural republic of the early 1800s–only Philadelphia and New York City had populations of more than 25,000 people[190]—became an industrial superpower during the 1800s. Its territory increased four-hundred percent from roughly 1,000,000

---

[189] Richard White, *Railroaded: The Transcontinentals and the Making of Modern America* (NY, NY: W.W. Norton & Company, 2012).

[190] J. Ellis, "The Growth of the United States During the 19th Century," *The Free Resource,* accessed September 23, 2013,

http://www.thefreeresource.com/american-history-the-growth-of-the-united-states-during-the-19th-century/.

square miles[191] to almost four million,[192] and its population grew ten-fold from seven million people in 1810, to seventy million by 1890.

With industrialization came urbanization: cities grew rapidly. John D. Rockefeller began life on a farm in rural upstate New York and wound up living in New York City. He became the richest man in America after founding and cornering the market of the new oil industry. Henry Ford was born into the rural world of the family farm and went on to found the automobile industry. He invented the first mass marketed car, the Model T, but had intended it for the rural market, promoting it with the line, "stronger than a horse and easier to take care of."

The demographic face of America of 1900 was unrecognizable from the more uniform and clearly drawn one of a hundred years earlier. The American social fabric was profoundly changed by the destruction of the native peoples, the emergence of African-Americans from slavery into a nominal citizenship, and the arrival, in huge numbers, of immigrants from Europe in the late part of the century; Polish farmers came to the steel mills of Pittsburgh, Serbians to the meat-packing companies in Chicago, and Slovaks to the car assembly plants in Detroit, among many other ethnic groups.[193]

The nation's energetic, even frenetic, pace of growth caused society to be in a constant state of significant change which brought both great opportunity and great anxiety. Many Christians came to believe that they were living close to the end of time when prophecies would be fulfilled with Jesus returning to judge the living and the dead. The Shakers, who believed that their Mother Ann Lee had fulfilled the

---

[191] "US Territorial Acquisitions," *United States History,* accessed 6, 2013, http://www.u-s-history.com/pages/h1049.html.

[192] Franklin K Van Zandt, "Expansion and growth of the United States," *USGS Publications Warehouse,* accessed October 2, 2013, http://pubs.usgs.gov/pp/0909/report.pdf.

[193] "Growth of Cities," *The First Measured Century,* accessed November 1, 2103, http://www.pbs.org/fmc/timeline/ecities.htm.

Second Coming, experienced a decade of visions and revival beginning in 1837.

Joseph Smith founded an indigenous form of Christianity after having a series of visions by which he came to believe that there had been an ancient Judeo-Christian civilization in America to which Jesus had preached after his Resurrection. He claimed to have found tablets recounting this lost history of Jesus Christ buried in the ground of upstate New York, in the 'burned-over' district, which he published as the *Book of Mormon.* The church he founded—which also sought a purer, 'restored' form of Christianity and saw itself as living in the 'Latter-Day'—spread rapidly and showed remarkable resilience and sustainability even in the face of violent persecution. He was killed in a skirmish in 1844, but the movement survived him—to grow and prosper under a new leader, Brigham Young.

The year 1844 was also important for a farmer in New York State who believed the time of the Second Coming had arrived: William Miller. After his personal conversion during the Great Awakening, Miller read and studied assiduously the time prophecies in the Bible for two years. He took the position that the Bible was internally consistent and, therefore, could be used reliably. Applying passages from the Book of Numbers and Ezekiel that a Biblical day was a year, he was thunderstruck by his discovery: Jesus was coming back in 1843-1844. Right then, he knew that he was being called to preach the coming Return. On the first Sunday of August, 1831, Miller, a simple farmer, clambered up to the pulpit for the first time, determined to call people to repentance in anticipation of the coming return of their Lord.

2.

On March 21st, 1844, William Miller looked out of his window. All he saw were clouds, trees, and blue spaces. The sky was empty.

March 21st was the Spring Equinox, the last day of the year 1843-44, during which Miller had predicted the return of the Son of God. Now, the year had ended, but it was the same old world that kept turning...the wind kept blowing...people continued going about their business...

A few days later, he wrote:

> "I am now seated at my old desk in my east room. Having obtained help of God until the present time, I am still look-ing for the Dear Savior...This time, as I have calculated it, is now filled up; and I expect every moment to see the Savior descend from heaven. I have now nothing to look for but this glorious hope...I hope I have cleansed my garments from the blood of souls. I feel that, as far as it was in my power, I have freed myself from all guilt in their condemna-tion...If God has anything more for me to do in his vine-yard, he will give me strength, open the door, and enable me to do whatever may be his will, for his glory and the best good of man."[194]

Miller had written a detailed chart of biblical prophecy for use in his preaching indicating the end times, but he had always been reluctant to give an exact date for Christ's return. He and the older Millerites believed that it was the *times* which were being revealed not a specific date or hour. He preferred to describe the time as "about the year 1843." and qualify all of his statements with "if there were no mistake in my calculation."[195] Miller was a humble man by nature. His follow-ers, though, increasingly pushed him to be more specific. At the 1842 annual general Conference of the Millerites, held each year in Boston since 1840,[196] the issue of the exact time of Christ's return came into prominence because they agreed that the time prophecies of the Old

---

[194] George R. Knight, *Millenial Fever and the End of the World* (Boise, Idaho: Pacific Press Pub. Association, 1993), 162.
[195] Knight, 126-7.
[196] Ibid., 85.

Testament clearly had an end point.[197] Miller concluded that Christ would return sometime in the Jewish year, March 21st, 1843-March 21st, 1844,[198] and he announced this in the January 1st, 1843, edition of the *Sign of the Times*, an Adventist publication.

The year 1843 opened with a great increase in the anticipatory fervor for the Second Coming.[199] The Adventist newsletter, the *Midnight Cry*, changed its subscription schedule to three month intervals, "if time should last".[200] Such was the interest that a talk by William Miller drew thousands in Washington DC, and another "convulsed" Philadelphia.[201] A comet crossed the sky in February and grew to its brightest degree in March,[202] seizing many with wonder about the meaning of the sign they were seeing in the heavens.

The Adventist leaders tended to have a more rationalist outlook and did not give too much credence to signs like a comet. Instead, they began a great push at the general Conference of May, 1843, to take Adventism west to Ohio, Iowa, and Missouri—the Western frontier of the United States in 1843 was the Mississippi River—and south. The South was not as receptive to the Adventist message as its leaders defended the status quo in the face in all reforms—especially abolition—and other forms of change. New periodicals were published in the Western cities. Soon Adventism was known throughout Britain and reached Norway and the Sandwich Islands by the summer.[203]

---

[197] Ibid., 128; David L. Rowe, *God's Strange Work, William Miller and the End of the World* (Grand Rapids, MI: Wm. B. Eerdman's Publishing Company, 2008), 176.

[198] Rowe, 176.

[199] Knight, 126-7.

[200] Ibid., 130.

[201] Ibid., 131.

[202] Donald K. Yeomans, "Great Comets in History," Jet Propulsion Laboratory/California Institute of Technology, accessed October 25, 2013, ssd.jpl.nasa.gov/?great_comets.

[203] Knight, 130-137.

Joshua Vaughn Himes, pastor of the Chardon Street Chapel in Boston, turned Adventism into a mass movement. He had been transformed after hearing Miller's preaching and asked him about spreading these teachings. Miller responded: "What can an old farmer do? I was never used to public speaking; I stand alone...."[204] Hines went into high-gear promoting these millennial teachings, and through his efforts, Adventism reached large audiences well beyond its original geographical region and attracted many new converts.[205]

This gathering excitement brought on a backlash. William Lloyd Garrison, the great abolitionist, was amazed that an uneducated man like Miller could convince such large multitudes but concluded that the "delusion has not long to run...let us rejoice." In early March, almost an entire edition of the *Tribune* of New York, the most influential paper in the country, published by Horace Greeley, a social reformer and abolitionist, was given over to refuting the claims of Miller.[206] The Hartford-based *Universalist*, called Millerites "deluded," "ridiculous," "fanatical," and "coarse."[207] The great evangelist Charles Finney reached out to Miller to try to dissuade him from his ideas. Joseph Smith, the prophet of Mormonism, expressed great surprise that some of his followers were drawn to Millerism. John Humphrey Noyes, the famous utopian socialist, described those among his followers who were attracted to Millerism as weak like "weathercocks" in a "popular tempest." Moses Stuart, a leading Biblical scholar, made fun of Miller by suggesting that April 1st was a day better suited to Miller's predictions.[208]

Mockery of Miller abounded. In a print ad, one of his mottos, "the time has come," appeared with angels flying around it, while a product, Wild Cherry medicine, was featured below these words. One

---

[204] Rowe, 159.

[205] Ibid., 158-165.

[206] Knight, 138.

[207] Ibid., 142.

[208] Ibid., 138-40.

cartoon showed Miller so busy preaching that he had forgotten to prepare himself for the end, and he is saying, "I had no idea it would be so hot." The use of 'ascension robes'—clothing owned by some Millerites to be worn on the day of Christ's Return—were lampooned with one article saying that if Adventist predictions were off by a thousand years, the robes could not be returned. Publications also described the movement as a folly in which people sold their property, gave up their wealth and circulated stories of followers wandering in the rain in their ascension robes, sitting alone in the woods, or standing on a wood pile looking for the Lord. Adventism was compared to yellow fever and came to be seen popularly as a form of insanity.[209]

With every passing day of 1843, the Adventist message became more strident in its challenge to Christians. A new generation of more aggressive Adventist preachers saw churches that rejected the imminent return of Christ as apostates, while hostility toward Adventism caused churches to distance themselves from Miller or actively reject his teachings. They stepped up their attacks on Adventist leaders by accusing them of lining their pockets with the contributions of believers while showing that they did not truly expect the end by the conduct of their lives. Miller himself was criticized for building a stone wall around his house which was unnecessary if the time of the end was at hand. Churches refused to allow Adventist preaching, dismissed preachers who had developed Adventist sympathies or, even worse, declared them to be heretics and threw them out of their congregations. Ministers who didn't renounce Adventism were "the few recalcitrant offenders...[who]...went on from bad to worse, till, like wandering stars, they disappeared in darkness." By the summer of 1843, the split between Adventism and established churches was becoming clear as leading Adventist preachers such as Rev. Fitch compared the churches which rejected Adventism to the "harlots" and "antichrists" of the Bible.[210]

---

[209] Ibid., 140-5.
[210] Ibid., 151-8.

The mockery, the attacks and criticisms, and, most of all, the condemnation from churches hurt Miller deeply. He had always seen himself as a Bible-centered Christian who wanted Christian fellowship for all and did not see his teaching as a new movement or the cause of separation and disunity.[211]

He grew increasingly ill. Miller preached away from home from October to March 1843.[212] By the summer, though, Miller's exhaustive efforts to raise the call of Christ's imminent return had taken their toll. He was sixty-one, his body shook with palsy and swelled with fluid, while rashes and boils burst out on his skin. In March, he collapsed with another attack of skin disease and had to be brought home in a wagon bed. The solitude and safety of his farm must have felt good to him. To his joy, his family and he gathered in the home and sang hymns and, soon, his children accepted his teachings and even became his travelling companions.

By October of 1843, Miller was well enough to rise up again and preach the coming end. In public, he appeared as an elderly squat farmer with a slight shake, and spoke in plain language like "a workman who needeth not be ashamed," ambling easily through the Scripture to unfold his points, gradually drawing his audience in. His preaching had become even more powerful with time, and people longed to hear him. He had become the genuinely-loved patriarch of the great movement he had launched.[213]

Looking up at the empty sky on March 21st, 1844, Miller knew he had done all he could do. God had not made Himself known. Miller's habitual self-doubt overcame him. The mainstream churches had rejected the message. He gave up an anguished cry; his friend tried to reassure him that God would "manage his own cause in his own way."[214]

---

[211] Rowe, 177-78.
[212] Ibid., 169.
[213] Ibid., 169-74.
[214] Ibid., 185.

As March disappeared into April, William Miller still held on to his faith:

> "I now am looking every day and hour for Christ to come, my time is full, the end of days are come, and at the end the vision shall speak and will not lie."[215]

3.

A few weeks after William Miller's great disappointment at seeing an empty sky, a young Muslim cleric in faraway Persia with the same deep spiritual yearning, walked towards the gate of the city of Shiraz. His spiritual teacher, Siyyid Kazim, the leader of the Shaykhis, a movement that interpreted Qur'anic prophecy about the end times in allegorical rather than literal terms, had passed away. Siyyid Kazim had taught him that God would make himself known through the return of a 'rightly guided one' who would arise to purify Islam and that they, the Shaykhis, whose allegorical interpretation of the Qur'an told them that time had come, must go out and seek him.

After his teacher's passing, this young cleric, Mulla Husayn, had secluded himself in the Great Mosque at Kufa, south of Baghdad, one of the oldest mosques in the Islamic world. His teacher had told him that he had to purify himself before beginning his quest. Though many of his fellow disciples were ignoring their teacher's command, Mulla Husayn was faithful to it. So he had prayed and fasted for forty days and forty nights, and when he was ready, he arose and went out on his search.

Mulla Husayn's prayers led him out of the holy city of Kufa, south by caravan to the Persian Gulf, east by boat to Persia, and then overland to his destination—Shiraz, the ancient city of poets and gardens. To enter Shiraz in those days, one had to pass through a gate, a beautiful large structure where people met up with one another. He and his companions carried with them no possessions except the same

---

[215] Ibid.

strong faith that drove William Miller forward. These were times of
revelation, and he believed he was about to see God's will in the world.

Mulla Husayn arrived in Shiraz on a hot and sunny afternoon. He
sent his companions ahead to find lodging. Then a young man walked
up to him and greeted him with great warmth. The gentle manner and
refined appearance of this young man astonished Mulla Husayn. He
wore a green turban which indicated that he was a siyyid, a descendant
of the prophet Muhammad. His name was Siyyid Ali Muhammad.
Mulla Husayn thought to himself that this young man must be one of
his fellow Shaykhis who had come out to greet him. Siyyid Ali Muhammad invited him to his home for dinner. Evening was approaching. He told Mulla Husayn not to worry about his companions who
had gone ahead: "Commit them to the care of God; He will surely
protect and watch over them."

Mulla Husayn followed the young Siyyid Ali Muhammad to his
house:

> "We soon found ourselves standing at the gate of a house of
> modest appearance. He knocked at the door, which was soon
> opened by an Ethiopian servant. "Enter therein in peace, se-
> cure" were His words as He crossed the threshold and mo-
> tioned me to follow Him. His invitation, uttered with power
> and majesty, penetrated my soul."

The two stepped into the refreshing little courtyard of the traditional
two-story Persian home and climbed up the stairs to the upper room.
There they prayed and began their discussion. Siyyid Ali Muhammad
asked Mulla Husayn about his quest. Mulla Husayn responded that
his teacher had told him to go forth and seek the Promised One of the
age. When he told the young Siyyid the signs of the person of the
Promised One, Siyyid Ali Muhammad said: "Behold, all these signs
are manifest in Me."

Shocked by this answer, Mulla Husayn thought about arguments as
to why this was impossible. He presented a theological essay he had
written and used it to test this young man. Siyyid Ali Muhammad

briefly looked over Mulla Husayn's complex and intricate points about the 'Promised One' in scripture. Then the young man revealed the hidden, deeper meanings which Mulla Husayn had neither seen nor understood in the sacred text. Siyyid Ali Muhammad's insights were completely original, and his words contained great power and authority. Soon, out of the blue, he offered to write a commentary on the Qur'anic chapter about Joseph, the son of Jacob. Mulla Husayn was stunned by this offer because his teacher had told him that only the Promised One would be capable of doing this. The words flowed effortlessly from Siyyid Ali Muhammad's mouth and pen:

> "The overpowering effect of the manner in which He wrote was heightened by the gentle intonation of His voice which accompanied His writing. Not for one moment did He interrupt the flow of the verses which streamed from His pen....I sat enraptured by the magic of His voice and the sweeping force of His revelation."

Mulla Husayn knew that he had found the object of his quest: the Promised One of God, the Renewer of the world. Siyyid Ali Muhammad proclaimed to him:

> "O thou who art the first to believe in Me! Verily I say, I am the Báb, the Gate of God, and thou art the Bábu'l-Báb, the gate of that Gate. Eighteen souls must, in the beginning, spontaneously and of their own accord, accept Me, and recognize the truth of My Revelation. Unwarned and uninvited, each of these must seek independently to find Me. And when their number is complete, one of them must needs be chosen to accompany Me on My pilgrimage to Mecca and Medina. There I shall deliver the Message of God to the <u>Sh</u>arif of Mecca. I then shall return to Kúfih, where again, in the Masjid of that holy city, I shall manifest His Cause. It is incum-

bent upon you not to divulge, either to your companions or to any other soul, that which you have seen and heard…."[216]

Mulla Husayn remembered that the revelation hit him like a "thunderbolt"; he was "blinded and overwhelmed":

> "…the knowledge of His Revelation had galvanized my being. I felt possessed of such courage and power that were the world, all its peoples and its potentates, to rise against me, I would, alone and undaunted, withstand their onslaught. The universe seemed but a handful of dust in my grasp. I seemed to be the voice of Gabriel personified, calling unto all mankind: 'Awake, for, lo! the morning Light has broken. Arise, for His Cause is made manifest. The portal of His grace is open wide; enter therein, O peoples of the world! For He Who is your Promised One is come!'"[217]

At dawn, May 23rd, 1844, (1260 AH), two months after William Miller's 'Great Disappointment', Mulla Husayn stepped back out into the street, a man transfigured by "a sense of gladness and strength."

Over the summer of 1844, one seeker after another like him found Siyyid Ali Muhammad, who came to be called the 'Bab', meaning the 'gate'. Most believed that the Bab was claiming to be the gate to the Hidden Imam but they came to see over the years that he was claiming to be both a new Divine manifestation and the precursor of a second major revelation. He was the 'gate' to the Divine world from which new revelation flowed.

The Bab taught that God made Himself known through His Primal Will, like the "Word" in the Gospel of John, and the creative Will described by Shaykh Ahmad, the founder of the Shaykhis. The symbol

---

[216] The above quotations and information are taken from Zarandi, 39-45.
[217] Ibid., 65.

of that Will was a woman, the Maid of Heaven. The Bab wrote: "I am the Maid of Heaven begotten by the Spirit of Bahá."[218]

In the new laws the Bab set forth for his followers, he provided for greater protections for women than had previously existed. He made divorce more difficult by requiring a twelve-month delay and ordered men not to harm women but, rather, to treat them with respect. He also allowed for greater social interaction between men and women. In some cases, his laws gave preference to women such as doubling the penalty for causing grief to a person when that person is a woman, and exempting women from the obligation of pilgrimage if fulfilling this required a dangerous journey.[219]

Now, his message was taken up by the extraordinary woman, Tahirih of Qazvin, who soon emerged as one of his foremost disciples and ablest teachers. Her search for truth had led her to the writings of the Shaykhi masters whose non-literal reading of the Qur'an told them that the time of the fulfillment of Islam was imminent. Her journey down this independent path brought her into direct conflict with the men in her family and the male clerical establishment.

By 1844, Tahirih was living in Karbila; this holy city and others in Iraq contained the sacred remains of some of the most important Imams of Shi'a Islam and was a frequent destination for Persian pilgrims.

She had come there hoping to study with the Shaykhi leader, Siyyid Kazim, having become convinced from his writings that the appearance of the Promised One of Islam was imminent. Her sister, daughter, and brother-in-law—who by then was a follower of Siyyid Kazim as well—, were all with her.[220]

---

[218] The Bab, quoted in Moojan Momen, "WOMEN iv. in the works of the Bab and in the Babi Movement," in the *Encyclopaedia Iranica,* edited by Ehsan Yarshater, accessed November 13, 2013, http://www.iranicaonline.org/articles/women-babi.

[219] Momen, "*WOMEN*".

[220] Mázandaráni, 313. According to Momen, "Usuli, Akhbari, Shaykhi, Babi." 329, her daughter

Tahirih's father had hoped that by going on such a pilgrimage, his daughter would give up her interest in these Shaykhi ideas which were causing such divisions within the family. But his visionary daughter could not be cowed by the men in her family into denying her conscience or restricting her spirit. In Karbila, she continued to study the Shaykhi texts, to correspond with Shaykhi leaders, and to teach others. This last act was most unusual because the teaching of religion had always been the prerogative of men. Had she been a man, her knowledge would have qualified her to be a mujtahid.[221]

By this point, her husband, humiliated by having such a strong and iconoclastic wife, harbored a great anger towards her. But it was her father-in-law, Mulla Taqi, who was the most venomous critic of the Shaykhi doctrines and his daughter-in-law's[222] involvement in promoting them. Though her father, Mulla Salih, did not approve of her behavior, he also objected to Mulla Taqi's tirades against the Shaykhis. After all, the Shaykhi leaders were all distinguished Muslim scholars. With the rift in the family widening, Tahirih moved out of her marital home and back into her father's house.[223] The cost of this break from her husband was the loss of a direct relationship with her sons. Her contact with them would forever be limited, and her husband would poison them against her.

The proclamation of the new day had become her calling.[224] In this ghazal, a form of lyric poetry traditionally used to express the pain and

---

was there as well.

[221] Amanat, "Qurrat al-'Ayn." 116; Hosseiny, *Hadrat-i-Tahirih*, 313, states that she received a license to teach Islam.

[222] Tahirih was both Taqi's niece and his daughter-in-law as she had married his son and was the daughter of his brother. Because of the primacy of the male in marriage, we will refer to her as his daughter-in-law.

[223] Ibid.

[224] Hatcher and Hemmat, 41-2; Amin Banani and Jascha Kessler trans., Anthony Lee, ed., *Tahirih: A portrait in poetry* (LA, CA: Kalimat Press, 2004), 124.

beauty of love and characterized by a melancholic mood, she proclaims the arrival of the new day instead, in joyous terms:[225]

> "Wake up, sleeper! Your lover's come for you!
> Rouse yourself, brush those cobwebs from your hair
>
> Gentle Love is here, and brings you kindness
> Miserable lover, your Love stands near
>
> Comfort awaits at the side of your bed
> Sit up, throw off your grief—not one more tear!
>
> Suffering, separate, lying there cold,
> embrace your lover, who loves without fear
>
> Wan and wasted, starved to death by the Fall,
> Get up! Get up! At last the Spring is here
>
> Our time's renewed, for life is always new
> Rise! Rise up! You corpse of that old, dead year!"[226]

Siyyid Kazim had passed away at the beginning of 1844, a short time before Tahirih arrived in Karbila.[227] His widow became totally devoted to her and invited her to stay in their home; the widow's love for her aroused the interest of other women.[228]

Soon she was giving classes in Siyyid Kazim's widow's home that attracted both men and women who wanted to hear the words of this most extraordinary woman.[229] Her reputation as a spiritual visionary spread through the personal networks of the women who attended her

---

[225] Banani and Kessler, 124.

[226] Ibid., 75.

[227] 'Abdu'l-Baha, *Memorials of the Faithful*, 192; Root, *Táhirih the pure*, 56.

[228] Zarandi, 193.

[229] Mázandarání, 313.

classes. When men came, she spoke from behind a curtain so as to conform to the cultural norms of propriety between men and women.

The Shaykhis, though, were divided in their purpose and did not have Tahirih's resolve. Shaykhism had begun as a movement which taught that the day of fulfillment was imminent, but it had now become a separate 'school' of thought among other such schools within Islam. This had not been the goal of its founders who had told their disciples to actively seek the Promised One.[230] With their passing the movement foundered as its adherents wavered in this mission. Tahirih was one of those disciples who actively sought the Promised One and did not want to spend her time in theological speculation. The day of God was an imminent reality for her, not an intellectual idol.

In the wake of Siyyid Kazim's passing in early 1844, a few of his disciples obeyed his instructions and began their search. Among these was Tahirih's brother-in-law, Mulla Muhammad Ali Qazvini. She gave him a letter written by her addressed to the Promised One. If her brother-in-law succeeded in finding him, he should give him the letter[231] and:

> "Say to Him, from me, the effulgence of Thy face flashed forth, and the rays of Thy visage rose high. Then speak the word, "Am I not your Lord?" and "Thou art, Thou art!" we will all reply."[232]

One night in the summer of 1844, Tahirih had a dream[233] in which she saw a young Siyyid—a male descendant of the Prophet Muhammad— dressed in black with a green turban, and his hands raised up in prayer.[234] The words he spoke stayed with her. Around the same time, her brother-in-law found the goal of his quest. He became a

---

[230] 'Abdu'l-Baha, *Memorials of the Faithful*, 192.

[231] Balyuzi, *The Bab*, 26; Hoseini, 314; Mázandarání, 314.

[232] Mázandarání, 314; Zarandi, 56.

[233] 'Abdu'l-Baha, *Memorials of the Faithful*, 190.

[234] Ibid.

believer in the Bab and gave him Tahirih's letter. The Bab immediately declared her to be one of his apostles as he did with two of her brothers-in-law. He gave them the title of "Letters of the Living."[235] meaning his chief disciples who would carry his message out to the people and of whom there would be eighteen. He was the Primal Point from which all came into being, and they were the Letters that originated from that Point. The Bab and the eighteen 'Letters' made nineteen, a 'vahid', or unity, signifying the unity of God; it is also the numerical value of the opening invocation of the Qur'an. This term was entirely new with the religion of the Bab.[236]

Though Tahirih never actually met the Bab in person, what confirmed her faith was reading a copy of the text revealed by him on the night of his declaration to Mulla Husayn which was brought to her by another of the Bab's Letters of the Living.[237] Tahirih recognized immediately that this commentary on the Qur'anic chapter about Joseph contained the very same words she had heard in her dream. She was now certain she had found the object of her spiritual search—the Promised One of the age as foretold by her Shaykhi spiritual teachers.[238]

---

[235] Tahirih's brothers-in-law, Mirza Muhammad Ali Qazvini and Mirza Hadi Qazvini, sons of Haji Mirza Abdu'l-Vahhab, her father-in-law/uncle, and Taqi's main rival in Qazvin, were Letters of the Living (H. M. Balyuzi, *The Bab*, (Oxford, UK: George Ronald, 1973), 26-7; Nabíl-i-Zarandi, *The Dawn-Breakers*, Translated by Shoghi Effendi, (London, UK: Bahá'í Publishing Trust, 1953), 55)

[236] The Editors, "Letters of the Living (*Huruf-i-Hayy*)," in the *Baha'i Encyclopedia Project*, edited by L. Bucknell, B. Fisher, F. Kazemzadeh, T. Lawson, H. Moayyad, G. Morrison, S. Quinn, M. Schweitz, R. Stockman, W. van den Hoonaard, accessed June 6, 2015 http://www.bahai-encyclopedia-project.org/.

[237] Mulla Ali Bastami (Balyuzi, *The Bab*, 58); the text was the "Ahsanu'l-Qisas" ("The Best of Stories") the commentary on the Surih of Joseph revealed by the Bab ('Abdu'l-Baha, *Memorials of the Faithful* (Wilmette, IL: Baha'i publishing Trust, 1971), 191)

[238] 'Abdu'l-Baha, *Memorials of the Faithful*, 193.

In this poem, she expresses the deep longing for nearness to God which drove her to become a seeker.[239] On another level of meaning, the poem below expresses her belief in the oneness of religion. The unusual form of this poem, a rondo in five stanzas, is uncommon in Persian poetry and imitative of a famous earlier Persian poem by Hafez in which a Muslim debates a Christian nun about the Church's Doctrine of the Trinity. The Muslim hears great church bells ringing and the Christians chanting the Islamic profession of faith in God and Muhammad. He decides that this belief in the absolute unity of God—not the mysterious division of God into three—is the true path. Christ and Muhammad's message is one. The seeker and God are one. The self is gone.[240]

> "Now from those locks must all my madness hang
> Your ruby lips have taught me love's sweet pang
> From head to toe your love about me sang
> Cut off from you, how loud my weeping rang
> I'm lost. You have destroyed my place
>
> Although you brought me sad adversity
> and I drank my cup of calumny,
> my soul burns in its frozen cavity,
> my heart lives on, that died in misery
> Your lips are my Messiah's grace
>
> You guard the vault where I am its treasure
> You keep the mine where I am its silver
> I am the seed, and you are the sower
> But whose body is this, if you're its owner?
>   What's this soul? You have filled its place

---

[239] Hatcher and Hemmat, *The Poetry of Tahirih*, 69.
[240] Banani and Kessler, *Tahirih, A portrait in poetry*, 138-9.

Your love has made of me a speck of dust
One single cup of wine—I'm drunk with lust
Since I have seized and hold your locks in trust:
Myself I praise—You I praise—I praise us!
   I lie lost in my arms' embrace

If my heart is yours, why would you tear it?
And if not yours, why should you impair it?
With each breath you feed the flame in it,
consuming what remains of me in it
   Make it your joyful dwelling-place!

When your love's fire grew incandescent,
Being and Having burnt from my essence
Heathen and Muslim from my heart were sent
Prostrate, I lie beneath your eyebrow's tent
   The very Ka'aba is my place

When the divine feather wrote upon the page
and pen kissed paper in love's knowledge,
when Nothingness heard not Being's homage
and His breath blew over Adam's image,
   my heart felt even then love's trace

When the divine hand molded Adam's clay,
your love sowed its seed in my breast that day,
your love became my foreknown, fated away
Not hell, not heaven can lead me astray
   You alone are whom I embrace

I am eternal, yet destroyed in mind
From this good cup I sip a lordly wine
In the valley of doubt I'm burnt to brine

A wanderer, to exile's wastes confined
	What may befall me in disgrace?

Since that day my heart cried out, *Behold Me!*
and I stepped in that street for all to see,
gadding about, a shameless debauchee,
He was all myself, all myself was he—
	His jewel set in my heart's palace

In the dust of my Ka'aba you now dwell
Your face lights the dark world with its dazzle
The waves of your hair my soul's manacle
The arch of your eyebrows my heart's idol
	Your locks my cross in sacred space

I'm the captive of his high holiness
I love his lovely heart's expressiveness
I walk through the valley of my madness
wanting no other but you to caress
	Love fills me with your sweet embrace

Then how much longer must I be restrained,
My feigned indifference to you still maintained?
How long must agitation be contained?
A prudish piety, how long ordained?
	My wares banned from the marketplace?

I'll drop my robe, my prayer mat I'll discard,
drink till I'm drunk, and none of them regard
My passion will fill their house, roof to yard
Mt. Sinai's flame grows bright, for I'm its bard
	By the tavern gate, there's my place!

Love's flag flies above my devastation
At Love's gate stands his annunciation
Truth brims my cup with intoxication
Estranged from myself, from every nation
      God bids run this noble race

The tavern's servant served us at the feast
Red wine was poured and poured and never ceased,
until the wine grew drunk and went to yeast
And all were turned to dust, even the least,
      Fermented by my wine's embrace

Night and day have we heard Love's voice proclaim:
It's Love that calls each being by its name
Whoever wants to make our way his aim
shall find that suffering's waves are not tame,
      nor will the shore give his foot place

I am the slave on your roof keeping time,
I am the frightened bird snared by your lime,
the nightingale silent in your night-time,
the axis that stands for your name, Sublime
Not I, not we—That agony's erased!"[241]

Tahirih set about translating the Bab's writings from Arabic into Persian for dissemination.[242] She saw it as her duty to teach others about the Bab's message and to remove any doubts about his claims. This poem reflects the belief that God reveals himself over time in ever greater degrees, and that those with insight must try to help others develop their inner vision such that they can see God in whatever form He makes himself manifest.[243] It is written in the form of a masnavi, a

---

[241] Ibid., 102-105.
[242] 'Abdu'l-Baha, *Memorials of the Faithful*, 193.
[243] Hatcher and Hemmat, *The Poetry of Tahirih*, 40.

Persian form of poetry in rhyming couplets used to express heroic, historical, and romantic themes. In this one, she extolls the qualities of the Bab such as 'beauty' and 'glory'.[244] The human presence of God leads us to His Divine Presence. His Beauty leads us to His Glory.[245]

> "He's come! He's here to tear our veils away
> He's here! He's come to show us God today
>
> Yet masters of the mind refuse to hear
> and heaven's song is wasted on their ear
>
> He's come to bring us life beyond all praise
> He lights this world: his voice is heaven's blaze
>
> Its fire burns our world with wild delight
> Stripped bare we stand we're made of purest light!
>
> Lift the veil, Tahirih! He's now exposed!
> His hidden mystery has been disclosed!
>
> And say: The Lord in glowing clothes is dressed!
> Praised be his beauty, and forever blessed!"[246]

4.

In October of 1844, a shop owner tacked up this sign on his store in Philadelphia:

> "This shop is closed in honor of the King of kings, who will appear about the 20th of October. Get ready, friends, to crown him Lord of all."[247]

---

[244] Banani and Kessler, *Tahirih, A portrait in poetry*, 112-3.
[245] Hatcher and Hemmat, *The Poetry of Tahirih*, 40, 152-3.
[246] Banani and Kessler, *Tahirih, A portrait in poetry*, 51.
[247] Knight, *Millenial Fever,* 208.

Six months earlier, in the spring of 1844, when Mulla Husayn and others found the Bab, and Tahirih was still seeking him, there had been a great a disappointment among the Millerites because Jesus Christ had not returned in the way they had expected. But in the early summer of 1844, Adventist preaching had picked up again because William Miller and his fellow Millerites remained committed to preparing souls for the return of Christ despite the spring disappointment.

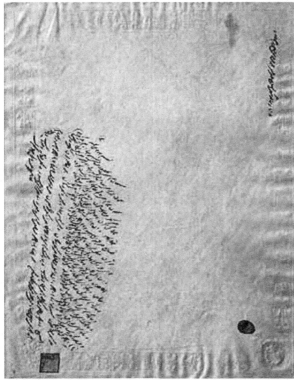

The Bab's Tablet to the Seventeenth letter of the living.

By late summer, 1844, eighteen individuals had become apostles of the Bab—Letters of the Living—while, at the same time, a powerful new spirit infused the Adventist movement with renewed hope.

At a late summer Adventist camp meeting in Exeter, New Hampshire, a preacher was going over the traditional Adventist teaching, but the crowd had no energy. It was hearing the same arguments that had been made before the spring disappointment. Then a woman in the audience interrupted the preacher and called for Samuel Snow to go up onto the platform to deliver a new message. Snow went up and claimed that Christ's actual date of return was October 22, 1844.[248]

His argument was based on familiar texts, but he had interpreted them differently. At the core of Adventist Biblical preaching was this parable of the Ten Virgins from the Gospel of Mathew which Snow used to make sense of the times they were living through:

> "At that time the kingdom of heaven will be like ten virgins who took their lamps and went out to meet the bridegroom. Five of them were foolish and five were wise. The foolish ones took their lamps but did not take any oil with them. The wise ones, however, took oil in jars along with their lamps. The bridegroom was a long time in coming, and they all became drowsy and fell asleep. At midnight the cry rang out: 'Here's the bridegroom! Come out to meet him!' Then all the virgins woke up and trimmed their lamps. The foolish ones said to the wise, 'Give us some of your oil; our lamps are going out.' 'No,' they replied, 'there may not be enough for both us and you. Instead, go to those who sell oil and buy some for yourselves.' But while they were on their way to buy the oil, the bridegroom arrived. The virgins who were ready went in with him to the wedding banquet. And the door was shut. Later the others also came. 'Lord, Lord,' they said, 'open the door for us!' But he replied, 'Truly I tell you, I don't know you.' Therefore keep watch, because you do not know the day or the hour."[249]

Snow used this parable to show that they were living in a 'tarrying time', a time of waiting, like the virgins who had fallen asleep. The tarrying time could last no longer than half a year because a prophetic day in the Bible counted as a year, and the virgins tarried for half a

---

[248] Rowe, *God's Strange Work*, 186.
[249] Matthew 25: 1-13 (New International Version).

day. This new date of October 20th, 1844, was the "midnight cry" that woke the virgins up.

Snow and others had arrived at this date by looking at the first century Jewish calendar and using it as a comparison to the modern times. In the traditional Jewish religious calendar, the High Priest blessed the believers on the Day of Atonement, the 10th day of the 7th month of the Jewish year, which fell on October 22nd. If Jesus is compared to the high priest then his appearance—itself a blessing to the faithful—would be on October 22nd. The year 1844 was the one predicted by Daniel's prophecy of the 2,300 days until the cleansing of the Temple.[250]

This prediction fired up fresh enthusiasm among the Millerites. While the older Adventist leaders were not sure about this exact date, they were delighted to see the renewal of excitement. William Miller, who preferred not to make specific calendar predictions, wrote an article in support of this new date only after much urging from his fellow Millerite leaders.[251]

Such was the excitement that by October many of the Millerites were giving away their worldly goods. Stores were closed—one store owner opened his shop and invited people to take whatever they needed—children were pulled out of school, debts were forgiven, household items were sold away, monetary investments were given up, crops were left to rot. To non-believers, it seemed as though insanity had taken hold of their Adventist neighbors.

But again, Jesus Christ did not come down from the sky. This time, the disappointment was crushing and final.

William Miller was roundly ridiculed. A neighbor wrote to him that "I should be ashamed to have my head seen in Publick had I sayed as much as you have and have it all prove false...," that Miller had been the cause of "...more suicide and more insanity in the last 5 or 6 years than has been known for 50 or 60 years before...," and that he was

---

[250] Rowe, *God's Strange Work*, 186-7.
[251] Ibid., 189.

"...one of those Class of things that has crept into houses and led astray silly wimin with sins...."[252] Even his brother in law encouraged him to leave preaching because "...folks in general will not believe what you say..." since "...what you believed as you thought the bible taught has fai[led] to come to pass."[253]

Other dates were put forward by different Millerites but none ever again caused widespread enthusiasm. Some of the Millerites fell away while others became more extreme in their beliefs and spiritualized all earthly events. The mainstream Millerite movement became a settled denomination, the Adventists, keeping intact some of its hopes and teachings.

The Millerites sang this hymn:

> "How long, dear Lord, our Savior
> Wilt thou remain away?
> Our hearts are growing weary
> Of Thy so long delay."[254]

5.

While the Millerites experienced bitter disappointment following the failure of their expectations, the Bab was boarding a boat bound for Mecca in that same month of October, 1844. This city on the Arabian Peninsula was the spiritual heart of Islam, and the Bab was going there to proclaim to the Muslim faithful that the time of fulfillment had arrived. He crossed the sea from Persia to Arabia with Quddus, one of the Letters of the Living, who then accompanied him on foot to the holy city.[255] There, next to the Kaba'a, the holiest shrine in Islam, the Bab proclaimed his message. Quddus gave a text revealed by the Bab to the ruler of Mecca who, busy with the management of pilgrims, only realized later the importance of its contents. They then journeyed

---

[252] Ibid., 193.
[253] Ibid., 188.
[254] Ibid., 196.
[255] Zarandi, 40.

to the tomb of Muhammad where they prayed intensely to the Prophet of Islam and his saints.

In Karbila, Tahirih seemed to have realized that the Bab was claiming to be the chosen messenger of a new Divine revelation, a greater claim than being the one who would purify Islam. He was now the source of authority, and his writings supplanted the Qur'an, the holy book which had guided the Shi'a for centuries. The instruction and the rule of the clergy were no longer necessary. This breathtaking claim was blasphemy to the Shi'a clerics.

She gave expression to these claims in the following poem in which she challenges readers to see the appearance of the Promised One of God in human form. In the Persian original, the poem is in the form of a ghazal, a song form with rhyming couplets, and she uses a poetical convention in which an author uses the same first line of a previous well-known poem. In this poem, she borrows a first line from a famous work by Rumi. The rest of the poem is a bold proclamation of the Bab's advent and station and a call for the believers to break from the clergy:[256]

> "Lovers! Creation veils his face no more!
> Lovers, look! He himself is visible!
>
> See! The face of God glows with glory;
> Look, lovers! Bright, pure, blinding, beautiful!
>
> Who made the cosmos turns earth green once more.
> Rise! Rise from that dark so miserable!
>
> The day of truth is here! Lies have turned to dust!
> Order, justice, law are now possible.

---

[256] Banani and Kessler, 127.

Smashed, the despot's fist! God's hand opens:
grace pours down—not sorrow, pain, and trouble

Minds in darkness now burn light with knowledge
Tell the priest. Shut your books! Lock the temple!

Hatred and doubt once poisoned all the world.
The bloodied cup holds milk now—pure, ample!

Let nations hear who's come to set them free:
Broken the chain, and smashed the manacle!"[257]

Tahirih taught the Bab's message boldly and publicly. She wrote long letters to all the leading clerics of Karbila in which she explained the true station of the Bab and exhorted them to abandon the effort to prevent the spread of his teachings. This was astonishing because not only was she a woman attempting to teach these prominent men who viewed women as inferior beings without souls, but she was doing it in writing. The written word in this time was the province of the highly educated male whose prerogative it was to instruct, to debate, and to explicate.[258]

In this early phase of the Bab's revelation, the central challenge facing the Shaykhis and Babis was to understand the true station and claims of the Bab. Tahirih saw that many of them had not grasped that revelation unfolded progressively[259] because they understood the Bab's teachings to be a continuation of the Shi'a tradition.[260] She believed, though, that the Bab was both the redeemer foretold by Shaykh Ahmad and Siyyid Kazim and the bringer of a new Divine revelation.[261] She had come to understand that a divine guide was necessary

---

[257] Ibid., 79.
[258] Shoghi Effendi, *God Passes By,* 73; Zarandi, 194.
[259] Mázandarání, v. 3, a1, 488.
[260] Conservative Shaykhis led by Gauhar, Amanat, "Qurrat al-'Ayn." 123.
[261] Ibid., 118.

in every age[262] and that God made His will known through him. There was no cessation of Divine revelation:[263]

"And day after day the cycle of the universe is in progress and 'there is no suspension in his emanation'. Praise be to God and our prayer and gratitude [to Him] that the Cause is everlasting."[264]

She reasoned that God's ways of testing the faithful were above the ways of men, and this knowledge could only be acquired intuitively. Only through inspiration—not through intellectual debate, human reasoning, or literal reading of the scripture—could other Shaykhis come to know the truth.[265]

Tahirih could let go of Shaykhism now since it had been fulfilled in her acceptance of the claims of the Bab. She had studied the Bab's writings, and so she realized that the Bab had not come to renew Islam by reviving the old traditions and institutions but by bringing a new divine revelation to reinvigorate the inner lives of people. Such a radical claim challenged Shia Muslim belief in the finality of Muhammad's revelation in God's plan and was a rupture with centuries-old traditions.[266]

Many Babis, though, continued to uphold the sharia, the Islamic law that had been developed over centuries, while still following the Bab as a divinely inspired reformer. The leader of these more conservative Babis in the region of the holy cities of Iraq did not approve at all of Tahirih's more radical interpretation[267] and of her public teaching,

---

[262] Ibid., 119; Mázandarání, vol. 3, 491.

[263] Ibid., 120-1.

[264] translated in Amanat, "Qurrat al-'Ayn." 119-20; Mázandarání, vol. 3, 494.

[265] Ibid., 119; Mázandarání, vol. 3, 486-8.

[266] Ibid., 122.

[267] Mulla Ahmad Hisari was the leader of conservative Babis of the holy cities of Southern Iraq (Abbas Amanat, "Qurrat al-'Ayn: The Remover of the Veil." Sabir Afaqi, ed., *Tahirih in history: Perspectives on Qurrat al-'Ayn from East and West* (Kalimat Press: LA, CA 2004), 123 f. 69); Mírzá Asadu'lláh Fádil-i-Mázandarání,

even going so far as to call her, in writing, the "Daughter of evil."[268] Tahirih reached out to him, but he did not reciprocate.[269] He was supported by a disaffected Babi back in Tahirih's hometown of Qazvin who actively attacked the authority and smeared the names of Mulla Husayn and Tahirih. Though she tried to reason with him in writing, he continued to side with those who opposed her.[270] Orthodox Shia clerics may well have encouraged these disagreements because they weakened the Shaykhis who were divided among themselves regarding acceptance of the Bab's message. They also feared the power of Tahirih's charisma to influence the hearts and minds of people. Her talent and complete conviction regarding the truth of the Bab helped her face the hostile Shia clerics, the conservative Shaykhis, and the conservative Babis.[271]

Despite this opposition which Tahirih faced in Karbila from 1844 to 1847, she gathered many fervent followers around her who, in turn, spread her teachings throughout the holy cities of southern Iraq. She spoke to large audiences from behind a curtain in Siyyid Kazim's house but was cautious when it came to the general public and involvement in any local squabbles and intrigues because she didn't want to invite unnecessary persecution of her followers.[272]

Her groups of students, called 'the Qurratiya', included both male and female and Persian and Arab. One of the Arab men became the first martyr for the new religion on Persian soil.[273] Women[274] were

---

Zuhúr al-Haqq, Volumes 1–4 (Tihrán, Iran: Bahá'í Publishing Trust, 1973), v. 3, 245, 253, 256)

[268] Amanat, "Qurrat al-'Ayn." 124 f. 73; Mázandarání, vol. 3, 256-7.

[269] Ibid., 125.

[270] His name was Jawad Valiyani (Amanat, "Qurrat al-'Ayn." 118)

[271] Ibid., 117.

[272] Ibid.

[273] Among these followers were Shaykh Salih Karimi, an Arab, who was the first Babi martyr on Persian soil; Shaykh Sultan, who went on to teach the Faith actively and followed Tahirih's instructions; and Shaykh Muhammad-i-Shibl, father of a high ranking Arab cleric in Baghdad (Zarandi, *The Dawn-Breakers*, 193).

attracted to her radical teachings and the possibilities that these created.[275] Her most devoted students carried these new ideas beyond Karbila.[276] The followers in the Qurratiya changed their habits to conform to Tahirih's dietary teachings such as abstaining from smoking or drinking coffee and even sought her blessing for their foods.[277] These more ascetic practices, though, bothered others in the group because they departed from the Sharia.[278]

Tahirih lost an important protector in early 1846, when Siyyid Kazim's widow passed away.[279] Meanwhile, the prominent conservative Shaykhi, Babi, and Muslim clerics continued their attacks on her, so she moved to the nearby town of Kazimayn.[280]

Once there, she was free again to teach, and she drew large crowds.[281] She challenged the prominent mullahs to a public debate but they declined.[282] Instead, conservative clerics spread slanderous rumors about her which made use of her iconoclastic teachings and behaviors to try to turn the Babis of Kazimayn against her.[283] Other mullas

---

[274] Khurshid Bagum (Shams al-Duha), wife of Mirza Mouhammad Ali Nahri; her sister, Mulla Husayn's mother, also a poetess; Mulla Husayn's sister, Bibi Kuchak; Siyyid Kazim's wife and her maid Kafiya. Later, more women would join: in Qazvin the three daughters of Haji Asadullah Farhadi—Khatun Jan, Shirin, and Sahiba; in Karbila, Zubayda Khanum—known as Firishtih, daughter of Fath Ali Shah and a poetess whose pen name was Jahan; the wife of Mahmud Khan; Shams-i-Jahan, daughter of Muhamad Riza Marzi, a poetess with the pen name of Fitna, who got to know Tahirih in Tihran when the latter was under house arrest (Martha Root, "Tahirih, The Pure, Iran's Greatest Woman," Bahá'í Library Online, Accessed October 1, 2013, http://bahai-library.com/martharoot_tahirih_pure_1938).

[275] Mazandarani, v. 3 314-5.

[276] Amanat, "Qurrat al-'Ayn." 117.

[277] Ibid., 121.

[278] Ibid., 118.

[279] Ibid., 149 f. 35.

[280] Ibid., 118.

[281] Ibid.; Mázandarání, vol. 3, 252.

[282] Hoseini, 200.

[283] Amanat, "Qurrat al-'Ayn." 124; Mázandarání, vol. 3, 257.

accused the conservatives of attacking her out of personal ambition.[284] Still, Persia was a deeply conservative society, and so these rumors had their intended effect. The Babis of Kazimayn decided to write to the Bab about Tahirih's teachings[285] because, as they understood it, "The Bab has not abrogated the old Shari'a and did not renew any command but increased observation of the religious injunctions...." [286]

By the time the Bab's reply had arrived in this region, Tahirih had already left Kazimayn.[287] His answer was read to a gathering of seventy Babis, and, in it, the Bab unequivocally supported Tahirih's understanding of his teachings and approved of her leadership of the Babis in the holy cities of Iraq. She was "a proof of God" and "none of those who are my followers repudiate her."[288] He referred to her as "the Pure," and "Siddiqih," the truthful,[289] showing his complete disapproval of the rumors of her immorality:[290]

> "Concerning what you have inquired about that mirror which has purified its soul in order to reflect the word by which all manners would be solved; she is a righteous, learned, active, and pure woman...."[291]

---

[284] Ibid.; Mázandaráni, vol. 3, 245-59.

[285] Siyyid Ali Bishir, the most learned of her opponents there, wrote the letter and Nawruz-Ali, a former attendant of Siyyid Kazim's, took it to the Bab in Mahku (Balyuzi, *The Bab*, 163; Mázandaráni, *Zuhúr al-Haqq*, 317).

[286] Baghdadi, Muhammad Mustafa. *Ar-Risalah al-Amriyyah*. (Treatise on the Cause). Appended to Ahmad Suhrab. *Ar-Risalah at-Tis``Ashariyyih*. Cairo: Matba`at as-Sa`adah, 1919/1338. Pages 102-128. Digitally republished, East Lansing, Mi.: H-Bahai, 1998. 109-110, quoted in Amanat, "Qurrat al-'Ayn." 124; H. M. Balyuzi, *The Bab*, 163; Mázandaráni, vol. 3, 317.

[287] According to Amanat, "Qurrat al-'Ayn." 151 f. 77, the Bab's reply came in mid-1261 AH.

[288] The Bab, quoted in Mázandaráni, vol. 3, 333.

[289] Balyuzi, *The Bab*, 163; Mázandaráni, vol. 3, 317; *A Traveller's Narrative Vol. 2*, translation by E. G. Browne (Cambridge, UK: Cambridge University Press, 1891), 311.

[290] Amanat, "Qurrat al-'Ayn." 124.

[291] Baghdadi, 110, quoted in Amanat, "Qurrat al-'Ayn." 124-5.

Some Babis renounced their faith, but most were able to accept the Bab's verdict.[292] The Bab reached out to the more conservative Babis and tried to reconcile them.[293] An additional test for the Babis of this region was that the Bab did not come to Karbila as expected after his pilgrimage to Mecca. Mulla Ali, the second Letter of the Living, had proclaimed the Bab's message to great public interest which aroused significant resistance from the authorities. When the Bab did not arrive in Karbila, many of his followers abandoned their faith.[294]

The Bab's tablet about Tahirih's station.

Through all of these intense attacks, Tahirih's love for the Bab remained constant. Her unwavering loyalty was grounded in her desire for reunion with God which she expresses in this, her most famous

---

[292] Siyyid Ali Bishir, Siyyid Taha, and Siyyid Muhammad Ja'far from Kazimayn, withdrew from the Faith. Most of the seventy stayed faithful (Mázandarání, *Zuhúr al-Haqq,* 318, citing Abu Fazl; Amanat, "Qurrat al-'Ayn," 125; Baghdadi, *Ar-Risalah al-Amriyyah,* 109-10).

[293] Amanat, "Qurrat al-'Ayn." 125.

[294] Mazandarani v. 3 235, 121; Moojan Momen, "Mulla `Ali Bastami, Letter of the Living." *Wendy and Moojan Momen.* http://www.momen.org/relstud/alibast.htm.

poem and the best example of her "bold and passionate"[295] poetical
personality. Its authorship was denied in her home country when, as a
part of a general attack on Babi/Baha'i history in the 1940's, a Persian
scholar questioned its authenticity:[296]

> "If ever I should behold you
> face to face,
> eye to eye,
> I would be bold to recount
> My heart's plaint
> point by point,
> Verse by verse.
>
> Like Saba the east wind,
> I have searched everywhere
> for your countenance
> from house to house,
> door to door,
> alley to alley,
> from quarter to quarter.
>
> Bereft of your visage,
> my two eyes have wept
> such bloody tears,
> Tigris after Tigris,
> stream upon stream,
> spring after spring,
> brook upon brook.
>
> Your bloom-like mouth,
> your face enveloped

---

[295] Banani and Kessler, 22.
[296] Ibid., 21-26.

with ambergris hair,
blossom to blossom,
flower to flower,
tulip to tulip,
fragrance to fragrance;

Your perfect brow,
your eyes, your beauty spot
have preyed on the bird of my heart,
sense to sense
and heart to heart,
feeling to feeling
and mood to mood.

My desperate heart
has knitted your love
to the very fabric of my being,
string by string,
thread by thread,
warp by warp,
and woof by woof.

Táhirih has searched
every layer of her heart
but found only you there,
sheet by sheet,
fold by fold,
cover by cover
over and over again."[297]

---

[297] Hatcher and Hemmat, 102-3.

FOUR:
TAHIRIH UNLOOSED

1.

"I plead with you!" Tahirih wrote imploringly to her father, "This humblest of people is your daughter. You know her, and she has been brought up and educated under your supervision. If she had, or has, a worldly love, that could not have remained a secret to you. If you want to inquire into her affairs, God who holds the scale and is the remover of veils would testify for her."[298]

Tahirih was defending herself against the rumors of her supposed immorality that had been spread by the mainstream Shia clergy who wanted to stop the growth of the Shaykhi movement, by her former fellow Babis who now rejected the Bab's claims, and by the more conservative Babis, who preferred a more gradual approach to revealing the Bab's claims. Her assertiveness in teaching her unorthodox views, gave those who opposed her, the material they needed to slander her.

So it was that around 1846-7, while still living and teaching in the holy cities of Iraq, she wrote the above refutation to her father. Her mission was "the declaration of the word of God," but this had been met with "accusations of disbelief and paganism." She reached out to her father: "Dear Father! So many times when I visit the holy shrine of the Imam, may peace be upon him, in the flood of my tears I pity you and pray for you that perhaps you may be saved," but also admonished him that "If you fail to recognize the cause, there will be no benefit for you in all your acts of devotion."[299]

She continued to fearlessly proclaim the promise and the power of the new day of God and concluded this poem by speaking in a divine voice and finishing with a quotation from the Qur'an:

---

[298] Amanat, "Qurrat al-'Ayn." 126.
[299] Ibid., 126, all the quotations in the paragraph.

"Hear this! My one and only Cause is true.
The words I speak mean victory for you.

Off with rags of law and pious fashion!
Swim naked in the sea of compassion!

How long will you drift through this world of war,
far from the safety of your native shore?

Sing, Be! Our Cause stands strong, both clear and plain:
"What comes from God returns to God again!"[300]

An angry mob attacked several of her followers and the house in which Tahirih was living.

A woman who was mistaken for Tahirih was saved from being murdered when Tahirih wrote to the governor, "I am at your disposal. Do not harm any other." The authorities then released the woman when they heard that Tahirih had been taken prisoner.[301] The Ottoman authorities wanted her released conditioned on a decision from the government in Baghdad, and, in the meantime, Tahirih was kept isolated under house arrest.[302]

Tahirih defended herself to the authorities stating that all she wanted was an open debate so that the truth of these matters could be established.[303] She reached out one more time to the leader of the conservative Babis, telling him she was willing to come to Baghdad to explain the true nature of the Bab's station and revelation.[304] Finally, she wrote to the authorities that "No word has come from either Baghdad or

---

[300] Banani and Kessler, 53.
[301] The woman's name was Shamsu'd-Duha ('Abdu'l-Baha, *Memorials of the Faithful,* 194). Tahirih was taken to the house of Hajj Mahdi Kamuna (Amanat, "Qurrat al-'Ayn." 125).
[302] Ibid.
[303] Amanat, "Qurrat al-'Ayn." 125-6, f. 86.
[304] Ibid., 126.

Constantinople. Accordingly we will ourselves proceed to Baghdad and await the answer there,"[305] and she left Karbila for Baghdad. On her way out, angry residents—stoked by clerics—threw stones at her.[306]

Karbila in the nineteenth century.

In this poem, she rejects the clerics as signs of the ignorance that marked the end of the age. Her husband and her father-in-law had constantly sought to contain her, and clerics of all persuasions attacked her in whatever town she taught. This rejection of Tahirih by the clergy was at every level—personal, social, and theological. While this poem is in the shape of a Persian love poem, the ghazal, she does not use any of the traditional imagery associated with this form. Instead she rebukes the clergy in very strong terms. At the end, though, she offers the hope of reconciliation in this new day:

---

[305] 'Abdu'l-Baha, *Memorials of the Faithful*, 194.
[306] Root, *Táhirih the pure*, 61.

"Look! Our guiding dawn breathes even now
The world with all its peoples is aglow

No canting priest now raves from the pulpit
No mosque hawks sanctimony to the crowd

No sheikh, no sham, no holy fraud prevails
The turban knot's cut to the root below

Freed from the fear of wicked whisperings
Mankind is rid of magic's foolish show

Ignorance is doomed by the search for truth
Equality's arm shall bring the tyrant low

Warring ways will be banished from the world
And Justice everywhere its carpet throw

New friendship must from ancient hatred spring
And far and wide the seeds of kindness sow"[307]

Tahirih arrived in Baghdad sometime in early 1847 and was installed in a new house.[308] She immediately resumed her public teaching in a space in the house that was provided to her.[309] She had translated important works by the Bab such as the *Qayyumu'l Asma*, the first book that he had revealed, and she had received a copy of the *Commentary on the Surih of Kawthar* and used all of these for her classes.[310]

Attempts to silence Tahirih multiplied as her influence spread. The leaders of the conservative Babis communicated their concerns to the

[307] Jascha Kessler, *Tahereh: A Persian Mystical Poet* (Unpublished manuscript: Santa Monica, CA, 1991), 10.
[308] She stayed in the house of Shaykh Muhammad Shibl (Balyuzi, *The Bab*, 162).
[309] Balyuzi, *The Bab*, 162.
[310] Ibid., 163; 'Abdu'l-Baha, *Memorials of the Faithful*, 193.

chief judge of Baghdad[311] that Tahirih's teaching and popularity among the people would lead to unrest.[312] The chief judge summoned Tahirih to an interview but found her to be innocent of heresy.[313] He wanted to be sure of this, though, so he sent her to the home of Shaykh Alusi, a cleric who had previously tried another of the Bab's disciples, Mulla Ali Bastami. Bastami had been one of the earliest of the Bab's 'Letters of the Living', his apostles. He electrified listeners with his teaching and had been the one to bring the commentary on the Surah of Joseph to Tahirih. His trial was the first between a Babi and the Muslim clergy, and the decision against him was the first time in modern history that a joint official warning was pronounced by both Shi'a and Sunni clerics. Subsequently, he was banished to the Ottoman Empire[314] where he died under uncertain circumstances, becoming the first martyr of the new faith. Tahirih's case was also referred to the court of the Ottoman Empire.[315] Knowing that Shaykh Alusi had banished Bastami, the chief judge was probably hoping to avoid any form of public trial which might cause unrest.

Later in his life, Shaykh Alusi remembered her this way:

> "Verily, I saw in her such a degree of merit and accomplishment as I rarely saw in men. She was a wise and decent woman who was unique in virtue and chastity ... there is no doubt about her knowledge."[316]

While he obviously admired her, he may not have clearly understood the claims she was making about the Bab. He interpreted her teaching to mean that the Bab was similar to the figure of the 'Perfect Man'

---

[311] Najib Pasha, a Sunni (Amanat, "Qurrat al-'Ayn." 127)

[312] Amanat, "Qurrat al-'Ayn." 127.

[313] Ibid.

[314] Baghdad and the other holy cities in Iraq were ruled over at this time by the Ottoman Empire.

[315] Balyuzi, *The Bab*, ch. 4; Momen, "Mulla 'Ali Bastami".

[316] Amanat, "Qurrat al-'Ayn." 127.

taught by Islamic mystics.[317] The 'Perfect Man' was the man in the beginning of creation who contained within him all the attributes of God but who had become separated from God because of his fall from grace. Muslim mystics believed that it was possible for a person to achieve this state again. The cleric interpreted Tahirih's claim to be that the Bab was this 'Perfect Man'. As the cleric seemed open to some form of dialogue, a meeting between Sunni clergy and Tahirih was convened in his home. In later years, the Bab wrote to him and called on him to recognize his station.[318]

A Jewish doctor, Hakim Masih, who was accompanying the King of Persia to the holy cities of Iraq, remembers being in a gathering of Muslim clerics in Baghdad as they debated with a woman who spoke from behind a curtain. Her arguments were so logical and expressed with such force and clarity that he was swayed by them and became a believer. Since he had never heard of the Bab, he thought that the woman was herself the Promised One. He was able to hear Tahirih speak three more times before he had to resume his journey with the Shah. When he returned to Tihran, he treated a prisoner who was a Babi and a survivor of Fort Tabarsi who taught him about Tahirih and the Bab. Through Masih's subsequent teaching, many Jews became Babis.[319]

During this time, Shaykh Alusi told Tahirih of a dream in which he was at the tomb of the Imam Husayn with other Shi'a mullas. The tomb opened, revealing the immaculate body of the Imam. The mullas tried to lift it up, but Alusi threw himself on the body to prevent them. Tahirih explained that the dream meant that he would free her

---

[317] Ibid, 128.
[318] Shaykh Kazim Samandar, Idid.; A.Q. Afnan, ed., "Biography of Tahirih." *Four historical narratives about Tahirih*, Third Conference of Alt and Culture (Landegg, Switzerland: Landegg University, September, 1991), 348-9.
[319] According to Martha Root, *Táhirih, the Pure* (Los Angeles: Kalimat Press, 1981), 62: "His son continued his work, and his grandchildren most of whom are physicians, are among the most cultured, capable, faithful Bahá'i workers of Tihrán today."

from the hands of the Shi'a clerics. Sometime later, Shaykh Alusi informed her that the Ottoman King had ordered her to be freed on condition that she leave Baghdad and return to Persia.[320]

The authorities decided that her teaching, combined with her popularity, constituted a threat to the established order and would exacerbate tensions between the different religious groups, especially Sunni, who were usually Arabs and Turks, and Shi'a Muslims, who were mostly Persian. Since Tahirih was Persian, they thought she should be sent back to challenge the clerics in her own homeland. Also, they did not want to make Tahirih a martyr for the Shi'a Persians who could then use her in the ongoing Shi'a-Sunni conflict.[321]

A representative of her family arrived in Baghdad to bring her back to Qazvin.[322] He spoke with the cleric in whose home she was housed and asked for the "chaste woman" who had been "overwhelmed with satanic temptations."[323] But he also observed in a letter to Tahirih's father that "The entire nobility and the 'ulama of Baghdad greatly respect her and confer on her highest praises."[324] In her letters to her father she had expressed her anger at the false rumors spread by former Shaykhi colleagues, and the representative assured her father in writing that "Whatever has been relayed to you and rumored [about her] is slander and fabrication."[325]

Tahirih left Baghdad around March, 1847, accompanied by Ottoman officials, about thirty of her followers, including Persians and Arabs—some armed, some on foot—and her female contingent, and

---

[320] 'Abdu'l-Baha, *Memorials of the Faithful,* 195.

[321] Balyuzi, *The Bab,* 163.

[322] Hajji Mulla Muhammad Hamadani (Amanat, "Qurrat al-'Ayn." 129).

[323] Mázandarání, v. 3, 304.

[324] Ibid.

[325] Abbud Salihi quoted in Amanat, 129; Nicolas, *Seyyed Ali Mohammed dit le Bab,* 274-6.

one of the chief judge's officers who had become attracted to the new teaching.[326]

The journey took about three months and wound east through the towns of Karand, Kirmanshah, and Hamadan. All along the way, she taught fearlessly about the appearance of a new revelation from God and met with both threatening resistance and enthusiastic acceptance.[327]

In the village of Karand, hundreds of the Turkic-speaking people gave Tahirih their allegiance and were willing to serve as her personal army.[328] In these villages of Western Iran, many people followed a religion from the 15th-century CE, called Ahl-e Haqq, which taught that God made Himself known through successive manifestations, so her message of a new manifestation of God may have resonated powerfully with them. Since the faith of these rural people had not become jaded like that of city dwellers, their hearts were open to the new teaching.[329]

Tahirih and her group arrived in Kirmanshah, the capital of the province with the same name on the Western border of Persia.[330] Many of the people in this city were Kurdish and also followed the

---

[326] Muhammad Aqa Yavar (Balyuzi, *The Bab*, 164). Martha Root gives additional details about Tahirih's departure from Baghdad: She left Baghdad with ten soldiers offered by the mufti for her protection with: "Kurshíd Bagúm, and the mother of Mirzá Hádíy-i-Nahrí; others were Siyyid Ahmad Yazdí, Siyyid Muhammad-I Báyigání, Siyyid Muhsin-i-Kázimí, Mullá Ibráhím Mahallatí, among the Persians; and among the Arabs were Shaykh Muhammad-i Shibl who arranged everything for her journey, hiring the mules and the places to sit, ordering the food and he paid all the expenses for the group as far as Kirmánsháh. Others from 'Iráq were his son Muhammad- Mustafá, Shaykh Sálih-i Karímí, Shaykh Sultán-i Karbilá'í, Darvísh Makú'í, Javád, 'Abdu'l Hádí-i Zahrawí, Husayn-i Hallawí, Siyyid Jabbáníz and others." (Root, *Táhirih, the Pure*, 62).

[327] Amanat, "Qurrat al-'Ayn." 130.

[328] According to Zarandi, *The Dawn-Breakers*, 194 f.2, 1,200 people volunteered to follow her.

[329] Ibid.

[330] Root, *Táhirih the pure*, 64.

Ahl-e Haqq religion; they resented the authority of the Shi'a Persians from the major cities who ruled over them. Tahirih spent forty days in Kirmanshah during which she met with the governor, his wife, and other prominent citizens[331] The clerics of the city received her respect-fully.[332] Once again, she challenged their leaders to a public debate.[333] Her presence and teaching began to generate excitement among the people, which worried the chief Usuli mujtahid[334] who, as a result, asked the governor to have her and her followers expulsed. The governor replied that she had offered to have a public debate or to undergo an ordeal in which both parties should pray to God that He show, through His Wrath, which party was in the wrong.[335] The chief mujtahid rejected both of these options, most likely because they were too risky with a person as talented as Tahirih.

An enemy of the governor—working with the local police chief and representatives of her family sent from Qazvin—organized an attack on the house where she and her companions were staying. The companions were beaten and their goods pilfered,[336] while she and a few close companions were put into a coach and sent out of the city into the desert without any provisions.[337] Tahirih wrote to the governor describing how they had been treated. He found out that the ulama were behind all of this and ordered the mayor to return all their belongings.[338] This was done, but she refused to return to the city.[339]

---

[331] Amanat, "Qurrat al-'Ayn." 130.

[332] Zarandi, 194.

[333] Amanat, "Qurrat al-'Ayn." 130; Baghdadi, 111-3.

[334] Aqa Abdullah i Bihbihani, (Balyuzi, *The Bab*, 164).

[335] This ordeal was called a 'mubahala'.

[336] According to Root, *Táhirih, the Pure*, 62, it was the Mayor of Kirmanshah who stirred up the attack against the Babis. Amanat, citing Baghdadi, 114-5, specifies that there were twenty-five Arab followers who were detained. Balyuzi, 164, specifies that there were four men from Qazvin and one local officer who carried out this attack. Also see: Balyuzi, *The Bab*, 164; Hoseini, 217.

[337] Root, *Táhirih the Pure*, 64.

[338] Ibid., 64.

[339] Mázandaráni, v. 3, 309.

Despite her family's wishes that she return immediately, Tahirih stopped in the important city of Hamadan, also in a Turkic-speaking area of the kingdom. There she once again challenged the clerical establishment. With the aid of women who were part of the local Turkish elite, she requested that the governor,[340] who was also the Shah's brother, invite clerics from the different Islamic sects to a debate. She set certain conditions: the substance of their debate must be based on prophecy, and the participants must refrain from indecent language and smoking. At such debates, the smoking of water pipes, even opium, was common, but she insisted on certain rules of purity just as the Bab had. In the debate, she explained the basic Babi doctrines that divine revelation was ongoing and progressive, that the Bab was giving a new teaching for a new age, and that the Babis were its recipients. The clerics chose as their spokesperson a great Sufi mystic.[341] Sufis believed that the source of human suffering was disconnection from the Creator and that all human beings had the potential to be re-united with Him. In every age there was one Perfect Man who reflected all the Divine Virtues so Tahirih's ideas concerning the Bab may well have both challenged and interested him. While the Sufi mystic treated her and her ideas respectfully, another mujtahid[342] launched a verbal attack against her. He was rebuked by the governor who then adjourned the debate.[343]

Tahirih's stay in Hamadan touched off conversions to the new faith in the important Jewish community there. By the turn of the century, Hamadan had the largest group of Baha'is of Jewish background in Persia.[344] In April, 1847, Mulla Lazar, son of the leading rabbi of Hamadan, hosted Tahirih in his home. His activities drew the anger of

---

[340] Khanlar Mirza Ihtisham al-Daula (Amanat, "Qurrat al-'Ayn." 131).

[341] Haji Mirza Ali Naqi (Amanat, "Qurrat al-'Ayn." 131).

[342] "Possibly Mulla Husayn Razavi Hamadani, son of al-Samad." (Amanat, "Qurrat al-'Ayn." f. 121, 154).

[343] Ibid., v. 3, 310.

[344] Mehrdad Amanat, *Jewish Identities in Iran: Resistance and Conversion to Islam and the Baha'i Faith* (I.B. Taurus: NY, NY 2011), 105.

other Jewish elders who lodged complaints about him to the King. Later, his writings were found to reflect Babi/Baha'i ideas though he never publicly identified himself as a Babi.[345] His father became concerned that her presence in a Jewish home might bring on anti-Jewish violence.[346] Zobaydeh Khanum, also known as Fereshteh, the daughter of the late King, Fath Ali Shah, hosted Tahirih after Mulla Lazar.[347] News of Tahirih's teaching in Hamadan travelled through the networks of the relatives of highly educated prominent women. One of these women, Sakineh Khanum, married the merchant Sayyed Ahmad Naraqi who became a Baha'i and developed an extensive knowledge of Babi and Baha'i history and Persian and Arabic literature.[348] Another prominent woman who came to be interested in Tahirih's teaching was Hajiyeh Khanum, the wife of the foreign minister of Persia.[349]

Later, a treatise written by Tahirih was presented to the chief mujtahid who had the messenger—himself a mujtahid—beaten and thrown out of his presence.[350] When the messenger was brought back to her barely conscious, she reassured him that his suffering—like that of the apostles of Christ and Muhammad—was a blessing.[351] She was moved to a village owned by the Turkish noblewomen of Hamadan, and then she left for Qazvin with her relatives.[352] She ordered the rest of her followers to go back to the holy cities of Iraq, though some of them continued on with her. Among those accompanying her back to

---

[345] Ibid., 175-6.

[346] Ibid., 95.

[347] Ibid., 235 n. 28.

[348] Ibid., 105.

[349] Ibid., 235, note 28.

[350] The chief mujtahid may have been Sayyid Abd al-Samad Razavi Hamadani (Amanat, "Qurrat al-'Ayn." f. 122, p. 154). The messenger was Mulla Ibrahim Mahallati (Amanat, "Qurrat al-'Ayn." 131). Balyuzi, *The Bab*, 163; Zarandi, 273.

[351] The Jewish rabbi was Hakham Ilyahu and his son, Ik'azar (Amanat, "Qurrat al-'Ayn." 132).

[352] Ibid., 165.

Qazvin were two men who were later martyred for the Bab, and her brother in law, one of the Bab's Letters of the Living.[353]

After three years away, Tahirih arrived back in Qazvin in July, 1847, to a family deeply divided by the Bab's claims, to religious communities in conflict, and to a town in economic distress. Her time in the holy cities of Iraq had not changed her heart and mind back to the traditional faith of her father; rather, she was acknowledged, by the Bab's own pen, as one of the leading teachers of the Babi Faith.[354] Greater conflict with her father-in-law and husband, both powerful clerics and keepers of the traditional order, was inevitable.

The writings of the Bab had arrived there prior to her return and had elicited a strong reaction, intensifying tensions between Shaykhis and Usulis. Some Shaykhis, Babis, and new converts from the merchant class enthusiastically greeted the reading of the new scripture. One cleric proclaimed them from the pulpit and called for opposition to the Usuli clerics led by Taqi.[355] The elderly leader of the Shaykhis in Qazvin, though, had not clearly accepted the claims of the Bab despite the encouragement of his sons to do so and had passed away in 1847.[356] Protection of the Babis and Shaykhis then devolved onto a prominent merchant family and their son, Muhammad Hadi.[357] Taqi and the conservatives rejected the writings of the Bab completely and as he stepped up his attacks on Shaykhi and Babi teachings, Muhammad Hadi and his family became their defenders.[358]

---

[353] The martyrs were Shaykh Salih and Mulla Ibrahim Gulpaygani, and her brother in law was Mulla Muhammada Ali, one of the Letters of the Living, apostles of the Bab. Siyyid Abdu'l-Hadi went with her as well (Zarandi, *The Dawn-Breakers*, 195). Balyuzi lists Mulla Ibrahim-i-Mahallati and Shaykh Salih al Karimi as companions who had come from Iraq (Balyuzi, *The Bab*, 165).

[354] Amanat, "Qurrat al-'Ayn." 133; Baghdadi, 117.

[355] Ibid., 134.

[356] Ibid., 133.

[357] The Farhadi family (Amanat, *Resurrection and Renewal*, 349).

[358] Amanat, *Resurrection and Renewal*, 350.

Hadi and his supporters had gone out to meet the Bab earlier in the year when he had passed near Qazvin on his forced march to the prison fortress of Mahku in the north and offered to rescue him which the Bab refused as he had on previous occasions.[359] From another village, the Bab wrote to Tahirih's father, father-in-law, and her maternal uncle.[360] His plans to meet the King had been thwarted by the Prime Minister who wanted to prevent the Bab's influence from reaching the royal court. Nevertheless, the Bab wrote to the King from his imprisonment in the remote fortress in Azerbaijan and boldly asserted his claim:

> "I am the Primal Point, from which have been generated all created things...I am the Countenance of God Whose splendor can never be obscured, the light of Go whose radiance can never fade...All the keys of heaven God hath chosen to place on My right hand, and all the keys of hell on My left...I am one of the sustaining pillars of the Primal Word of God. Whosoever hath recognized Me, hath known all that is true and right, and hath attained all that is good and seemly...The substance wherewith God hath created Me is not the clay out of which others have been formed. He hath conferred upon Me that which the worldly-wise can never comprehend, nor the faithful discover."[361]

Cut off from contact with the Bab due to this imprisonment, Hadi became more radical and believed that violent conflict with the authorities was inevitable—he had already had to free a sympathetic cleric who had been beaten by Taqi for his preaching.[362] He began to make weapons in his home.[363] Adding great stress to the tensions in

---

[359] Ibid.; Mazandarani, v.3, 95-96.
[360] Hoseini, 230.
[361] Shoghi Effendi, *The World Order of Bahá'u'lláh: Selected Letters*, "The Dispensation of Bahá'u'lláh." 126.
[362] Mázandarání, vol. 3, 347-8.
[363] Amanat, *Resurrection and Renewal*, 350; Mázandarání, vol. 3, 374.

Qazvin was the fact that there had been a significant downturn in the economy which had hit the merchants hard. Land, as a result, became a greater source of wealth in Qazvin. Since Taqi owned much of the land in the area, he had conflict with the merchant families against whom he, as a religious judge, issued unfavorable verdicts.[364]

As Tahirih approached Qazvin, several of her family members came out of town to greet her. They wanted her companions to leave, but she refused. The family members then led her to her father's house.[365]

Tahirih's family held a council on her first night back. Her father told her that if she had been born a man and declared herself to be the Bab, he would have believed her, but he couldn't understand her devotion to the "Shirazi lad" as he referred to the Bab.[366] He wanted to keep peace in the family by maintaining a middle course between his daughter's radical teachings about the Bab and the strong conservative reaction against them from other family members.[367] Some men in the family were by now Babis,[368] including her youngest uncle on her father's side, Mulla Ali, although he did not want to acknowledge this publicly.[369] She responded to her father that she had come to her faith through reasoned consideration. Her uncle Taqi flew into a fury when she said this. He cursed the Bab and then struck her. She uttered the prophetic warning that she saw his mouth filled with blood.[370]

Tahirih spent her days in her father's house chanting and praying, while her family pressured her to abandon her Babi beliefs and followers.[371] She moved to her brother's house where she held classes for

---

[364] Ibid, 348-9.

[365] 'Abdu'l-Baha, *Memorials of the Faithful*, 197.

[366] Root, *Táhirih the pure*, 69; Nicolas, *Seyyed Ali Mohammed*, 276.

[367] Zarandi, *The Dawn-Breakers*, 96.

[368] Mulla Abd al Wahhab Qazvini, Mulla Hadi, Mulla Muhammad Ali (Amanat, "Qurrat al-'Ayn." 133; Mázandaráni, *Zuhúr al-Haqq*, vol. 3, 304).

[369] Ibid., vol. 3, 309-310.

[370] Root, *Táhirih the pure*, 70; Nicolas, *Seyyed Ali Mohammed*,276.

[371] Amanat, "Qurrat al-'Ayn." 134.

women.[372] She was in constant correspondence with the Bab who asked his followers to go proclaim his message in the provinces, so she implored them to do so. By this time, the Bab was imprisoned in the stone fortress of Mahku in the far northwest of Persia. The Babis discussed whether his imprisonment was only a prelude to a widespread persecution of Babis and whether the time had come to break him out of Mahku.[373]

Tahirih's estranged husband sent a message to her asking that she return to their home. She replied that she could have changed his unbelief into belief had he stood by her, but he hadn't. Now, because he had rejected the religion of God, she was casting him out of her life forever and, in so doing, taking the male prerogative of divorce upon herself. This angered her husband and his father, Taqi, and added to their resolve to accuse her of being a heretic. They set out to undermine her in every way.[374]

Taqi resented the calumny whispered in public about the Baraghani house—his respected and wealthy family—and became even more aggressive in his attacks.[375] Babis were insulted in public and humiliated by having their turbans unwound and used to drag them about.[376] Her father did not believe these rumors and continued to deny them and, later that year, he was publicly shamed in a meeting of the top mullahs in Qazvin when one cleric recited a verse which mocked his house by saying that the hens in his house crowed like cocks. Many years later, the humiliation would drive him out of Qazvin; he would die in the region of the holy cities of Southern Iraq in 1866.[377]

Taqi denounced the new teachings from his pulpit in the mosque. He referred to the first Shaykhi teacher, Shaykh Ahmad, as the

---

[372] 'Abdu'l-Baha, *Memorials of the Faithful,* 197.

[373] Nicolas, *Seyyed Ali Mohammed,* 276-7.

[374] Root, *Táhirih the pure,* 70; Zarandi, 195.

[375] Amanat, "Qurrat al-'Ayn." 136; Zarandi, 195-6.

[376] Zarandi, 196.

[377] Momen, "Usuli, Akhbari, Shaykhi, Babi." 333.

embodiment of "error."[378] This so angered a sincere young Shaykhi that he resolved to kill Taqi.[379] The young man entered the mosque in the evening and waited until sunrise to stab Taqi while he performed his dawn prayers.[380] He then went up the stairs to the roof of the mosque leaving Taqi's bloodied body on the mosque floor in the semicircular niche in the wall that indicated the direction of Mecca towards which the faithful prayed. From the rooftop, he watched as people rushed into the mosque. When they couldn't find the attacker, they turned on each other.[381] Innocent Babis were subsequently arrested.[382] The attacker was bothered by this and gave himself up to the governor.[383] He confessed to the killing, but he wasn't believed, even after an elderly lady who worked in the mosque was brought in and testified that she had seen him. Finally they brought him to the death bed of Taqi who identified him.[384] Ironically, he escaped prison and wound up perishing in the armed conflict between the Babis and the military at Fort Tabarsi.[385] Taqi was around eighty years old at the time of his death.[386]

The shocking murder of a high ranking cleric like Taqi gave the enemies of Tahirih the perfect pretext with which to destroy the Babi

---

[378] Amanat, "Qurrat al-'Ayn." 136; Zarandi, 196.

[379] Mirza Abdullah Salih Shirazi (Root, *Táhirih, The Pure, Iran's Greatest Woman*, 10; Amanat, "Qurrat al-'Ayn." 136).

[380] Nicolas, *Seyyed Ali Mohammed*, 278; Zarandi, 197; description of the killing, Root, *Táhirih the pure*, 73.

[381] Zarandi, 197.

[382] 'Abdu'l-Baha, *Memorials of the Faithful*, 198.

[383] According to Samandar Qazvini, quoted in Root, *Táhirih, the Pure*, 74, the killer burst in while Tahirih was being interrogated to confess; Amanat, "Qurrat al-'Ayn." 137.

[384] Zarandi, 197.

[385] According to 'Abdu'l-Baha, *Memorials of the Faithful*, 197-9, he was put in chains and sent to Tihran. Seeing that the innocents were still persecuted, he escaped prison to the house of Riza Khan, the son of the Master of the Horse to Muhammad Shah. After some time, he went with Riza Khan to Fort Tabarsi. They were martyred there.

[386] Samandar, 131.

community of Qazvin, one the largest in Persia at the time.[387] Her husband, Mulla Muhammad, and his associates rounded up prominent Babis. Homes of Babis were raided and ransacked.[388] The house of the merchant family who had become the protectors of the Babis was pillaged twice.[389] Women were also attacked.[390] Tahirih and her maid were forcibly removed[391]from her father's house by a mob. The governor interrogated Tahirih who defended herself eloquently. The governor then threatened to brand them, and Tahirih's maid was about to be tortured when news arrived that the killer had turned himself in.[392] There was no evidence that Tahirih had played any role in this crime, so she was released into complete confinement in her father's house. Her husband and one of her cousins, though, plotted to poison her food.[393] No one was allowed to visit her except a faithful friend[394] who made excuses like washing Tahirih's clothes so she could bring her news and food. Tahirih did not eat the household food in case it had been poisoned.[395]

Though Tahirih's innocence made it impossible for her husband to punish her, he was able to destroy several of the leading Babis of Qazvin. These were the first public executions of the followers of the new faith in Persia and included the first Babi—one of Tahirih's Arab

---

[387] Amanat, "Qurrat al-'Ayn." 137.

[388] Haji Siyyid Asad'ullah and his son Mihdi's house was ransacked; he was a faithful believer whose daughter was a sister-in-law to Tahirih (Root, *Táhirih, the Pure,* 75). Mulla Mushin known as the 'Babi killer', and government agents raided the homes of known Babis (Samandar, "Biography of Tahirih." 54).

[389] Amanat, *Resurrection and Renewal,* 350,

[390] Samandar, 54.

[391] Katiya (Amanat, *Qurrat al-'Ayn,* 137).

[392] According to Mázandarání, *Zuhúr al-Haqq,* and Root, (*Táhirih, the Pure,* 74), Tahirih's maid was about to be branded. According to Root, *Táhirih, the Pure,* 74, they were saved when Tahirih turned in prayer towards Mahku where the Bab was imprisoned.

[393] Hoseini, 238.

[394] Khatun Jan the eldest daughter of Haji Asad'u'llah (Root, *Táhirih, the Pure,* 75).

[395] Samandar quoted in Root, *Táhirih the pure,* 74-75.

followers—to be killed on Persian soil.[396] The killings were carried out with great cruelty by mobs in the streets who were incited by clerics[397] while government officials did nothing.[398] The future persecutions of Babis and Baha'is in Persia followed the pattern in Qazvin—the clerics accused Babis and incited mob violence while the civil authorities allowed the bloodshed to take place to appease the powerful clergy.

Tahirih challenged the injustices being perpetrated by her estranged husband, Mulla Muhammad, who had now succeeded his father as the Imam Jumih of Qazvin. She sent him a message from the Qur'an which stated that only unbelievers rejected God's light when it appeared. She wrote that if she was not delivered from him in nine days, this would be a sign that she had been wrong:

> "'Fain would they put out God's light with their mouths; but God only desireth to perfect His light, albeit the infidels abhor it.' (Qur'an, 9:33). If my Cause be the Cause of Truth, if the Lord whom I worship be none other than the one true God, He will, ere nine days have elapsed, deliver me from the yoke of your tyranny. Should He fail to achieve my deliverance, you are free to act as you desire. You will have irrevocably established the falsity of my belief."[399]

Mulla Muhammad ignored the message.

Mirza Husayn Ali, the prominent Babi leader, was in Tihran and decided that the time had come to remove Tahirih from the threat of violence in Qazvin. He summoned the very trusted Muhammad Hadi

---

[396] Balyuzi, *The Bab*, 166.

[397] They were taken before the king of Persia in Tihran. The first Babi to be executed on Persian soil was one of Tahirih's Arab followers, Shaykh Salih Karimi, who was blown out of the mouth of cannon in Tihran (Zarandi, *The Dawn-Breakers*, 200; Mázandarání, *Zuhúr al-Haqq*, 261; Shaykh Kazim Samandar, A.Q. Afnan, ed., "Biography of Tahirih." *Four historical narratives about Tahirih*, Third Conference of Alt and Culture (Landegg, Switzerland: Landegg University, September, 1991, 56).

[398] Amanat, "Qurrat al-'Ayn." 138.

[399] Zarandi, 203.

Farhadi, protector of the Shaykhis and Babis of Qazvin,[400] for the task.[401] Hadi was given a sealed letter to be taken by his wife—disguised as a beggar woman—to the house where Tahirih was being kept.[402] According to the plan, Tahirih was secretly brought to the home of Sheikh Kazem Samandar and then to that of a carpenter who was a good friend of Hadi's.[403] Her captors realized she had escaped. People were searching everywhere for her, going so far as to pillage the home of one of her faithful followers.[404] Several of those loyal to her went over to throw out the mob.[405] Hadi and a trusted servant brought Tahirih to the city wall, near the gate where an attendant with three fast horses sent by Mirza Husayn Ali was waiting for them. After going over the walls, they proceeded to a nearby slaughterhouse where they mounted the horses.[406] The group of the two veiled women—Tahirih, her servant, and Hadi, —then rode ninety miles to Tihran through the cold October night, leaving the major road and taking a less-travelled one through the villages of Kolah Darreh and Isdhtibard to avoid

---

[400] Root, *Táhirih the pure*, 75; Balyuzi, *The Bab*, 167.

[401] Balyuzi, *The Bab*, 167. 'Abdu'l-Baha, *Memorials of the Faithful*, 199, calls him "Hadi Qazvini." husband of Khatun Jan; according to Samandar, quoted in Root, *Táhirih, the Pure*, 75, Khatun Jan was the eldest daughter of Haji Asadullah, of the Farhadi family. She was the one who secretly visited Tahirih. This Hadi had left Qazvin before the agitation but was sent back there by Baha'u'llah to rescue Tahirih.

[402] Samandar, 58; Zarandi, 203; according to Mazandarani, 376, Hadi's wife was disguised as a washerwoman.

[403] His name was Hasan Najar (Root, *Tahirih, The Pure, Iran's Greatest Woman*, 10; Samandar, "Biography of Tahirih." 83).

[404] His name was Haji Asad'ullah Farhadi, father-in-law of Muhammad Hadi Farhadi. (Mazandarani, *Zuhur'ul-Haqq*, vol. 3 373; Root, *Táhirih, The Pure, Iran's Greatest Woman*, 10, 76; Samandar, "Biography of Tahirih." 58)

[405] Shahzade Khanum, daughter of Muhammad Ali Mirza Maqfour, and others went to Asad'ullah's house, and with Sadiq Khan Ajudan's help, kicked out the mob (Samandar, "Biography of Tahirih," 58).

[406] The trusted servant's name was Quli, Nicolas, *Seyyed Ali Mohammed*, 278; the Gate of Shahzade Hossein (Samandar, "*Biography of Tahirih.*" 58; through a 'breach in the wall' (Nicolas, *Seyyed Ali Mohammed dit le Bab*, 287); Samandar quoted in Root, *Táhirih the Pure*, 76.

detection.[407] They stopped at one of the two shrines to holy figures a couple of miles to the west of the capital.[408] Tahirih and her group were able to rest in the garden, while a messenger went into town to let Mirza Husayn Ali know they had arrived.[409]

Tahirih was brought to the home of Mirza Husayn Ali and led into the upper room.[410] Beds had been made for all the tired companions, though the humble messenger did not want to dirty them with his shabby clothes. The following day they went to meet Mirza Husayn Ali in a little village outside of the city.[411] She was safe for the time being. Back in Qazvin, her deliverance made such an impression on her brother that he came to believe that there was divine power in this new faith.[412]

Tahirih's voice seems to have become more strident by this time, possibly because, after years of preaching, exhorting, teaching, and writing, her proclamation of the Bab was still almost constantly rejected by authorities. One evening in Tihran, Vahid, who had given up his position as one of Persia's highest-ranking clerics by becoming a Babi, was visiting the home of Mirza Husayn Ali in Tihran while Tahirih was there. She listened to Vahid speaking about signs and prophecies in the scripture. Suddenly, she interrupted Vahid with a plea mixed with rebuke:

---

[407] Samandar, "Biography of Tahirih." 58; Root, *Táhirih the Pure*, 76; one of Tahirih's attendants on her flight, Naib Quli, said that as soon as they were out of the city, they left the main road and went on the one of Zah'ra of Qazvin, (Nicolas, *Seyyed Ali Mohammed*, 278).

[408] Ibid, 58; according to Nicolas, *Seyyed Ali Mohammed*, 278, they arrived in Enderman, near the Shazade Abdu'l Azim; Root, *Táhirih the Pure*, 76.

[409] According to Samandar, 58, Tahirih rested while Aqa Hadi went into the city and told Karbala'i Hasan Tajere Qazvini that Tahirih had arrived. Karbala'i Hasan Tajere Qazvini came out to the garden of Imam Zadi where she was staying. Quli didn't know him and hit him but Tahirih told him to stop. She brought fruits out and shared the food with him.

[410] 'Abdu'l-Baha, *Memorials of the Faithful*, 200.

[411] Samandar, "*Biography of Tahirih*," 58.

[412] Zarandi, 204.

"Let deeds, not words, testify to thy faith, if thou art a man of true learning. Cease idly repeating the traditions of the past, for the day of service, of steadfast action, is come. Now is the time to show forth the true signs of God, to rend asunder the veils of idle fancy, to promote the Word of God, and to sacrifice ourselves in His path. Let deeds, not words, be our adorning."[413]

This strong admonition from Tahirih showed the growing urgency in the spiritual movement underway in Persia.

2.

During these same years, a movement spontaneously erupted out of the 'Burned-Over District' of New York which brought thousands of women into the public arena for the first time: spiritualism.

This mass movement began in the unlikeliest of places: the bedroom of two teenage girls. The Fox sisters lived with their parents in the village of Hydesville, NY. Their mother, Margaret, an outgoing woman in her fifties, and her husband John, a very introverted and serious Methodist, had moved to this region to build a new house and finish raising their two youngest daughters, the last important task of their lives. So they found themselves in this small temporary house near the site of their future home. They had accumulated neither land nor money and were worried about setting up a life for their girls which could include marriage.[414]

One unseasonably cold evening in the late March of 1848, Kate and Maggie Fox huddled together in their bedroom out of fear. For several nights they had been hearing the sounds of knocking. The first time this happened, their parents had gotten up and searched for the source of the sounds:

---

[413] 'Abdu'l-Baha, *Memorials of the Faithful*, 200.
[414] Barbara Weisberg, *Talking to the Dead, Kate and Maggie Fox and the rise of spiritualism* (NY, NY: HarperCollins, 2004), 12-3.

"It sounded like someone knocking in the east bed-room, on the floor…as if the chair moved on the floor; we could hardly tell where it was…It was not very loud but it produced a jar of the bedsteads and chairs, that could be felt by placing our hands on the chair, or while we were in bed. It was a feeling of tremulous motion, more than a sudden jar."[415]

The knocks continued every night. On the eve of April 1st, a new snow blanketed the ground. The girls were sent to bed.

After the girls had climbed into bed that night, they sat up and snapped and clapped with their hands, and these were followed by a corresponding number of raps. Then their mother asked questions aloud such as the age of her daughters, and the raps gave the answer. The girls were now clinging to their mother. After doing this with several different questions, their mother went to get her neighbor who went to get her husband who went to get more neighbors to come over. Men who were night fishing in a nearby river came up to see what was going on. A very skeptical man asked the 'spirit' about itself. It had been a peddler who had come through the area years earlier carrying five-hundred dollars; after the skeptic named many people from town, the spirit indicated that a Mr. John Bell—who had lived in that same house—had killed him. The spirit seemed to know intimate details about all the people in the area.

Night after night, as winter changed to spring, people came to the house to ask the spirit 'yes/no' questions about all kinds of details. Most of the raps seemed to come from the bedroom on the east side. The husband responded to the growing local criticism of blasphemy in his house by saying that he had no idea what caused the raps and assured skeptics that they had searched every inch and crevasse of the house.

The local newspaper, *The Western Angus* wrote on April 12th:

---

[415] Ibid., 17.

"The good people of Arcadia, we learn, are in quite a fever, in consequence of the discovery of an 'underground' *ghost*, or some unaccountable noise. Picks and bats were at once brought into requisition, and on digging down about four feet, a stream of pure water gushed forth and filled up the 'ghost' hole."[416]

Despite skeptics and mockery, many first hand testimonies about the strange sounds in the Fox home were given and all of them were similar. Beliefs in ghosts, spirits, and witchcraft were prevalent throughout society, especially in this area. The 'burned over' district, bounded by the Finger Lakes and Lake Erie, was the geographical heart of the Second Great Awakening. Rochester, the largest city in this area, was becoming a center for social reform movements especially abolition and the women's movement.

The Fox phenomenon continued. Efforts were made to separate the sisters from each other but, even then, the raps seemed to follow them. They were brought to the home of their older sister in the city of Rochester. After their arrival, objects seemed to move and doors slam, and so the terrified girls moved out. A sober Congregationalist minister came over to investigate these strange occurrences. Several families had gathered and, when they were all sitting in the parlor, the table moved, and raps were heard. An explosive scene unfolded including one in which a mother asked the spirits if her daughter had been wicked, and she then accused her young daughter of antagonizing the spirits and demanded that she repent. The girl fell to her knees crying acknowledging that she had done wrong—though she didn't know what she had done—and protesting that she didn't know how to repent. The Congregationalist minister could not understand the nature of these events, though he felt there was a comingling of the spiritual and material worlds. Throughout the episode, Kate Fox was

---

[416] Ibid., 22.

the medium—the delicate person through whom the spirit communication took place.[417]

Soon, meetings were being held regularly called séances, spirit circles, or sittings, with Kate as the medium. Many people came to inquire about relatives or to test the 'spirits'; those who had lost children—a common occurrence—were especially eager to know about the condition of their little ones in the next world.

Protestant, especially Calvinist, churches painted terrifying visions of hell, and preachers threatened 'fire and brimstone' to warn sinners about their impending eternal damnation. From the opposite direction, science was calling immortality into question. Society itself was also changing. The sense of a close-knit community was being lost as individuals and families moved more for work in the dynamic and changing economy, intensifying grief and the need for reassurance when a profound loss was suffered. There was also an increased individualism with each deceased person being thought of as unique and special. During these years, cemeteries became much more elaborate as people came to spend time in them and dwell on the lives of their loved ones.[418] The rapid changes in American society shook the personal faith of many, and spiritualism provided evidence of the continuation of life after death and the well-being of loved ones who had passed on.[419]

News of the Fox sisters' communication with spirits and spiritualism went across the North and East like wildfire. Christian churches were certain that the phenomenon of the Fox sisters was the work of the devil and his demons.[420]

Soon Americans in all regions were sitting around their parlors attempting to reach those in the world beyond. Within months, women emerged who were considered 'mediums'. This movement was entirely

---

[417] Ibid., 44-54.
[418] Ibid., 56.
[419] Braude, *Radical Spirits,* 4.
[420] Weisberg, *Talking to the Dead,* 68.

democratic—anyone could be a medium if they could convince others that they could channel spirits of the dead—, and there were no restrictive creeds, dogmas, or organization to hold people back. As a result, its rapid spread was entirely popular—people participated completely voluntarily and no priests or official missionaries were sent out. Spiritualism was easily accepted among black Americans who had held on to their African beliefs in ancestor worship. The role of the medium came to be seen as feminine—adolescent girls were the most believable mediums to people—with the primary trait being passivity, so that the spirit could work through the woman without the medium's will interfering. So spirit communication became associated with the "woman's tongue" and 'spiritual' meant 'feminine'.[421]

As the demand for mediums increased, professional ones emerged. The movement was woman-centered and highly individualistic and stood in contrast to the established churches. As a result it helped bring focus to the position of women in the country. Spiritualists saw that, "woman has been so long subject to customs degrading to herself, that neither she nor the men are sensible where, and to what extent, they [equal rights] exist!"[422] They became committed to working for the emancipation of women from constraints imposed on them by the established order such as unjust marriage laws and limited education, and for women's advancement in such areas as health and education. This rejection of the status quo also extended to the abolition of slavery. Spiritualists connected freedom for women with freedom for all.

Spiritualism's practitioners and followers became an important force for social change in the United States, and women were at its center.[423]

American women were soon going to hold the first convention in Seneca Falls, NY, to begin the very long and arduous process of extending the right to vote to women in the United States.

---

[421] Braude, *Radical Spirits*, 19-29.
[422] Elizabeth Kingsbury quoted in Braude, *Radical* Spirits, 56.
[423] Ibid., 56-7.

At the same time, in Persia, the Babi leaders were gathering to discuss the true nature of the claims of the Bab and what those meant for the laws of Islam which had guided them for centuries, a gathering in which Tahirih would help them cast the past away forever.

It was the summer of 1848.

FIVE:
1848: THE SENECA FALLS CONVENTION, THE
CONFERENCE OF BADASHT

1.

In the darkened sitting room of his house in Johnstown, NY,[424] Judge Cady sat alone, bent over in grief next to the casket containing the remains of his son. This son had been the last great hope for the aging judge's family. Now no one was left to carry on the family name; all of his hopes for the future were dashed. His eleven-year old daughter, Elizabeth, came into the dark parlor. She knew this last brother had held more of her father's affection than she and her three sisters combined. She climbed up on his knee. Her father mechanically put his arm around her. She rested her head on his chest. She wondered what she could say or do to make him feel better. A long silence passed. He heaved a great sigh and said, "O my daughter, I wish you were boy." Wanting so much to make her father feel better, the little girl threw her arms around him and exclaimed, "I will try to be all that my brother was."[425]

Judge Cady, on this morning in 1826, was unconscious of the fact that he was wrapped in the arms of a young daughter who would become one half of a duo that would effect deep, widespread, and permanent social change in American society.

Judge Cady was a highly educated and well-respected judge who upheld the institutions of his society and a conservative man who accepted the social roles assigned to men and women but also fair–minded enough to realize that his daughter had real ability and should

---

[424] Sally McMillen, *Seneca Falls and the Origins of the Women's Rights Movement* (Oxford, UK: Oxford University Press, 2008), 9.

[425] *Not For Ourselves Alone – The Story of Elizabeth Cady Stanton & Susan B. Anthony,* directed by Paul Barnes and Ken Burns, 1999, USA: Florentine Films, WETA.

be given a quality education. So Judge Stanton sent Elizabeth to the Troy Female Seminary in Troy, NY, run by Emma Willard. Elizabeth spent much of her time there at the home of her cousin, an enthusiastic supporter of the social reform movements of the time, especially abolitionism. In his home, she participated in all the discussions and met, for the first time, escaped slaves. Soon she fell in love with Henry Stanton, a tall, handsome abolitionist who championed the rights of slaves even in front of pro-slavery crowds. They married over her

Elizabeth Stanton.

father's objections. Elizabeth changed one aspect of the marriage vow—the word "obey" was dropped. She did not take her husband's first name, "Mrs. Harry Stanton," as was the custom but kept her own original family name instead, the name by which she would go down in history: Elizabeth Cady Stanton (1815-1902).[426]

By the mid-19th century, American women were being pulled in two directions—one towards rights and freedoms and a public role for women as exemplified in the reform movements, spiritualism, and the revivals, and the other—and by far the most prevalent—towards the

---

[426] Ibid.

ideal of true womanhood which held that a woman was the guardian and caretaker of the home, the place where all of the nation's morals were shaped.

Reformers themselves were deeply divided about the proper extent of women's roles in public. Even Rev. Lyman Beecher, who preached forcefully for years against slavery, did not believe in a public role for women.[427] His daughter, Harriet Beecher Stowe, wrote the most popular American novel of the 19th century, *Uncle Tom's Cabin*, which was largely responsible for turning mainstream public sentiment against slavery. The novel popularized the idea that the most powerful moral educator of society was a loving Christian mother who created a Christian home environment.[428] So virtue was always in the context of the home.[429] Women shouldn't get too 'out there'; as Rev. Lyman Beecher stated:

> "There *is* generally, and should be always, in the female character, a softness and delicacy of feeling which shrinks from the notoriety of a public performance. No well-educated female can put herself up, or be put up, to the point of public

---

[427] Ellen Beecher, a descendant through marriage of the Beechers, became a Bahá'í, and her granddaughter, Dorothy Baker, was an important teacher of the Bahá'í Faith in the 20th century. According to a book on the Bahá'í Faith and Christianity: "Ellen Tucher Beecher, affectionately known as "Mother Beecher." was another distinguished early Bahá'í....Her husband was a relative of Harriett Beecher Stowe, and Ellen was an early advocate of women's rights in the Christian church. When she heard about the Bahá'í Faith, she immediately embraced it, and 'Abdu'l-Bahá began corresponding with her in 1897....She raised her granddaughter, Dorothy Baker, to become an outstanding Bahá'í leader. Dorothy met 'Abdu'l-Bahá when she was thirteen years old, and she eventually became the first woman to chair the National Spiritual Assembly of the Bahá'ís of the United States." (Brian Lepard, *In the Glory of the Father* (Wilmette, IL: Bahá'í Publishing Trust, 2008), 58).

[428] Braude, *Sisters and Saints*, 48-52.

[429] Brekus, 153.

prayer, without the loss of some portion at least of that female delicacy, which is above all price."[430]

The home was the sphere where women could play that role. The public sphere—politics, business, public-speaking and preaching—was for men who only had to point to the rough and tumble of public life with its violence, aggression, and drinking, to prove this. Voting, for example, often took place in saloons.[431]

So by tradition, law, and the standard interpretation of Scripture, women in mid-19th century America were in an inferior position. They had little access to education, few if any career paths, no right to own property in a marriage, no right over their bodies in marriage, no right to speak in traditional public forums, and no right to change any of this by the exercise of the most basic right of a citizen—the right to vote.

Free black women in the northern United States lived with all of these restrictions as well as a racial segregation which resulted in most women working as domestic servants and living in poverty as single mothers. Enslaved black women in the South lived with all of these deprivations and the brutality of slavery which made them completely vulnerable to their masters. Harriet Jacobs, for example, went into hiding out of fear of her master and escaped slavery in 1842. She had been a slave in the land of the free, black in a white society, and a woman in a world ruled by men.[432]

Social restrictions placed on American women had some similarities with those for women in Persia, the most limiting one being that men made all the important decisions in a woman's life. But in the United States, American women had a greater degree of public freedom in moving about and the legal framework of the United States contained the concept of individual rights such that a woman could even conceive of a day when she might have the 'right' to vote. The American

---

[430] Ibid.
[431] McMillen, *Seneca Falls*, 24.
[432] Ibid., 11.

economy was also undergoing an industrial revolution which greatly impacted the very ideas of work and family while Persia remained an agrarian based economy ruled by a king and priests invested in keeping the populace uneducated.

By the mid-19th century, changes were underway in the area of women's rights in the United States. Cumbersome divorce laws that were disadvantageous towards women were easing as divorces were moved from the overburdened legislatures to the court system where cases proceeded much more quickly. Property rights for married women remained a very contentious issue as they were closely related to the right to participate in government.[433] More women worked in textile and shoe factories as the nation industrialized though they were paid less than their male counterparts.[434] Women were the backbone of many volunteer efforts in churches and, by mid-century, were participating and playing important roles in all the major social reform movements: the American Society for the Promotion of Temperance (1826), the American Peace Society (1828), the American Anti-Slavery Society (1833), and the American Female Reform Society (1834)[435] which fought rampant prostitution—there were an estimated ten thousand prostitutes in New York City alone and thousands of Chinese women were virtually enslaved having been brought from China for use by the men out West.[436]

There were two events which helped to galvanize women reformers into focusing on the specific issue of gaining the right to vote: the Council of Congregational Ministers of Massachusetts' Pastoral letter of 1837, and the London Anti-Slavery Convention of 1840. The unintended result of both of these was to motivate several women to

---

[433] Ibid., 28-9.
[434] Ibid., 30.
[435] Virginia Bernhard (Editor), Elizabeth Fox-Genovese (Editor), *The Birth of American Feminism: The Seneca Falls Woman's Convention of 1848* (St. James, New York: Brandywine Press, 1995), 3.
[436] McMillen, *Seneca Falls*, 44.

organize the first ever women's suffrage convention in the United States in Seneca Falls, NY, in the summer of 1848.

The Congregational Church's Pastoral letter of 1837 was written as a reaction to the most controversial speaking duo of the American reform era—the Grimke sisters. That year, the sisters were on a speaking tour of New England advocating forcefully for abolition as they always did. Their powerful presentations elicited vehement negative reactions. On this tour, they not only attacked slave-owners and their supporters, they also went after the many Northern business interests that benefitted from slave labor. This was all too much for the Congregational ministers in Massachusetts who issued a Pastoral letter in July, 1837, to steer their flock clear of the Grimke sisters and "the dangers which at present seem to threaten the female character with wide spread and permanent injury". It went on to clarify that "the power of woman is her dependence," and that "God had ordained her weakness and need of protection". When women stepped out of their appropriate place by doing things like speaking in public, "her character becomes unnatural."[437]

The pastoral letter infuriated women like Lucy Stone (1818-1893). While she listened in church to it being read aloud, she poked her sister every time she heard something that offended her so much so that by the end, her sister's side was sore. Stone had been born into the Congregational church, but this pastoral letter began her separation from it and the start of her own trailblazing journey of self-discovery. She became the first woman in Massachusetts to hold a Bachelor's Degree, having earned it from Oberlin College, the first institution of higher learning in American history to admit women and African-Americans;[438] even Oberlin, though, did not allow her to give the Commencement address.![439] There, she discovered that she had real

---

[437] Ibid., 63.
[438] "Oberlin College and Conservatory," *About Oberlin,* accessed October 1, 2013, http://new.oberlin.edu/about/.
[439] Braude, *Radical Spirits,* 91.

oratorical skills, and she put these to use by speaking out for women's rights and against slavery, her parents having nurtured in her strong abolitionist views. She gave her first talk on women's rights in 1847, in her brother's Massachusetts church. She was then hired by William Lloyd Garrison's Massachusetts Anti-Slavery society as one of its advocates; Garrison remembered her "conversational tone...She is always earnest, but never boisterous, and her manner no less than her speech is marked by a gentleness and refinement which puts prejudice to flight".[440]

The Congregational church's pastoral letter of 1837 showed the resistance that mainstream churches had towards women teaching and preaching. The principal leaders of the emerging women's movement saw these churches as major impediments, the strongest opposition coming from clerics whose "readings of the Bible are intensely inimical to the equality of women with men."[441]

The second event which caused the convocation of a woman's rights convention in the U.S. was, unintentionally, the 1840 London Anti-Slavery Convention. Organized by a Quaker, this Convention's purpose was to fight slavery on a worldwide scale—the British had already outlawed it in general. Eight American women went as representatives of their anti-slavery societies, including Elizabeth Cady Stanton, who was the new bride of Harry Stanton, an active abolitionist. Women in Europe, though, did not participate in such gatherings.

The American delegation also included one of the most respected and well-known women of the time, Lucretia Mott (1793-1880), who had founded the first female anti-slavery society in the world. Meeting her created a completely new consciousness in Stanton.[442] Mott had been born into a Quaker family on Nantucket Island, MA, and

---

[440] Carol Lasser, "American National Biography Online: Stone, Lucy," *American National Biography Online*, accessed September 24, 2014, http://www.anb.org/articles/15/15-00663.html.
[441] McMillen, *Seneca Falls*, 64.
[442] Burns and Barnes, *Not For Ourselves Alone*.

learned of the horrors of slavery from the stories told about it in her home. The equality of men and women was also practiced within her own family. Her sea captain father was often away for his trading business so her mother, who also ran a small shop, made the decisions for the household. Lucretia attended the coeducational Nine Partners School when the family moved to Boston and went on to teach there and to marry the school superintendent's grandson, James Mott. Their Quaker marriage vows included the promise to be loving partners and made no mention of female obedience. So strict were they in their commitment to abolition that they refused to use any products made from slave labor such as cotton and sugar. James Mott even changed his business from cotton to wool, a very courageous act when the norm among northerners was still to be involved in businesses which were tied into the slave system. They had six children, five of whom survived into adulthood, and their marriage lasted 57 years.[443] Over the years, Lucretia spoke at Quaker meetings and became a Quaker minister.[444] Frederick Douglass remembered her oratorical skills:

> "In a few moments after she began to speak I saw before me no more a woman, but a glorified presence, bearing a message of light and love. Whenever and wherever I have listened to her my heart has always been made better and my spirit raised by her words."[445]

Encountering the strength of Lucretia Mott's convictions was a turning point for Elizabeth Stanton. They forged a strong and long-lasting work relationship, despite their differences. By the time they had their first in-depth discussions while strolling on the streets of Boston, Mott was Stanton's senior at forty-seven years of age to Stanton's twenty-five. Mott had a serious disposition, dressed plainly

---

[443] Bernhard and Genovese, 6.
[444] McMillen, *Seneca Falls*, 35-36.
[445] Ibid., 37.

and had graying hair, while Stanton had a youthful appearance and wore her hair in ringlets.[446]

The London Convention would not allow any women to take the floor. Ninety percent of the male delegates voted against seating

Elizabeth Cady Stanton and Susan B. Anthony.

women despite the best efforts of Wendell Philips, an American delegate who gave much of his life to the advancement of women's rights.[447] Instead, the women were relegated to sitting in the galleries behind a curtain. And so it was there, while walking the streets of

[446] Bernhard and Genovese, 7; McMillen, *Seneca Falls*, 82.
[447] McMillen, *Seneca Falls*, 73-5.

London together and discussing the affairs of women, that Mott and Stanton decided to hold a convention for the rights of women when they returned to the United States.[448]

The holding of a convention would be long delayed because the Motts lived in Philadelphia with their six children while Stanton moved with her husband and children to the small town of Seneca Falls, NY, to have greater financial stability. When Stanton lived in Boston, she had been in regular association with the leading reformers of the day, so the small town pettiness and isolation of Seneca Falls was difficult for her. In addition, she found the day-to-day chores of managing a household with three small boys suffocating. This made her far more empathetic to what she saw as the drudgery of the lives of ordinary women. Stanton and Mott corresponded with each other but were not able to realize their plans.[449]

In the intervening years, there were some important intellectual contributions in the United States on the subject of women's rights. In 1845, *Women in the Nineteenth Century,* by Margaret Fuller (1810-1850), was published. Fuller was one of the most well-known women in America. Her father had actively encouraged her education such that by the age of nine she could read Latin and wrote him letters in that language. She edited an important magazine for the Transcendentalist movement, associating freely with famous literary figures of the time. She became the country's first female journalist when the *New York Times* hired her in 1844. Her essay, while not advocating for giving the right to vote to women, introduced bold ideas to the American public such as the elimination of public and private spheres of activity for men and women, female self-reliance, women's education that went beyond training on how to be good wife, and the rejection of what she saw as a self-indulgent ideal of the 'female at home' promoted in books for women. Her contributions to the women's movement were cut short by her death in a shipwreck off the

---

[448] Bernhard and Genovese, 7.
[449] Ibid.

coast of Long Island. In the same year as Fuller's essay, Elisha Powell Hurlbut's *Essays on Human Rights and their Guaranties* came out. As a judge, Hurlbut concentrated his arguments on the legal rights and protections denied to women and asked the question, "Hath not a woman a *right* to be regarded as a free moral agent?" Later, in November of 1845, Samuel J. May Jr., a Unitarian minister, became the first minister of a mainstream denomination to publish a sermon in support of a woman's right to vote, *"The Rights and Condition of woman."* In this sermon, he acutely observed: "Women are coaxed, flattered, courted, but they are not respected by many men as they should be; neither do they respect themselves as they should...These circumstances operate powerfully to depress, and oppress women—to make them too dependent—to leave them at the mercy of men." To May, the solution was equal justice for all.[450]

A few years after these important public contributions to the advancement of women, Lucretia Mott and her family went for a visit to Waterloo, NY, located only a few miles from Seneca Falls, NY.[451] On the afternoon of July 13, 1848, five women had tea together including Stanton, Mott, and Mary Ann McClintock, and, moved by Stanton's impassioned words on the lives of women, decided to follow the call and hold their convention. That day they convinced a local Methodist minister to allow them to use his church, the Wesleyan Methodist Chapel of Seneca Falls.

The town of Seneca Falls was benefiting from its proximity to the newly built Erie Canal on which goods could be shipped to the Atlantic seaboard and to a railroad which connected the town to the cities of Syracuse and Rochester. These were both part of the rapid development of transportation going on all over the United State. There were now twenty-four small factories, six churches, four hotels, and a newspaper in Seneca Falls.[452] In addition, the town was in the

---

[450] McMillen, *Seneca Falls*, 77-9.
[451] Bernhard and Genovese, 7.
[452] Ibid., 9.

middle of the area of New York State which was a center of reform activity and was home to famous reformers. Seneca Falls and its region reflected the changing times both economically and morally.

The day after the tea party, July 14, 1848, the *Seneca County Courier* ran this announcement:

> "WOMAN'S RIGHTS CONVENTION - A Convention to discuss the social, civil and religious condition and rights of women, will be held in the Wesleyan Chapel at Seneca Fall, N.Y., on Wednesday and Thursday, the 19th and 20th of July, current, commencing at 10 O'clock A.M."
>
> During the first day, the meeting will be exclusively for women, who are earnestly invited to attend. The public generally are invited to be present the second day, when Lucretia Mott of Philadelphia, and other ladies and gentlemen, will address the Convention."[453]

Lucretia Mott was the principal organizer of the Convention, while Elizabeth Cady Stanton was its driving intellect. It took place five days after this announcement ran.

On the morning of July 19, 1848, the bumpy country roads around Seneca Falls, NY, were crowded with carts and horses coming to the Wesleyan Church. But when the organizers arrived, they found the church locked. The minister could not be found, so Stanton's young nephew was hoisted into the dusty church to open it from the inside. The Seneca Falls Convention began at eleven a.m.. This gathering, which began the journey of American women towards getting the right to vote, was opened by a man, James Mott, Lucretia Mott's husband, so as not to offend public sensibility. He took turns presiding with Thomas McClintock, Mary Ann McClintock's husband. Stanton's

---

[453] "Report of the Woman's Rights Convention," *Women's Rights,* accessed January 1, 2014.
http://www.nps.gov/wori/historyculture/report-of-the-womans-rights-convention.htm.

husband, Harry, while generally supportive, objected vehemently to the inclusion of the demand for the right to vote in the Convention's proceedings, so he left for Albany on the pretext of business. He was also worried that the Convention would become a cause for mockery of his wife. Stanton's father, Judge Cady, travelled to Seneca Falls fearing his daughter had gone insane, while his eldest daughter wept

Lucretia Mott.

over her sister's involvement in such a gathering.[454]

Only women were supposed to have been in attendance that first day, but forty men showed up anyway. There were attendees from the various mainstream denominations, the largest single block being Quakers. Stanton and Mott were the first two to address the Convention, though this was a time when women were usually denied the right to speak to "promiscuous assemblies"—meaning ones which included both men and women.[455] Stanton had never even spoken in front of an audience before, and still she spoke courageously:

---

[454] Bernhard and Genovese, 10.
[455] Braude, *Radical Spirits*, 90.

"... we are assembled to protest against a form of government existing without the consent of the governed - to declare our right to be free as man is free, to be represented in the government which we are taxed to support, to have such disgraceful laws as give man the power to chastise and imprison his wife, to take the wages which she earns, the property which she inherits, and, in case of separation, the children of her love; laws which make her the mere dependent on his bounty ... And, strange as it may seem to many, we now demand our right to vote according to the declaration of the government under which we live ...

All white men in this country have the same rights, however they may differ in mind, body, or estate ...

The right is ours. Have it, we must. Use it, we will. ...

... Verily, the world waits the coming of some new element, some purifying power, some spirit of mercy and love. The voice of woman has been silenced in the state, the church, and the home, but man cannot fulfill his destiny alone, he cannot redeem his race unaided. There are deep and tender chords of sympathy and love in the hearts of the downfallen and oppressed that woman can touch more skillfully than man ...

The world has never yet seen a truly great and virtuous nation, because in the degradation of woman the very fountains of life are poisoned at their source...."[456]

After Stanton and Mott had spoken, the draft of the Declaration of Rights and Sentiments was read aloud. This document had been prepared by the organizers in advance of the Convention and written by Stanton. It followed the format of the Declaration of Independence, with an introduction that began "We hold these truths to be self-

---

[456] Elizabeth Cady Stanton, "Elizabeth Cady Stanton: Seneca Falls Keynote Address," *Great American Documents,* accessed July 5, 2013, http://www.greatamericandocuments.com/speeches/stanton-seneca-falls.html.

evident," but then made the bold assertion "that men and women are created equal." This was followed by a list of grievances about the position of women in society which included the unjust status of women in property, marriage, and divorce laws, their limited access to college educations or professional opportunities, the passing of laws into which women had had no input, and the denial of the right to vote, among others. These injustices, according to the Declaration, caused women "to lessen her self-respect, and to make her lead a dependent and abject life."[457]

The afternoon session began with Stanton reading a series of eleven resolutions which expressed the specific changes that needed to be made to improve the status of women. These resolutions made the point that all laws which prevent the full equality of women to men and inhibit the development of the potential in women were against "the great precept of nature." That evening, Lucretia Mott placed these demands in the larger context of reform in general and encouraged men to become partners in this effort.[458]

The following day, the audience had grown considerably as word spread of the exciting and bold ideas being discussed at the convention. The morning began with a reading of the previous day's minutes including the eleven resolutions. The only resolution to encounter opposition was the following:

> "Resolved, that it is the duty of the women of this country to secure to themselves their sacred right to the elective franchise."[459]

Stanton argued passionately for the right to vote, pointing out that "drunkards, idiots, horseracing rum-selling rowdies, ignorant foreigners, and silly boys."[460] all could vote—but not women. Other partici-

---

[457] McMillen, *Seneca Falls*, 91.
[458] Ibid., 92.
[459] Ibid., 93.
[460] Bernhard and Genovese, 11.

pants, including Lucretia Mott, found this a difficult resolution to adopt.[461] Quakers like her sought to avoid the partisanship of politics and to exercise moral authority in the spheres of life other than the public sphere of politics. This way was seen as the truer, more spiritual and peace-oriented way rather than the divisive world of partisan politics. Women's moral superiority in the private sphere should not be given up or sullied by politics. Some attendees thought that the husbands and fathers could adequately represent the interests of their families at the ballot box and that the right to vote, therefore, was unnecessary. Frederick Douglass, who had been born into slavery and escaped its horrors, rose up to speak on behalf of the resolution:

> "In this denial of the right to participate in government, not merely the degradation of woman and the perpetuation of a great injustice happens, but the maiming and repudiation of one-half of the moral and intellectual power of the government of the world."[462]

The moral weight that Douglass' life and work gave to his words helped the resolution to pass. Douglass would always remember his contribution to the Seneca Falls Convention proudly. All the resolutions of the Declaration had been passed by the convention.[463]

That evening, the last issue for the convention was the signing of the Declaration. The question arose as to whether both men and women should sign it. The convention decided that both would sign but on separate sheets of paper; sixty-eight women and thirty-two men committed their names in ink. A quarter of them were Quaker, most lived in the general area.

But only one of these signatories lived to see the right to vote for women become part of the United States Constitution in 1920. At the

---

[461] Ibid.
[462] McMillen, *Seneca Falls*, 93-4.
[463] Ibid., 94.

close of the Seneca Falls Convention on July 20, 1848, the long struggle for women's suffrage was just beginning.

2.

By the summer of 1847, a year before the Seneca Falls Convention, the Bab's influence had spread throughout Persia, and this brought a backlash from the clergy and the government, both of whom had vested interests in not allowing this powerful new religious movement to upset the established order. In the United States, a person could make religious claims without direct interference from the government, but, in Persia, religious claims could bring on the accusation of heresy, and heresy was a crime. In addition, this was a time of political unrest with the government having to put down a large revolt in the important eastern province of Khurasan.[464] The Prime Minister gave the order to banish the Bab to a remote part of northwestern Persia near the border with Russia, where he was incarcerated in the fortress of Mahku, a stone structure with four towers that sat like a grim lookout on the top of a mountain. A lone path connected its front gate to the town of Mahku at the foot of the mountain. The Araxes River, which marked the border between Persia and Russia, flowed below. From this remote stone castle, the Persians could watch the border with the Russian Empire.[465]

The people of this area were Kurds who followed the Sunni form of Islam and were at odds with their Shi'a Persian rulers. As the local farmers went to their fields, they often stopped to look up at the stone fortress hoping to receive a blessing from the holy man being kept within. Soon, the Prime Minister, through local spies, was reading of the effect of the Bab's presence on the warden and others around him.[466] After seeing the Bab in a vision walking outside the castle, the warden relaxed all the rules pertaining to the prisoner and allowed the

---

[464] Zarandi, 177.
[465] Ibid., 170-1.
[466] Ibid., 181.

growing stream of visitors to come in and meet him.[467] Mahku was becoming a center of attraction, and the Bab saw his imprisonment in the path of God as the essence of freedom—and himself as the incarnation of God's will:

> "All that belongs to the Chosen One is in heaven. This solitary room (wherein I am) which has not even a door, is today the greatest of the gardens of Paradise, for the Tree of Truth is planted herein. All the atoms of which it is composed cry out, 'In truth, there is no other God but God, and there is no other God beside me, the Lord of the Universe.'"[468]

A bitterly cold winter took hold of this remote and mountainous region. From his dark and cold stone room,[469] the Bab began to reveal his Holy book, the Bayan (the 'Utterance').

The Bab was also preparing the way for a second manifestation of God. He was "only the foreshadowing of Him whom God shall make manifest," and his followers "must realize what should be done for Him whom God shall make manifest, when he will appear, so that he will be spared what is happening to me on this day."[470]

The Prime Minister read a letter from the Russian Minister expressing his concern about the presence of a person as influential as the Bab on the border with Russia and his desire to see the Bab removed further away from the Russian border.[471] In April, 1848, the Prime Minister had the Bab moved south to the prison fortress of Chihriq located in an even more remote Kurdish region. This confinement was supposed to have been stricter—the Bab referred to Chihriq as the "Grievous Mountain"—but soon the officer in charge was moved by the Bab's holiness as were the local people. Important clerics in the region became his followers. After having seen the Bab in a dream, a

---

[467] Ibid., 173-4.
[468] Ibid., 172.
[469] Ibid., 176.
[470] Ibid., 172.
[471] Balyuzi, *The Bab*, 132.

seeker travelled all the way from India, greatly impressing the local people with the strength of his convictions.[472]

The authorities in Tihran decided that the time had come to put the Bab on trial in the city of Tabriz, the regional capital. All along the road to Tabriz, the Bab's presence generated excitement as stories of his miraculous deeds were spread among the people.[473] The city of Tabriz was in a state of anticipation about the upcoming trial which was being attended by the most prominent clerics of the area and the future king. Without being asked, the Bab sat in the seat of honor. When questioned about his claim, he answered:

> "I am, I am, I am, the Promised One! I am the One whose name you have for a thousand years invoked, at whose mention you have risen, whose advent you have longed to witness, and the hour of whose Revelation you have prayed God to hasten."[474]

This extraordinary statement astonished the clerics who then responded with a series of very specific questions on obscure issues not related to the Bab's claim but meant to trip him up and embarrass him. When asked about his proofs, the Bab answered that his own word was the "…most convincing truth of the Mission of the Prophet of God."[475] Then a cleric asked that he describe the trial in Qur'anic language, and just as the Bab began to do so, he was cut off by his questioner who mocked him for a mistake he had made in Arabic grammar—the Bab wrote and spoke his own highly unconventional Arabic. At that point the Bab uttered the Qur'anic verse, "Far be the glory of thy Lord, the Lord of all greatness, from what they impute to Him, and peace be upon His Apostles!"[476]

---

[472] Zarandi, 219-221.
[473] Ibid., 226-7.
[474] Ibid., 229.
[475] Ibid., 230.
[476] Ibid., 231.

He then got up and walked out of the trial which descended into an argument among the clerics. Some of the prominent clerics thought the Bab had been treated disrespectfully. The only outcome of this episode was that the Bab was later whipped like a criminal. News of the trial's proceedings spread throughout Tabriz, and the reputation of the Bab grew. The authorities took him away and isolated him back in the mountain fortress of Chihriq.[477]

During the days when the Bab was incarcerated in the castle of Mahku, Tahirih had been spirited away from the persecutions in Qazvin that had been unleashed against Babis following the murder of her father-in-law. Though she had been cleared of any involvement, she was still very vulnerable, and so the most prominent Babi in Tihran, Mirza Husayn Ali, sent his men to extricate her from danger. For several years now, Tahirih felt intuitively that Mirza Husayn Ali had a high spiritual station and would play a great role in the future.[478] She was fully aware that the Bab had written that he was preparing the way for a second Divine manifestation that would follow him. Mirza Husayn Ali had been born into a wealthy noble family but had shown from an early age great sensitivity towards the poor which was very unusual in that society. As he grew to manhood, he turned down all offers of high political and social rank, and instead, adopted a life oriented towards service. He had unreservedly accepted the claims of the Bab and developed a great reputation for spirituality and integrity.

In some of her poems she may have been referring to Mirza Husayn Ali and his station when she used the word 'Baha', meaning 'glory', the title by which he would later be known. In this poem, she expresses her devotion to the manifestations of God—she makes reference to the Bayan, the Bab's Holy book, and uses symbolism related to Moses and Muhammad—and she also uses the name 'Baha' as a personal name thereby indicating the spiritual station of Mirza Husayn Ali:

---

[477] Ibid., 232-233.
[478] Ibid., 204-5.

"His Bayan's words erased my fantasy
And no else but him do I now see

A'la's name stands firmly in his name
Just as God's light shone from the sleeve-like flame

Greatest of masters, O, most lordly of lords
His garden is a heaven beyond words

Thrones in heaven called Baha, ranked so high
Their seats exalted far beyond the sky

God, O God! Who are, and always were
Almighty, Eternal, Grace without peer

Cast a kind glance on one who is alone
And grant new life to this decaying bone

That I may freely tell your mysteries here
And make your deepest, inmost meanings clear

I can think of no other goal but you
I will adore and praise no one but you

You spoke the secret: oneness is always one
Must I keep circling heaven like the sun?

Baha's loved one loves, and is loved, O Lover
Draw to yourself this slave, this sufferer

Harmony stands on this rug of power
Let gentle kindness now forever flower"[479]

In another passage, she refers to Baha'u'llah as the "Abha Beauty"—a variation of the name 'Baha'—who had "pierced the veil of night," and that the "souls of his lovers" were dancing in the light that had "flashed from his face."[480]

Protected by Mirza Husayn Ali, Tahirih spent some time in hiding in and out of his home in Tihran.[481] In the home's beautiful main room, with its multicolored windows and vibrant carpets, she may have been able to teach classes to seekers. Because she could not stay indefinitely in this one home, she was transferred to the residence of the minister of war. He had been deported out of the capital after having fallen out of favor with the King—though he later became Prime Minister—and his sister, a supporter of Mirza Husayn Ali's, was living in their mansion.[482]

In early 1848, the Babi leaders were making preparations to go east in response to the Bab's call that his followers go to the province of Khurasan. Mirza Husayn Ali sent a message asking them to gather at the village of Badasht near a main road in that province.[483] This province had special significance in terms of the Shi'a Muslim belief in a figure known as the 'Mahdi'. This tradition in Islam taught that a messianic figure, the Mahdi, would emerge at the end of time to signal the day of judgement, but he does not appear in the Qur'an, and the beliefs about him changed over the centuries. 'Mahdi' seems to have originally meant a liberator who would bring the Arab tribes of

---

[479] Kessler, 14-5.

[480] Zarandi, 205.

[481] Amanat, "Qurrat al-'Ayn." 138, states that she was in and out of Tihran for several months; Zarandi, 205, states that Baha'u'llah had decided to send her to Khurasan after "a few days".

[482] David S. Ruhe, *Robe of Light, the Prophetic Years of the Supreme Prophet Baha'u'llah 1917-1852* (Oxford, UK: George Ronald, 1994), 82.

[483] Ruhe, *Robe of Light*, 83.

Southern Arabia back to their ancient glory, like the idea of a 'Messiah' for Jews, a king who would liberate the Holy Land. This idea then merged with beliefs about righteousness against corrupt rulers, the resurrection of the dead, the day of judgement, and, in Shi'a Islam, the occultation of the last Imam as well. Over the centuries, there were many claimants to being the 'Mahdi'—from rebels, to founders of dynasties and Sufi mystics, who emerged in Persia, Central Asia, and the Sudan, among other places.[484] In the Sunni tradition, the 'Mahdi' seems to have been thought of more as a ruler in this world; in the Shi'a tradition the Mahdi is the return from occultation of the twelfth Imam who would then redeem Islam. The Babis understood the station of the Bab generally in this way, though it became clearer with time that the Bab was claiming much more—that he was the bringer of new Divine Revelation and the forerunner of a second Manifestation of God, referred to as "the One Whom God will make manifest." One of the prophetic traditions regarding the Mahdi is that he would appear in the Eastern province of Khurasan riding in front of an army that had a black flag as its standard.[485]

In addition to the turmoil in Khurasan caused by the revolt, Mulla Husayn and Quddus, two of the Bab's most important apostles, had been spreading the new teachings there, and this was beginning to upset the established order. Such large numbers of people were coming to meet the two in Mashhad, the capital of the province, that the local police chief had become alarmed. Government troops were still stationed right outside of the city because of the recent rebellion. The prince in charge of the army invited Mulla Husayn to his camp as a way of quieting the tensions in the city. Before going out, Mulla Husayn met with Quddus who told him that he was leaving for the province of Mazindaran in the west and that he would look for Mulla

---

[484] Said Amir Arjomand, "Islam in Iran vi., the Concept of Mahdi in Sunni Islam," *Encyclopaedia Iranica* XIV (Fasc. 2), Dec. 2007, 134–136.
[485] Zarandi, 253.

Site of the historic meeting at Badasht.

Husayn to appear later carrying a black standard at the head of an army of the faithful.[486]

The Bab instructed Mulla Husayn to initiate this episode by raising the black standard in Khurasan and journeying westward. The Bab moreover issued a general call to his disciples to rally to the black standard.[487]

On the road to Mashhad lay the village of Badasht where the Babi leaders finally met up.[488]

Tahirih travelled there with the aid of Mirza Husayn Ali's brother.[489] She and her personal servant[490] rode through Tihran's northern gate. This had to be done cautiously because the city's gatekeepers were on the alert for any woman without a pass. Seven or eight miles outside of the city, they came to a large house in the middle of an orchard at the foot of the mountains whose owner had vacated it after a dispute. Its

---

[486] Ibid., 208-10.

[487] Moojan Momen, *The Social Basis of the Babi Upheavals in Iran (1848-1853): A Preliminary Analysis* (United States of America: Int. J. Middle East Stud. 15, 1983, 157-183), 161.

[488] Amanat, "Qurrat al-'Ayn," 138.

[489] Mirza Musa.

[490] Her name was Qanitih (Zarandi, *The Dawn-Breakers*, 205).

elderly caretaker was there and agreed to look after the two women as they made preparations for the long journey east. Tahirih set out for Khurasan with a group that included her personal servant and Hadi, the Babi who had rescued her and now served as her protector, along with several others. They took the main east-west highway that followed the southern foothills of the Alborz Mountains and was just above the arid region to the south with its vast expanse of salt. With no trees, dust from all the other travelers riding donkeys, horses, and camels filled the air.[491]

To avoid suspicion, Mirza Husayn Ali followed a few days later. He rode with several other Babis and the supplies needed for the gathering. On such an overland journey one could cover fifteen to twenty miles a day. Mirza Husayn Ali made good time so as to reach the place of provisioning and find a suitable spot for the gathering. By late June, 1848, he had covered the four-hundred kilometers to Shah-rud, the town midway between Tihran and Mashhad, the capital of Khurasan. This town was at the juncture of the roads which went east to Mashhad and north to the sea and was used as a place of assembly for groups of travelers who wanted to band together for protection against Turkmen tribesmen. Mirza Husayn Ali rented three gardens to the south[492] in Badasht, a small rural village. The area had been a resort for the nobility. There were several small gardens with a large open area in the middle where the Babis could gather to meet.[493] One was for himself, another for Quddus, and a third for Tahirih;[494] other believers

---

[491] Ruhe, *Robe of Light*, 83-4.

[492] Ibid., 84.

[493] Root, *Táhirih the pure*, 81.

[494] 'Abdu'l-Baha, *Memorials of the Faithful*, 200; Zarandi, 211; according to 'Abdu'l-Baha, (*Tablets of Abdu'l-Baha Abbas* v. 4 16 and 20), there were two gardens and the tent of Baha'u'llah was pitched in the square with the tents of other Babis.

pitched their tents near them.[495] Each garden had a large tent with mats and carpets; Tahirih's was protected by Hadi who had accompanied her out of Tihran. There was a stream which ran through the great open field.[496] Summer had come and, with it, the flowering of fruit trees with the majestic mountains as a backdrop.[497]

Eighty-one Babis eventually gathered at Badasht in the beginning of the summer of 1848.[498] Quddus, the 18th Letter of the Living of the Bab, arrived after hearing about the location of the gathering from Babis whom he had met on the road.[499] Mirza Husayn Ali had brought him over in secret from Shah-rud after his long ride from Mashhad. Mulla Husayn, the first Letter of the Living, had been detained by the authorities in Mashhad, and Vahid, one of the most prominent clerics in the kingdom to become a Babi, was unable to attend. Several other Letters of the Living stayed in smaller tents on the property.[500] Most Babis at Badasht were from Khurasan, Mazandaran, and Qazvin.[501]

With the Bab now imprisoned and largely cut off from them, the Babis had come together as a result of the Bab's command and Mirza Husayn Ali's efforts. There had been extensive correspondence between the Bab and Mirza Husayn Ali regarding preparations for this gathering.[502] Its main purpose was to determine the true nature of the Bab's revelation. The contents of the Bab's holy book, the *Bayan*, were not widely known as it had just been revealed during his imprisonment in Mahku that previous winter of 1847-48. Babis may also have

---

[495] According to Balyuzi, *The Bab*, 168, the area in which the generality of believers stayed faced the three gardens. The believers pitched their tents in the middle court ('Abdu'l-Baha, *Memorials of the Faithful*, 200).

[496] Ibid.

[497] Ruhe, *Robe of Light*, 84.

[498] Mázandarání, 111; according to Shaykh Abu Turab quoted in Zarandi, 211.

[499] Zarandi, 207.

[500] Ruhe, *Robe of Light*, 85.

[501] Amanat, "Qurrat al-'Ayn," 138.

[502] Shoghi Effendi, *God Passes By*, 31.

wanted to consult on what should be done about the Bab's imprisonment.[503]

The Babis did not have unity of understanding about the Bab's station and mission, and his claims relative to Islam and the traditions of the past. Was he announcing a new Revelation or was he the promised reformer of Islam? If this was a *new* Revelation, *what* were its teachings and *who* were its leaders? Quddus was seen as the exponent of the more conservative view, while Tahirih expressed a more iconoclastic view.

Tahirih had already challenged the Babis in the holy cities of Iraq with her understanding of the station and teachings of the Bab. She clearly believed this was a new revelation, and that they were living in an 'in-between' time; the Shari'a and the law of prayer were now replaced by the new law. One day, Quddus and other believers were meeting in the tent of Mirza Husayn Ali, who was ill, when Tahirih entered their gathering without her veil and proclaimed that "the Trumpet is sounding! The great Trump is blown! The universal Advent is now proclaimed!"[504] These were words from the Qur'an and the Book of Isaiah. She, Tahirih, a woman, was that trumpet blast.[505]

The Babis were shocked by this display because they regarded Tahirih as the holy Fatimih, Muhammad's daughter, and to look upon her face was blasphemous. Some may have remembered the Islamic tradition in which Fatimih appears unveiled on the Day of Judgement and were thus shaken by the realization that the time had come.[506] Quddus sat with a furious expression on his face. One Babi even cut

---

[503] Ibid..

[504] The Qur'an, Surah 74:8 and 6:73, quoted in 'Abdu'l-Baha, *Memorials of the Faithful*, 201.

[505] According to Shaykh Abu Turab quoted in Zarandi, 213; 'Abdu'l-Baha, *Memorials of the Faithful*, 201; Shoghi Effendi, *God Passes By*, 33-4.

[506] Shoghi Effendi, *God Passes By*, 32.

his own throat as a gesture of atonement for having looked on the face of such a holy person.[507]

They looked to Mirza Husayn Ali for guidance in this moment of crisis, and he told them to read the Surih of the Inevitable from the Qur'an:

> "When the Day that must come shall have come suddenly...Day that shall abase! Day that shall exalt...."[508]

In the poem below, Tahirih uses the image of the veil—which she did often—to symbolize that which comes between the seeker and the beloved, depicted here as the famous lovers from Persian literature, Layli and Majnun. In this poem, the veil is burned away.

> "His drunken eyes have wasted all the land!
> Whoever gazes at him cannot stand!
>
> He turns his head, and one glance from his eyes
> will turn to sand the wisdom of the wise
>
> Madder than Majnum, Layli's tent he flees
> to throw his heart at any opened hand
>
> The goldsmith's tent glows bright from his fire-brand
> All veils now burn away at his demand
>
> He holds the flame Moses could not withstand
> It's not that bush—so why fear his command?

---

[507] According to Shaykh Abu Turab quoted in Zarandi, 213. According to Zarandi, 213, the Babi who cut his throat was 'Abdu'l-Khaliq-i-Isfahani. 'Abdu'l-Baha calls him 'Ismael', *Tablets of Abdul Baha*, v. 4 17 and 21.
[508] The Qur'an, Surah 56, quoted in 'Abdu'l-Baha, *Memorials of the Faithful*, 201; Balyuzi, *The Bab*, 168.

So come, and fill my cup! That's my demand!
I'll spill his secrets—I know them first-hand

Open your eyes! Gaze at us if you can,
and see the face of God! Do you understand?

Naked glory fills our universe and
like the sun sheds light on every land."[509]

Tahirih appeared radiant and peaceful despite the hostile reaction of
some of the Babis. She spoke about this new time using Qur'anic
language. She concluded by looking at Mirza Husayn Ali and Quddus
and saying:

"'Verily, amid gardens and rivers shall the pious dwell in the
seat of truth, in the presence of the potent King.'"[510]

She then declared herself to be the word of this revelation:

"I am the word that the Qa'im will utter, the word that shall
put to flight the chiefs and nobles of the earth."[511]

And she encouraged those assembled to celebrate this day:

"This day is the day of festivity and universal rejoicing, the
day on which the fetters of the past are burst asunder. Let
those who have shared in this great achievement arise and
embrace each other."[512]

Tahirih's actions divided the Babis. Some now doubted the truth of
the Bab, and a few even left the Faith.[513] Some saw her as the source of
authority, while others believed Quddus to be the true representative
of the Bab and still others saw the whole episode as a Divine test.

---

[509] Kessler and Banani, 77.
[510] Quran 54:54, 55, quoted in Zarandi, 213.
[511] Ibid, 213; Shoghi Effendi, *God Passes By,* 32-33.
[512] Ibid., 214.
[513] Ibid., 215; 'Abdu'l-Baha, *Memorials of the Faithful,* 201.

Tahirih challenged Quddus by referring to him as a "pupil" whom she had to instruct.[514] During a debate with him, she tried to show the weaknesses of the more conservative view. Her followers, inflamed with the idea of the end of the old order and the beginning of a new one, discarded their prayer rugs and broke their prayer seals as idols. She told the more conservative Babis that if they thought she was a heretic, they should try to bring her back to the true path.[515]

But it was Mirza Husayn Ali's wisdom which held the Babis together and guided them to a new understanding of the Bab's revelation. Though no written record survives of the proceedings, the Babis came to understand that the Bab's revelation was a new Revelation. Now, every day of the gathering, another law of Islam was abrogated.[516] Each abrogation was followed by a vigorous discussion among the Babis. Mirza Husayn Ali steered the course of these events.[517] He was able to

---

[514] Ibid., 214.

[515] In one version based on an eyewitness account, she interrupted Quddus's prayers, waving a sword, and called on him to stand up to the important clerics who had opposed him in his hometown because it was the time for martyrdom (Mázandarání, vol. 3, 325-6).

[516] According to Shaykh Abu Turab quoted in Zarandi, 211; Mázandarání, vol. 3, 111.

[517] Shoghi Effendi in *God Passes By*, 31-2, writes that this public conflict between these two Letters of the Living of the Bab was pre-arranged to lessen the shock of the coming break with Islam: "Quddús, regarded as the exponent of the conservative element within it, affected, in pursuance of a pre-conceived plan designed to mitigate the alarm and consternation which such a conference was sure to arouse, to oppose the seemingly extremist views advocated by the impetuous Táhirih." Zarandi, quoting Shaykh Abu-Turab gives a very dramatic account of the conflict between the two and adds this footnote (f, 1, 212): "According to the "Kashfu'l-Ghitá," a decision had been previously arrived at between Quddús and Táhirih, in accordance with which the latter was to proclaim publicly the independent character of the Revelation of the Báb, and to emphasise the abrogation of the laws and ordinances of the previous Dispensation.
Quddús, on the other hand, was expected to oppose her contention and strenuously to reject her views. This arrangement was made for the purpose of

create unity among the Babis. He revealed one tablet on each of the twenty-two days which was then chanted aloud by a Babi hailing from his home district of Nur and which gave new names to individual Babis; he didn't tell anyone he was the author. He was now Jinab-i-'Baha', meaning 'Glory' or 'Glorious One'; there was no objection to him having this title because of the respect in which he was held by the other Babis. Tahirih was now known by this name which meant the "Pure One"; prior to that she had been known by other names, including the descriptive phrase "Qurratu'l-Ayn." meaning the 'solace of the eyes', used by Siyyid Kazim to indicate her status as a favored disciple, and by her father.[518] From this day forth, the Babis called each other by these new names. The Bab, at his trial in Tabriz which was happening at the same time as the conference of Badasht, declared that this was indeed a new revelation and a break with the past.[519] In tablets to his followers, he used the new names they had been given at Badasht.[520]

The conference at Badasht and Tahirih's role in it were given this tribute in the history of the early Baha'i Faith, *God Passes By*, by Shoghi Effendi, head of the Baha'i Faith (1921-1957):

> "A little over four years had elapsed since the birth of the Báb's Revelation when the trumpet-blast announcing the formal extinction of the old, and the inauguration of the new Dispensation was sounded. No pomp, no pageantry marked so great a turning-point in the world's religious history. Nor was its modest setting commensurate with such a sudden,

---

mitigating the effects of such a challenging and far-reaching proclamation, and of averting the dangers and perils which such a startling innovation was sure to produce. (211.) Bahá'u'lláh appears to have taken a neutral attitude in this controversy, though actually He was the prime mover and the controlling and directing influence throughout the different stages of that memorable episode."

[518] Hoseini, 176.

[519] Shoghi Effendi, *God Passes By*, 33; Nicolas, *Seyyed Ali Mohammed*, 280; Ruhe, *Robe of Light*, 85.

[520] Ibid., 32; according to Shaykh Abu Turab quoted in Zarandi, 211.

startling, complete emancipation from the dark and embat-
tled forces of fanaticism, of priestcraft, of religious orthodoxy
and superstition. The assembled host consisted of no more
than a single woman and a handful of men, mostly recruited
from the very ranks they were attacking, and devoid, with
few exceptions, of wealth, prestige and power. The Captain
of the host was Himself an absentee, a captive in the grip of
His foes. The arena was a tiny hamlet in the plain of Badasht
on the border of Mazindarán. The trumpeter was a lone
woman, the noblest of her sex in that Dispensation, whom
even some of her co-religionists pronounced a heretic. The
call she sounded was the death-knell of the twelve hundred
year old law of Islám."[521]

After Badasht, the Babis went back out into the world greatly
changed, having let go of many of their old religious habits which had
guided their families for centuries[522] such as the law of prayer.[523] Many
of the Babis were mullas with beliefs shaped by their Shaykhi understanding of Shi'a Islam. They tended to be more open-minded than
other clerics and had to be very courageous even to be associated with
the Bab's heretical spiritual message. By breaking with the past at
Badasht, they were leaping into the unknown. They would have to be
educated in the precepts of the new faith, which would be accom-
plished through the study of the Bab's writings and the teaching by
prominent Babis such as Jinab-i-Baha, Tahirih, and others.[524]

At Badasht, Tahirih had stepped well outside the boundaries of
female propriety, compelled by the powerful spiritual forces which she
believed to have been released into the world because of the Bab's
revelation. Her gender was not a limitation, but rather, according to
this poem, a source of power. In it, she uses traditional imagery found

---

[521] Ibid., 33-34.
[522] Zarandi, 215.
[523] Mázandaráni, vol. 3, 111.
[524] Ruhe, *Robe of Light*, 90.

in Persian poetry of perfumed hair, gazelles, and dawn, in an unexpected way—to celebrate her own strength as a woman:

> "Just let the wind untie my perfumed hair,
> my net would capture every wild gazelle.
>
> Just let me paint my flashing eyes with black,
> and I would turn the day as dark as hell.
>
> Yearning, each dawn, to see my dazzling face,
> the heaven lifts its golden looking-glass.
>
> If I should pass a church by chance today,
> Christ's own virgins would rush to my gospel."[525]

---

[540] Banani and Kessler, 49.

SIX:
THE MARTYRDOM OF TAHIRIH

1.

The Conference of Badasht made it clear that the Bab was claiming to be the bringer of a new revelation with a new Divine law. The Bab was the manifestation of God's will, the Bayan was his holy book, the Babis were the new sacred community—and all of this was to prepare the people for a second Divine outpouring by a figure prophesied by the Bab as 'Him whom God shall make manifest'.

Such a claim went far beyond any prophetic expectations in Shi'ism and marked the fulfillment and end of the Islamic age. This was heresy and significantly increased the danger from the clergy for Babis, especially as news of the gathering at Badasht spread.

The Bab was kept isolated in the northern province of Azerbaijan. He was moved from the stone fortress of Mahku to Chihriq farther away from the Russian border out of concern for the effect his presence was having in that sensitive region. Chihriq was another stone citadel that sat atop a gloomy rock mountain.

After the conclusion of the conference of Badasht, Tahirih and Quddus headed north with Jinab-i-Baha and others. They stayed away from the main east-west highway, possibly to avoid detection. The northerly route wound along the Mojen River through a high mountain pass into the Nika River valley which went all the way to the Caspian Sea. Tahirih and Quddus were now completely reconciled, so much so that they rode together in a howdah, a carriage strapped on the back of a camel. Tahirih composed and chanted poems aloud in praise of the new day; the sound of her voice echoing in the valley may have helped inspire her fellow believers.[526]

The group came to the village of Niyala where local villagers attacked the band of Babis. Jinab-i-Baha later recalled the unexpected assault:

---

[526] Ruhe, *Robe of Light*, 91.

"We were all gathered in the village of Niyala and were rest-
ing at the foot of a mountain, when, at the hour of dawn, we
were suddenly awakened by the stones which the people of
the neighbourhood were hurling upon us from the top of the
mountain. The fierceness of their attack induced our companions to flee in terror and consternation. I clothed Quddus
in my own garments and dispatched him to a place of safety,
where I intended to join him. When I arrived, I found that
he had gone. None of our companions had remained in Niyala except Tahirih and a young man from Shiraz, Mirza
Abdu'llah. The violence with which we were assailed had
brought desolation into our camp. I found no one into
whose custody I could deliver Tahirih except that young
man, who displayed on that occasion a courage and determination that were truly surprising. Sword in hand, undaunted
by the savage assault of the inhabitants of the village, who
had rushed to plunder our property, he sprang forward to
stay the hand of the assailants. Though himself wounded in
several parts of his body, he risked his life to protect our
property. I bade him desist from his act. When the tumult
had subsided, I approached a number of the inhabitants of
the village and was able to convince them of the cruelty and
shamefulness of their behaviour. I subsequently succeeded in
restoring a part of our plundered property."[527]

Jinab-i-Baha's courageous leadership helped extricate the Babis from
this attack. He had sent Quddus in disguise to the apostle's hometown
of Barforush and put Tahirih and her servant under the protection of
another Babi. Tahirih then went to Barforush in September, 1848,
and stayed in the home of a mullah who supported the Bab, even
preaching in his mosque.[528]

---

[527] Zarandi, 215-6; 'Abdu'l-Baha, *Memorials of the Faithful*, 202.
[528] Mázandarání, 326-7; Amanat, "Qurrat al 'Ayn." 143. The mulla was Mulla
Muhammad Hamza Shari'atmandar.

Tahirih began a long period of wandering now, a homeless apostle. In this poem, she becomes a pure heart who goes from complete destruction to restoration through her attraction to the Beloved. The heart is freed from death through the Beloved and consumed in the fire of love for him:

> "This heart, this heart, it thinks of only you.
> This heart, I swear, it sings for only you.
>
> Wounded and bleeding, enchanted, undone:
> this heart, I swear, it sings for only you.
>
> The musk in your hair, the spell of your face:
> this heart, I swear, delights in only you.
>
> And just to be in heaven standing there,
> this heart finds its rightful place in glory.
>
> The moonlight of your eyes, and drenched in fire:
> dark clouds now flee from this heart's ecstasy.
>
> Be kind, generous! Take pity, take care!
> End this heart's pathetic agitation.
>
> Driven from everything, drawn just to you:
> freed from death in tasting your affliction.
>
> Let sparks fly! This heart's father is the fire.
> This joyful heart will burn hot with desire."[529]

Tahirih spent the remainder of 1848 and all of 1849 under the protection of Jinab-i-Baha in the province of Mazindaran where his family owned land and homes in the district of Nur.

---

[529] Banani and Kessler, 95.

The province of Mazindaran was called the "verdant isle" by the Bab
because of its greenery and flowers, the result of having numerous
rivers and mountain torrents running through it into the Caspian Sea.
The Alborz Mountains rose up in the southern part of the province
and dropped dramatically into the coastal plain of the Caspian Sea in
the north. This plain was so fertile it could grow sugar cane; during
Roman times tigers used for the coliseum shows roamed the lush
ground. The Caspian Sea was filled with valuable sturgeon. The
overall climate of Mazindaran was moderate.

Jinab-i-Baha's father was a former governor of Luristan province and
quite wealthy. He owned several villages and homes in the mountain
district of Nur, an estate in the foothills north of Tihran, and a large
multi-home complex in the northern section of the capital. He had
built a large mansion in the village of Takur located in the province of
Nur. The villagers had seen Jinab-i-Baha grow up there as a boy and
respected the whole family as owners who treated them justly. The
village had been exempted from taxation by the King as a sign of the
honor in which he held Jinab-i-Baha's father.

Jinab-i-Baha eventually made his way back to his ancestral village
from where he guided the affairs of the dynamic new religion. Takur
sat in a dramatic setting. Mountain peaks soared north of the village
and the Nur river valley opened to the south; the river flowed east to
the Haraz River through a canyon with a sheer rock cliff which had a
sloping mass of rock fragments at the foot of the cliff. The village of
forty to sixty families sat next to a stream which roared to life when
snow melt ran down from the mountain peaks when the weather
warmed; such a torrent once destroyed the family home. The stream
plunged into the Nur river valley. This typical mountain village was
made up of simple stone and brick buildings, all built at different
angles from each other, with rocky lanes meandering between them.
Mirza Buzurg's large house dominated the village, sitting on the site
where the brook came into the river valley. The two story rectangular
mansion of brick and stone had a large central hall with stained glass

windows and gardens behind its walled enclosure. The arch above the
gateway had an inscription: "When thou enterest the sacred abode of
the Beloved, say: "I am at thy command. This is the home of Love;
enter with reverence. This is holy ground; remove thy shoes when thou
enterest here."[530]

Rasht Rudkan Fortress.

While Jinab-i-Baha, Tahirih, and Quddus were travelling north after
Badasht, other Babis went east to join Mulla Husayn in the province
of Khurasan. In July, 1848, Mulla Husayn rode west out of Mashhad
holding up a black standard in fulfillment of the Bab's wishes and the
well-known prophecy drawn from Islamic tradition that the Mahdi
would ride out of Khurasan under the Black Standard.[531]

Mulla Husayn wore on his head a turban that the Bab had sent him
befitting his role as the representative of the Promised One. He
proclaimed the message of the Bab at every stop. He chose a few
converts each time to join his large and growing group of companions

---

[530] Ruhe, *Robe of Light*, 40-1.
[531] Momen, *The Social Basis*, 161.

on their journey but warned them of the sacrifices they would have to make which scared some away.[532] Crossing over into the next province of Mazindaran, he had over three-hundred people with him.[533] They were from all walks of life and came from over ten different provinces

Baha'u'llah's residence in Takur.

of Persia; most were minor village clerics mixed in with urban workers, merchants, peasants, and over a dozen high-ranking clerics.[534]

As they neared the town of Barfurush, a very large and angry crowd confronted them after having been incited by the local mujtahid who warned that these Babis had come to destroy Islam and had to be stopped. There was a brief skirmish in which Mulla Husayn's reputation as a fierce warrior grew. The intensity of his faith seems to have transformed Mulla Husayn from a religious scholar into a warrior. Once in town, Mulla Husayn reprimanded the people for their mistreatment of the Babis, and the local leaders came to offer their acquiescence, but as they were leaving, the Babis were treacherously attacked by soldiers on the orders of a leading cleric. Mulla Husayn led the Babis to a local shrine dedicated to the saint named Shaykh

---

[532] Zarandi, 235-7.
[533] Momen, *The Social Basis,* 161.
[534] Ibid., 162-6.

Rud Fortress, Mazindaran.

Tabarsi, one of the transmitters of the Islamic traditions. There, the Babis built a simple fort and set up camp.[535]

The Babis were frequently attacked by local people while they built the fort. One day, Jinab-i-Baha arrived at the site of the shrine and greeted the Babis, spoke at some length with Mulla Husayn, offered them his encouragement and blessing, and asked that they go and bring Quddus to this site because his presence would make the group complete and inspire the other Babis. He then set off back to Tihran. Quddus had been under house arrest in another town, and his arrival some days later brought great joy to the Babis. He was greatly revered by them; Mulla Husayn called himself Quddus' "lowly servant." Then the Babis gathered together to chant the writings of the Bab and passages from the Qur'an which they believed referred to them as the spiritual heroes of the end times.[536]

With the fort complete, the leading cleric in the region wrote a letter of alarm to the newly enthroned King of Persia, Nasir al-din Shah, warning him that there was a rebellion brewing in the region and that troops were needed. The untrained but determined Babis, though,

---

[535] Zarandi, 237-48.
[536] Ibid., 250-257.

were able to repulse the attacks of the professional soldiers. Meanwhile, Jinab-i-Baha attempted to reach Tabarsi but was turned back and beaten at the town of Amul. Army reinforcements arrived, and the fort was ringed by barricades. Despite the overwhelming odds in favor

The village of Vaz in Mazindaran where Tahirih was arrested.

of the army, the standoff continued through the winter of 1848-9 with Mulla Husayn leading four different sorties which routed and terrified the soldiers. The fourth time, on February 2nd, 1849, he was killed. The grieving Babis managed to continue their struggle with inspiration from Quddus. Despite their dwindling food supplies, the onset of hunger, cold, and the constant cannon fire, the Babi resistance did not give way. Finally, officials lured the Babis out by swearing on a Qur'an that they were guaranteed their safe passage. Quddus responded faithfully to the oath. A few of the Babis were taken as slaves; the remainder, save for Quddus, were massacred. He was brought to his hometown of Barfurush where he suffered an appallingly cruel martyrdom at the hands of a street mob. In his dying moments he asked for forgiveness for his tormentors.[537]

---

[537] Ibid., 259-298.

After hearing about the Babis gathering at Tabarsi, Tahirih had wanted to disguise herself as a man and join Mulla Husayn and the others—she even gave away a ring to one of the ladies of Nur[538]—, but Jinab-i-Baha discouraged her from going.[539] She spent 1849 under his protection living in various towns and villages in Mazindaran. She may have spent much of the year in one farmhouse near the village of Vaz, south of the town of Amul.[540] The Prime Minister of Persia considered Tahirih a wanted Babi rebel, so government agents were on the lookout for her. Near the year's end, she was found by government agents who killed her host on the spot.[541]

In January, 1850, Tahirih was brought to Tihran as a prisoner. This sprawling capital city of over one hundred thousand people lay over a flat plain. The foothills of the Alborz Mountains rose up in the north. Long paths connected it to the villages and countryside. The new king had taken down the old walls which measured four miles around. He had the main palace compound, government buildings, and the major bazaars built north of the city. The wealthy also constructed their mansions with private gardens up in the foothills where the weather was mild and where they were in closer proximity to the royal family. Jinab-i-Baha's father had an estate there named 'the abode of the birds'. Their main family home was a compound of seven mansions near the Shimiran gate. The vast majority of people lived in the south part of Tihran which was a jumble of one to three story buildings of brick and stone cut by uneven and mostly unpaved streets and alleys. This section of the city was poor and crowded with streets filled with

---

[538] Mázandarání, 327.

[539] Root, *Táhirih the pure,* 88; according to Mazandarani, 327, Tahirih did attempt to get to Tabarsi but was arrested and taken to Tihran. The authors believe that the sequence of events as described in this narrative are more likely because they fit clearly into the overall timeline whereas the Mazandarani version does not.

[540] Mázandarání, 327; Amanat, "Qurrat al-'Ayn." 143. According to these sources she was the guest of Aqa Nasrullah Gilardi.

[541] Amanat, "Qurrat al-'Ayn." 157 f. 179.

the stench of animal and human waste and was especially noxious during the dry, hot, and dusty summer months. The lives of people in these areas could be quite short. Though Jinab-i-Baha began his own family in a rented house near the Shimiran gate, he and his new wife spent much time serving the poor in south Tihran.[542]

Tahirih's arrival in Tihran began the last phase of her life. She was a high profile prisoner who came from a very prominent family of clerics. After Jinab-i-Baha, she was the most prominent and influential of the Bab's followers at a time when the faith of the Bab was spreading rapidly and violent persecutions had begun. She was soon summoned to an interview with the highest authorities in the kingdom— the Prime Minister and the King.[543]

Tahirih may have received an offer of marriage from the king and, in response, she penned a rejection in the form of a poem. In the first part of this poem, she writes of the joy experienced by the followers of the Bab in giving up their lives for him; then, she lays bare her own willingness to be a sacrifice to him. Infidels, symbolized here as Chinese and Turkmen cities, cannot draw the Muslim faithful away, but he, the Beloved, can. He draws Tahirih towards him.[544] She then contrasts the Bab's mystical power with the king's lust for 'empires'. She is content with sacrifice on the spiritual path:

> "The raptures of yearning for you have constrained with the
> chains of sorrow and calamity
> All the broken-hearted lovers,
> who gladly give up their lives in the path of your love.
> And if out of caprice or cruelty
> my Beloved be intent on slaying me, stainless though I be,

---

[542] Ruhe, *Robe of Light*, 24, 50-2; Homa Irani Behbahani, Ph. D; Fakhri Khosravi, M. Sc, *Iranian Garden: A Place of Coexistence: City-Nature-Landscape Case Study: Tehran Gardens in 19th Century*, http://www.academia.edu/, 82.

[543] Amanat, "Qurrat al-'Ayn," 143; Qazvini, *Samandar*, 368; Hoseini, 315; Root, *Táhirih the pure*, 95-96.

[544] Hatcher and Hemmat, f. 287, 184.

I will be patient under his sword,
And indeed I will content myself with whatsoever contents him.
At dawn that cruel charmer of mine
Deigned to approach my bed,
And when I saw his face,
it was as if the morning itself had dawned.
No musky scent in all Khotan
can match the fragrance of his tresses!
No infidel in all Khatá possesses
such seditious eyes as those of my beloved!
But you, O King, ignorant of wine's ecstasy and love's longing,
can but pace behind the pious ones, the ascetics.
And what can I do when you doubt or disdain
the holy motives of the sanctified ones?
You desire only a woman's dangling ringlets,
the well-bred steed, the silver studded saddle.
Your entire life you have been ungrateful to the poor,
have abhorred the destitute in your midst.
For you there exist empires only—Alexander's pomp and glory;
for me, the ways and the habit of the dervish suffice.
You adore kingdoms? Take them.
As for me, this chastisement is bounty enough.
So pass beyond this interlude—this notion of 'I' and 'we',
dwell in your kingdom of nothingness.
When you enter therein,
you will indeed have attained your heart's desire."[545]

She was placed under house arrest in the home of the mayor of Tihran, Mahmoud Khan.[546] Because of her connection to Jinab-i-Baha whose family had links to the highest levels of government, and her own personal fame, and, possibly, because of the king of Persia's

---

[545] Ibid., 108-9.
[546] Shoghi Effendi, *God Passes By*, 74; Zarandi, 455.

favorable opinion of her, Tahirih was able to visit certain other homes with permission.[547] She may even have been visited by the Prime Minister. He was deposed in July, 1851, banished, and executed, possibly a victim of the constant palace intrigue that surrounded the Queen mother.[548]

House of the Mayor in Tihran, in which Tahirih was under house arrest at the end of her life.

The wife of the Mayor became an enthusiastic devotee of Tahirih. Many women of high social rank in Tihran came to listen to the learned guest.[549] Tahirih most likely explained the Bab's claims to them. If she also had showed them how the Babi Faith could greatly improve the position of women in society, this may have had repercussions in their homes.[550]

---

[547] Ruhe, *Robe of Light*, footnote, 111; Balyuzi, *Bahá'u'lláh: The King of Glory*, 63-4.

[548] Samandar, 368.

[549] 'Abdu'l-Baha, *Memorials of the Faithful*, 202; Zarandi, 455.

[550] Nicolas, *Seyyed Ali Mohammed*, 446.

Among the women who were attracted to Tahirih and her message was a prominent poet, Shams-i-Jahan, the grand-daughter of the second king of the Qajar dynasty, Fath Ali-Shah.[551] She had been able to make a pilgrimage to Mecca. Once she heard of Tahirih's presence in Tihran, she was determined to meet her. In a series of poems written later, she described their first encounter. She set out one day with her servant for the home of the mayor without telling anyone. Arriving at the mayor's compound, she stepped into the inner court-yard and crossed over to the building where Tahirih was being held on the second floor. As she got close, she said a prayer beseeching God that if Tahirih's teachings were true, she would be allowed to see her. A second floor window opened in which Tahirih appeared "like a brilliant sun" and called down to her. Overcome with emotion, the princess began to cry while Tahirih smiled. The princess asked her about her imprisonment, and Tahirih answered that it was because she proclaimed the truth. The princess came to understand that the 'truth' spoken of had to do with the teachings of the young Siyyid from Shiraz. Abruptly, though, their exchange was cut off by men who were meant to be guarding Tahirih, and the princess went home longing to resume their conversation on these spiritual questions.[552]

The high esteem in which Tahirih was held by the prominent women of Tihran and the excitement she generated among them were evident on the evening of the wedding feast held for the mayor's son. The house was festooned with decorations, and singers and musicians were brought in for the celebratory occasion. The women, who included princesses and wives of important government officials, came dressed in all of their finery. The celebration got under way with music playing and food being served. The women sent a message to the mayor—men and women were segregated from one another—asking that he allow Tahirih to come and speak to them. Shams-i-Jahan remembered Tahirih entering with great dignity and speaking with

---

[551] Amanat, "Qurrat al-'Ayn." 143 f. 179.
[552] Jinab-i-Avarih, *Star of the West* vol. 14, No 12 (1924): 359-360.

such power that the women forgot the wedding. She moved them to tears with expressions of her trials and tribulations and then comforted them with humorous stories. She finished by walking among them chanting her poems. After this night, even the maids and helpers in the home became deeply attached to Tahirih.[553]

The clerical order of Persia, though, had determined by now to destroy the Babi faith. After the heartbreaking loss of many of his apostles, the Letters of the Living, and other devout followers at Fort Tabarsi and other places, the Bab may well have known that his own days were now approaching their end. He sent letters of instruction to important disciples calling on them to carry out specific missions. In early June of 1850, the Bab sent a special locked coffer to his most important disciple, Jinab-i-Baha, containing letters, seals, pens and pen-cases, and rings. He wrote one message on a scroll of delicate blue paper in calligraphy so refined that it appeared not only completely free from error but also to have been written in one stroke in the form of a pentacle with five hundred verses containing three-hundred and sixty derivations of the word 'Baha'.[554]

The Prime Minister[555] stoked the effort to destroy the insurgent faith. The time had come to kill it at its head, and so he signed the Bab's death warrant. On July 9th, 1850, in a public square in the northeastern city of Tabriz, the Bab, the former young merchant who had caused a spiritual revolution by proclaiming to be the revealer of a new holy book and a manifestation of God and the forerunner of another manifestation of God, was shot to death by firing squad along with a young believer who had begged to ascend with him.

The Bab had described himself once in majestic yet mystical language:

---

[553] Abdu'l-Baha, *Memorials of the Faithful*, 202; Shoghi Effendi, *God Passes By*, 74.

[554] Effendi, *God Passes By*, 69.

[555] Mirza Taqi Khan.

"I am the Mystic Fane, which the Hand of Omnipotence hath reared. I am the Lamp which the Finger of God hath lit within its niche and caused to shine with deathless splendor. I am the Flame of that supernal Light that glowed upon Sinai in the gladsome Spot, and lay concealed in the midst of the Burning Bush."[556]

The Bab had made his claims known gradually; only with time did Babis come to realize their breadth. Shoghi Effendi, the future head of the Baha'i Faith, explained that, from the later Baha'i perspective, the Bab was "...one of the self-sufficient Manifestations of God, that He has been invested with sovereign power and authority, and exercises all the rights and prerogatives of independent Prophethood...," and "...That He is not to be regarded merely as an inspired Precursor of the Bahá'í Revelation, that in His person,...the object of all the Prophets gone before Him has been fulfilled...."[557]

This poem may give us an idea of Tahirih's emotions during this painful period. Here, she returns to a theme often expressed with great power in her poetry—separation from the Beloved:

"I am lost in the heartland of your love,
and yet you do not even seem to care

Look down in pity at this foreigner,
you truest ruler of the kingdoms here,

and tell me, love, how have I sinned, and where?
And why, my idol, does your love prepare

with each breath banish me, strip me bare
like some murderer exiled to nowhere?

---

[556] The Bab, *Selections from the Writings of the Bab*, (Haifa, Israel: Bahá'í World Centre, 1982) 74.
[557] Shoghi Effendi, *Dispensation*, 121.

I have waited for you day after day.
I'm weary now. I'm wasted, worn away

to bone, a flute that sighs away my care—
sorrows sung to the wind, and lost in air.

Is there a mind that knows your perfection?
A passion to utter your perfection?

A path that leads me to your perfection?
Beyond you, nothing, and no direction

And when the wandering wind reaches you,
it carries our tormented words to you

Look at these tear-filled eyes, this pallid face—
Can you refuse them? Whom would it disgrace?

Will you not come at daybreak to my bed,
with kindness ravish me, and end my dread?

Lift me, love, on the wings of my desire
Lift me to you, to safety in your fire

Only take me up, away from this place
Set me down in the place that is no place

Yet keep me close to you, far from strife,
since in this empty world, I have no life "[558]

---

[558] Banani and Kessler, 92-93.

2.

During his stay in the holy cities of Iraq in 1851, Jinab-i-Baha continued to actively and fearlessly proclaim the teachings, station, and claims of the Bab, despite the execution and the terrible persecutions which had descended on the Babi faithful. He searched for those individuals who were open to hearing the message and continued to encourage and uplift his fellow Babis. The time of the fulfillment of the Bab's revelation was approaching when the Bab had promised a second divine outpouring soon after his own.[559]

In late 1851, Mirza Aqa Khan-i-Nuri, a neighbor of Jinab-i-Baha from the province of Nur with whom he had stayed many times in his mansion in the mountains, was appointed the new Prime Minister. He was able to invite Jinab-i-Baha to return to Persia and expressed the hope for reconciliation with the Babis. Jinab-i-Baha spent that summer directing the affairs of the faith from the foothills near Tihran.

Then disaster struck: several Babis, acting out of a desire to avenge the execution of the Bab and against the expressed warning made to them by Jinab-i-Baha not to engage in any such action, attempted to kill the King of Persia on August 15th, 1852. In their deranged grief they followed through with their half-formed plan which included defective weapons. The King was traumatized by the attack and unleashed a brutal persecution of the Babis on a far greater scale than ever before, greatly encouraged by his mother who carried a deep fear of the Babis and especially Jinab-i-Baha.

Having forsaken any form of protection, Jinab-i-Baha was taken on foot and in chains down to the capital under a broiling sun and past the shouts and jeers of people on the road. Tihran was in a frenzy. Troops were sent up into the mountains around this time to attack his village of Takur and destroy his home to prevent a feared Babi uprising there.[560]

---

[559] Ruhe, *Robe*, 128.
[560] Ibid, 146-7.

The authorities also turned on Tahirih who had been under house arrest in Tihran. She had continued to actively teach the message of the Bab both in person and in writing. Because of the conditions of her arrest, she had to sneak out notes and letters to others. Lacking a pen, she dipped strands of a broom in vegetable juice and wrote them on paper grocery bags.[561]

Two important clerics charged with ascertaining her beliefs summoned her to a series of interviews.[562] They concluded that her views were heretical and that she should be put to death, even though killing a female heretic was contrary to Islamic tradition. This sealed her death sentence.[563] She may also have received this sentence because of her influence among the noblewomen of Tihran, who, in showing interest in Tahirih's teachings, may have created a liability for their husbands in this period of intensified persecutions of the Babis. Even the Prime Minister—against whom the queen mother plotted for influence and power—would have wanted to distance himself from anything related to Babis, especially if women in his household had become interested in the radical teachings.[564]

This poem may have been written at the time of her interrogations by the two clerics in Tihran and takes the form of a riddle, something

---

[561] Amanat, "Qurrat al-'Ayn." 143; Mázandarání, 328.

[562] Ruhe, *Robe* 150; according to Shoghi Effendi, *God Passes By,* 74, there were seven interviews; Root, *Táhirih the pure,* 145 f. 39, recorded: "The grandson of Táhirih who lives in Tihrán told me in March, 1930: "I heard from my own father that Nasiri'd-Din Shah asked three important Mullás to come and speak with Táhirih. At this discussion they asked her, 'what are the proofs of your Faith?' From the Qu'ran she proved it. The mullás tried their best to go against her, but they were not able to answer her. The Sháh wished a second discussion to be arranged, but in the second meeting the Mullás did not permit Táhirih to come. Rather with great haste they begged the government to have her put to death. Nasiri'd-Din Sháh did not wish Táhirih to be persecuted".

[563] Shoghi Effendi, *God Passes By,* 74, describes the clerics as the "deputies of the Grand Vizier"; the clerics were Mulla Ali Kani and Mulla Muhammad Andarmani.

[564] Amanat, "Qurrat al-'Ayn." 143, 158, f. 185.

very uncommon in Persian poetry. In the second couplet she may well be referring to her interrogators when she writes of the "moralist and the priest." The riddle is full of contradictions with complex clues and surprising turns and includes some of her concepts of union and separation—"You betray while you promise the union of love -/How can there be one man who swears two vows?"; and, unity and duality—"...one man who swears two vows ...," "...one slave with two names...." In the use of a riddle and these surprising turns, Tahirih seems almost playful in tone:[565]

"That mole on your lip, those two curls above:
One seed, two springs—and my poor heart is snared!

A priest, a judge, and I—we talk of love,
but what is there that I can teach two fools?

Your face, your curls, turn day to night, my dove:
One day that is night—two nights in a day?

The grape-vat swells with the vintner's child of
the vine. The bastard—one dad, and two moms!

Cupbearer! Where's your wine? Up, Moonface! Move!
Bill them for two—I'll pay for mine in cash!

Two eyes, and I'm drunk. I've lost my heart's trove:
lost in the Turk's two cups—yet why one wine?

Your eyebrows' sword slew thousands, then you drove
whole nations mad—like me—just with your eyes!
You broke your promise, the union of love!
Can any man who swears two vows be good?

---

[565] Banani and Kessler, 120-1.

Call me your watchdog, but still I won't move.
I am your servant: one slave with two names!"[566]

The attempted killing of the King allowed him,[567] his Prime Minister, and clerics to finally eliminate this woman who had stood up to them for so long. So in the week after the attempted assassination, the violence unleashed by authorities finally found Tahirih.

One day, the wife of the mayor came up to her room to see her. The room was redolent with perfume. Tahirih turned to her and told her that she was going to meet her beloved—the time of her martyrdom was coming soon. When that time came, she wished her body to be placed in the ground and covered over. The wife of the mayor became filled with anxiety upon hearing this; she had grown to truly love her guest. Tahirih then gave her a package, and said that a woman would arrive three days after her death and that she was to give it to her. She instructed her not to allow anyone else into her room because she wanted to fast and pray now while waiting for the appointed hour. The wife of the mayor, in fear over the loss of the woman she loved, went repeatedly up to her room to listen for sounds. She could hear Tahirih chanting.

Tahirih's execution took place in the middle of the night less than one week after the attempted assassination of the king. Three hours after sunset, soldiers cleared the streets in the area around the mayor's house. No one must witness this movement, so they created a corridor through the streets between the house of the mayor to the gardens where the execution was about to take place. They were ordered to fire on anyone who approached. Such orders reflected the sordid nature of the act they were carrying out.

At four hours after sunset, soldiers arrived at the door of the mayor's house and demanded that Tahirih come with them. The frightened

---

[566] Ibid., 69.
[567] Hoseini, 315.

mayor's wife approached her room trembling. Tahirih emerged dressed in her finest clothes, veiled and perfumed as though she were going to an event of the greatest importance.

Before going downstairs, she gave the mayor's wife the key to a chest of her belongings and told her that these objects were to help her to remember her gladness at the hour of martyrdom. Tahirih asked that the son of the mayor accompany her to make sure that the soldiers did not handle her body or remove her clothing after her death, and to act as a go-between for her.

Downstairs, the soldiers waited with a horse for the prisoner. A cloak was put over her for a disguise should anyone still be out in the streets or looking through a window.

Though heavily armed, the soldiers feared attack from Babis as they rode through the dark streets. They reached the Ilkhani garden outside the gate of the city. There, an army officer and his soldiers were drinking. The son approached the officer who ordered that Tahirih be executed. The son went with two men and gave them her handkerchief to be used for this purpose. Among her last public words, she issued this powerful prediction: "You can kill me as soon as you like, but you cannot stop the emancipation of women."

After the men had strangled her, the mayor's son and several others lowered her body into an empty well and covered it with stones and dirt. The men then all dispersed.[568]

Behind them, they left the body of one of the most extraordinary women in the spiritual and cultural history of Persia. The shame of their act that night and her sacrifice reverberated down through time. The Baha'i history, *God Passes By*, remembered her influence:

> "Many and divers are her ardent admirers who, throughout the five continents, are eager to know more about her. Many are those whose conduct has been ennobled by her inspiring

---

[568] 'Abdu'l-Baha, *Memorials of the Faithful*, 203-204; Shoghi Effendi, *God Passes By*, 75; Zarandi, 455-459.

example, who have committed to her memory odes, or set to music her poems, before whose eyes glows the vision of her indomitable spirit, in whose hearts is enshrined a love and admiration that time can never dim, and in whose souls burns the determination to tread as dauntlessly, and with that same fidelity, the path she chose for herself, and from which she never swerved from the moment of her conversion to the hour of her death."[569]

Garden of Ilkhani, Tihran, where Tahirih was murdered.

Back at the mayor's mansion, his wife leaned over the chest containing the few items Tahirih had left behind in this world:

"As I gazed upon her earthly belongings, I mused over the circumstances of her eventful life, and recalled, with a throb of wonder, her intrepid courage, her zeal, her high sense of duty and unquestioning devotion. I was reminded of her literary attainments, and brooded over the imprisonments, the shame, and the calumny which she had faced with a fortitude such as no other woman in her land could manifest. I pictured to myself that winsome face which now, alas, lay bur-

---

[569] Shoghi Effendi, *God Passes By*, 76-7.

ied beneath a mass of earth and stones. The memory of her passionate eloquence warmed my heart, as I repeated to myself the words that had so often dropped from her lips. The consciousness of the vastness of her knowledge and her mastery of the sacred scriptures of Islam, flashed through my mind with a suddenness that disconcerted me. Above all, her passionate loyalty to the Faith she had embraced, her fervor as she pleaded its cause, the services she rendered it, the woes and tribulations she endured for its sake, the example she had given to its followers, the impetus she had lent to its advancement, the name she had carved for herself in the hearts of her fellow-countrymen, all these I remembered as I stood beside her chest, wondering what could have induced so great a woman to forsake all the riches and honours with which she had been surrounded and to identify herself with the cause of an obscure youth from Shiraz. What could have been the secret, I thought to myself, of the power that tore her away from her home and kindred, that sustained her throughout her stormy career, end eventually carried her to her grave? Could that force, I pondered, be of God? Could the hand of the Almighty have guided her destiny and steered her course amidst the perils of her life?"[570]

But, to Tahirih, this death was life itself, separation from her Beloved was the real death. Her Beloved's words had been her salvation and now her death meant reunion with him. Martyrdom was the last gift she could give to express her love for the Bab:

"I will lay my head in the dust before your face.
My idol, this is the holy law I embrace.
You are the Ka'aba that I long to circle 'round.
A river of tears falls from my eyes to the ground.
So don't ask me why I'm drunk. Just look at your eyes!

---

[570] Zarandi, 458-9.

Don't tell me that I've lost my mind. Look at your face!
O Lord of the worlds! Bend his heart, so unbending!
Or else, release me from this grief where I am drowned.
No life flows from my soul, my tomb brings no ending.
To be with you is life, and separation death.
As I lay dying, your lips moved to speak a word
Of care, and that is the one thing that gives me breath."[571]

---

[571] Banani and Kessler, 73.

SEVEN:
SPIRIT, SPIRITUALISM, AND SUFFRAGE

1.

At a Sunday service in 1833, the minister invited anyone who wanted to be united with the church to come forward. A nine year-old girl, Antoinette Brown (1825–1921), walked up. Astonished at seeing someone so young come forward, the minister asked her two simple questions, and the church voted to accept her. She remembered later that deep sense of knowing her calling: "I was as deeply and truly religious at that time, though but nine years of age, as I have ever been at any age."[572]

The Brown family had settled on the frontier in Western New York, the 'Burned-Over District' where new religious movements such as the Millerites, the Latter Day Saints, and the Shakers were thriving, and passionate revivals were a regular feature of the spiritual landscape. They attended a liberal Congregational church where God was presented as a loving presence that was both near and accessible.[573]

Antoinette was both spiritually oriented and fortunate enough to have a father who gave her an education. He sent her to the Monroe Academy where she was taught a more rigorous curriculum than most girls received which included mathematics, French, composition, and rhetoric. At fifteen, she was hired to be a teacher in a small district school. A farmer came to pick-up 'Ms. Brown' on her first day, having torn out the old planks from his old farm wagon and replaced them with a carriage seat. Her real ambition, though, was to become a minister. To do this, she knew she needed more education but did not want to go to a school which taught only home-making skills.[574]

---

[572] Elizabeth Cazden, *Antoinette Brown Blackwell, A Biography* (Old Westbury, NY: The Feminist Press, 1983), 3.
[573] Ibid., 7-9.
[574] Ibid., 13-16.

She set her sights on Oberlin College, run by the great preacher Charles Finney, a family friend; its catalogue announced that the college educated "the female character by bringing within the reach of the misjudged and neglected sex all the instructive privileges which hitherto have unreasonably distinguished the leading sex from theirs."[575] Her childhood then came to an abrupt end with the passing of her sister and brother from tuberculosis and her mother from a serious illness due to physical exhaustion from having given birth so many times in a row.[576]

After an arduous journey by canal and wagon, she arrived in the flat, swampy land where Oberlin stood. The college was infused with Finney's sense of moral urgency, and the school was aflame with the abolitionist cause. There were several African-American students and ten percent of the town's population was African-American—some escaped slaves, some free persons. Though female students were allowed to take demanding academic courses, they were not allowed to speak in public settings. Even the school's Ladies Board did not approve of this and so were very displeased when Lucy Stone spoke at a public celebration. Inspired by Stone, some female students started their own Ladies Literary Society and met clandestinely in the home of a black woman to practice their public speaking skills on topics such as "Egotism" and "The Qualifications to be a Minister's Wife."[577]

Brown's road to the ministry was to be a difficult one even in a place like Oberlin; a professor there wrote that it was "improper" for women to become lawyers and ministers.[578] Even Mrs. Finney and the Ladies Board discouraged Brown in her study of theology because she could never be wise enough to compare to the "great men of the past."[579]

---

[575] Ibid., 16.
[576] Ibid., 17-18.
[577] Ibid., 21-32.
[578] Ibid., 35.
[579] Ibid., 36.

Brown continued with her theological studies and applied to Oberlin for a license to preach. Though she was refused official sanction, the college did not try to stop her public speaking, and she organized lectures on popular topics like 'Temperance' in nearby churches aided by the support of other students. As her days at Oberlin drew to a close, she was unsure about her next steps. She did not apply for ordination from the College because she knew this would be very difficult and preferred to be ordained by a church congregation who wanted her as its pastor. When she graduated at age twenty-five, her name was not included on the list of graduates because a woman was not supposed to study theology in any official capacity. Still, Brown was looking forward towards the future.[580]

Soon after graduation and encouraged by her good friend Lucy Stone, Brown presented a refutation of the Biblical foundation for the prohibition of women speaking in public at the National Women's Rights Convention. Her talents were validated by the Convention, so Brown decided to try to make her living as a public speaker. In those times, lectures were a source of evening activity for people as there were no radios, televisions, or movies. Soon, with the help of friends from the Convention, Brown was lecturing throughout New England, Ohio, Pennsylvania, and New York.[581]

On a speaking trip through central New York State, the village of South Butler offered her a position as pastor in its church. They had been unable to hire a minister and had even taken on a black preacher for a while. After considering the offer for several months, Brown agreed to take the position. She rented rooms in a physician's home and enthusiastically set to work giving two sermons on Sundays and carrying out her pastoral duties. Antoinette Brown had become the first woman to be ordained a minister in the history of the United States.[582]

---

[580] Ibid., 50-52.
[581] Ibid., 57-62.
[582] Ibid., 73-82.

Ironically, some of her important female friends in the women's rights movement did not support her religious avocation because they thought of religion as a mighty barrier; this caused her much distress, and she began to doubt some of her own religious convictions.[583] While she participated in reform meetings, she found the squabbling between factions discouraging; once, she was drowned out by hecklers at a women's rights convention.[584]

Olympia Brown.

Olympia Brown (1835-1926) idolized Antoinette Brown and also sought ordination. She had been strongly encouraged by her mother to pursue her education. After enrolling in Mount Holyoke, she found that there were low expectations for female students from the professors.[585] Eventually she changed to another progressive school, Antioch College. Even there, less was expected of women; women were not invited there as lecturers. As a reaction to this, she asked her idol, Antoinette Brown, to come and speak.[586]

---

[583] Ibid., 86.

[584] Ibid., 80-82.

[585] Charlotte Cote, *Olympia Brown: The Battle for Equality* (Racine, WI: Mother Courage Press 1988), 34.

[586] "Biography," *Olympia Brown Papers*, ca.1849-1963; item description, dates. A-69, folder #. Schlesinger Library, Radcliffe Institute, Harvard University, Cambridge, Mass.

Antioch's president at the time was the legendary American educator Horace Mann. Olympia Brown received an excellent education there, despite the restrictions on women, so much so that her entire family moved to Antioch to enable all of her siblings to attend the school.[587] Olympia pursued the goal of becoming a minister. Theological schools such as the Unitarian Theological School in Meadville, Pennsylvania, did not admit women because the trustees thought this was "too great an innovation."[588] She chose St. Lawrence University in Canton, New York,[589] a regularly established theological school whose president "did not think women were called to the ministry. But I leave that between you and the Great Head of the Church,"[590] and became its first female graduate.[591]

She achieved this distinction in 1863, ten years after Antoinette Brown. Whereas, Antoinette Brown was ordained by a single congregation, Olympia Brown was ordained by a whole denomination, the Universalists—the one in which she had been raised.[592] She preached for forty-eight years[593] and also pastored churches in Massachusetts, Connecticut, and Wisconsin.[594] On the subject of women in the ministry, she asserted that "…no profession is so well suited to women in their various relations of wife, mother, or housekeeper as the ministry."[595]

---

http://oasis.lib.harvard.edu/oasis/deliver/~sch00054

[587] Noble, Laurie Varter, "Olympia Brown," *Dictionary of Unitarian and Universalist Biography*. Unitarian Universalist History and Heritage Society, accessed May 5, 2013, http://uudb.org/articles/olympiabrown.html.

[588] Olympia Brown, *Acquaintances, Old and New* (Milwaukee: S.E. Tate, 1911), 27.

[589] Ibid.

[590] Noble.

[591] Ibid.

[592] Ibid.

[593] Brown, *Acquaintances, Old and New*, 31.

[594] "Brown, Olympia, 1835-1926. Papers, ca. 1849-1963: A Finding A".

[595] Brown, *Acquaintances, Old and New*, 31.

Olympia Brown lived a long and productive life, speaking at women's conventions, writing books, working for the equal rights for women, and laboring for reform. She lived well past 1880, when there were one-hundred and sixty-five ordained female ministers with parishes.[596]

The time of the preaching women had arrived.

2.

By the mid-1800s, American women were making themselves felt as movers in public life through their participation in reform movements and spiritualism. Even more remarkable was the appearance of a few women who had a broad impact through their personal teaching, speaking, and formulation of new ideas which caught on with the general public. Their struggles and successes reflected the powerful changes wrought by the great awakenings.

One such woman was Ellen G. White (1827–1915) whose thought and writings shaped an entire Christian denomination, the Seventh-Day Adventists, which had its historical roots in the preaching farmer from New York, William Miller.

1863 was an important year for White.

Born into a farming family of eight children, she grew up in the small city of Portland, Maine. She was severely injured on her way to school when a classmate threw a rock at her which hit her in the head. Three years later, in precarious health, she entered the Methodist church at a revival during which she asked to be baptized by immersion. Around this time, the family became convinced by the teachings of William Miller on the Second Coming. While worshipping with a small Adventist group, she had a vision of Adventists entering the City of God. She then travelled to the small scattered groups of Adventists—who were by now quite divided and discouraged—to tell them of

---

[596] Cazden, 227.

her visions. Some took this as a teaching sent from God through Ellen.[597]

Ellen married James White, an Adventist preacher, in 1846. The young couple struggled economically, and James had to work multiple jobs. She continued to have visions which showed her new commandments regarding the keeping of the Sabbath. Ellen bore a son but soon began travelling and preaching again to Adventist groups, feeling compelled to do so by a powerful sense of calling. James began printing a semi-monthly paper, *The Present Truth*, which gave an outlet for Ellen's writings. Her articles offered guidance, admonitions, and prophecy regarding the church and its future. Her first book, *A Sketch of the Christian Experience and Views of Ellen G. White*, came out in 1851.

After some years of great struggle, the Whites moved to Battle Creek, Michigan, where the Adventists built them a home. The community spread the Adventist teachings using Ellen's writings. She and her husband covered many miles in all kinds of weather to serve their faith. By 1860, the White family had grown by six children, and their Adventist work begat an administrative structure, the General Conference, in 1863.

In June of that year, White had a powerful vision which led her to teach the importance of health and health reform, including the founding of an institute to care for the sick. She advocated new ideas about healthy eating and a balanced diet in a time when a good meal meant meat and gravy, and she eschewed the use of tobacco. She wrote three books on this important topic when almost no one paid any attention to it. People, she believed, lived frenetic lives supported by

---

[597] Arthur L. White, "Ellen G. White: A Brief Biography," *The Ellen G. White Estate, Inc.,* accessed November 4, 2013. http://www.whiteestate.org/about/egwbio.asp.

stimulants, whereas "sleep and repose" were "nature's great restorers."[598]

In addition, White wrote important works on education in which she stressed that children had to be educated to rule their passions by being engaged as thoughtful beings and not by being trained by rote.[599] They must not be taught in an oppressive way because this

Ellen White and Family.

prevented them from developing inner-directed self-discipline.[600] Also, parents and teachers themselves must demonstrate the moral capacity to be successful in this important work.[601]

White wrote on many subjects including music, theology, the end times, and the nature of salvation. Her influence in shaping the teachings and organization of the church came primarily from her

---

[598] Ellen G. White, "Proper Education," *The Health Reformer* v. 7, # 9 (1872): 284-6.
[599] Ibid., 284.
[600] Ibid., 284.
[601] Ibid., 284.

prodigious written outpouring which, though not considered Scripture, was greatly valued by Adventists. During her lifetime, she wrote some five-thousand articles and forty books; she may well be the most translated female writer in history due to the worldwide missionary work of the Seventh-Day Adventist Church.

In this period, there arose another American woman who was very interested in the relationship between faith and health, who wrote prolifically, who lived through deep pain in near constant uncertainty and poverty to finally find her calling—to develop and teach a 'spiritual science' of health. She became the only woman ever in history to found a major Christian denomination, the Church of Christ, Scientist: Mary Baker Eddy (1821–1910).

As a little girl, Mary remembered going through her grandmother's trunk in 1820s-30s rural New Hampshire and taking out an old rusty sword, a yellowing news article on the death of George Washington, sonnets written by a female relative and accounts of the doomed Covenanters, a Presbyterian Scottish sect. Her grandmother was a living link to New Hampshire's frontier past and she loved to read–too much so for her husband's liking. Mary's memory of sitting in an old rocking chair with her, reliving the frontier days, remained a constant one throughout her life, so much so that she always tried to keep a rocking chair in her possession.[602]

Mary was the last of six children whose mother maintained a warm and loving home and whose father was very severe. In her teens, he moved the family to the prospering town of Sanbornton Bridge near Concord, New Hampshire, which had a growing textile industry. She retained fond memories of her early childhood and wrote down four stories from it that later elicited considerable reaction. In one story, she took a pin and poked her father with it as he led family prayer in his usual declamatory manner, prefiguring how she would later stand up to men in her adult life and seek to get out from under her father's domination. Mary was the bookish one in the family and was always

---

[602] Gillian Gill, Mary Baker Eddy, (Cam bridge, MS: Perseus Books 1998) 5.

willing to debate her father in theology. He may even have tried to hide books from her when he became concerned that she preferred reading more than playing outside with other children.[603]

In another episode, Mary remembers being eight years old and hearing a voice calling her but it wasn't her mother's. Her mother then read to her a Bible story in which the child Samuel hears a voice and exclaims "Speak, Lord, for thy servant heareth"—the words of commitment to God. When Mary answered the voice with the words of Samuel, it went quiet. She later told a related story of being twelve years old and at her church confirmation, when she came down with a fever because of the repulsion she felt for the doctrine of predestination. Her mother urged her to pray, and, after doing so, Mary emerged fully cured, much to the doctor's amazement. These two stories showed to her later followers that she had a mystical connection with God even as a child.[604]

The fourth important story from her childhood was a conversation with her mother in which she asked if her mother believed in eternal punishment. Her mother, who had taught her daughter to say, "I am sorry and will not do so again," answered that she supposed this teaching was true.[605] Mary responded:

> "What if we repent and tell God 'we are sorry and will not do so again'—will God punish us? Then He is not as good as my mother and He will find me a hard case."[606]

Mary loved her mother dearly, and her mother's devotion formed in her mind a concept of God that had female attributes as well as the traditional male ones. Her concept of the Divine would always have a strong female principle.

---

[603] Gill, 36.
[604] Ibid., 9-11.
[605] Ibid., 13.
[606] Ibid.

She also adored her other brothers George and Albert but saw little of her eldest brother, Samuel, because he had moved to Boston. George never lived up to his talents because of his excessive use of alcohol and tobacco. Mary's passionate teaching against these two substances may well have had an emotional connection to the loss of the promise of George's life. Her second brother, Albert, also left the religious path and put himself through law school. He made his way into politics, patronized by the Pierce family which later produced a president. Just as his star was rising, and he was poised to enter Congress, he died of a kidney ailment. Still only a teenager, Mary grieved deeply for her beloved brother and in some profound way, may have determined to follow him in public achievement.[607]

Mary's father was very stern, hard-working, and frugal, and had a very strong Protestant work ethic which may have made life hard for his three sons. Even as the family prospered materially after its move, the father still drove his daughters to church in the old work wagon instead of a new chaise much to his teenage daughters' embarrassment. He did not allow his daughters to attend dances, but he did support his daughters' education. He was very involved in local school matters, including planning the school itself, and sent his daughters to an excellent local school after the family moved.[608]

One of the main challenges of Mary's life was sickliness, which ran in the family but hit her the hardest. While there is no evidence of hysteria in her youth—a common criticism by her detractors—she did suffer a broad range of back pains, colds, and indigestions, which were not unusual for that time. Some have posited that these constant illnesses were a way of her skirting around her father's rules; suspiciously, in letters between the sisters, complaints about being ill were followed by an account of some pleasurable activity they were able to engage in as a result of not having to work due to illness. The romantic and fashionable ideal of a young woman at the time was that of a

---

[607] Ibid., 17-21.
[608] Ibid., 31.

passive and sickly creature with a pale countenance. There is evidence that she and her sisters vied for being the sickest. Mary's constant state of illness seems to have been a pattern among American women; Catherine Beecher noted that most of the women she knew were invalids. Physical illnesses of various kinds remained a constant in her life making her increasingly despairing of medicine.[609]

After her sisters left home, Mary may have been kept back to help her mother. Her sickliness did not really allow her to be a teacher, so she turned to writing. In the 1840s, journalism was a possible—though very difficult—professional path for women. Fortunately, her family supported this aspiration and soon her poems were being published. She had also become a physically attractive young woman. A description based on her neighbor's account was published much later:

> "As a young woman she was slim, alert, and graceful. Of me-dium height, she had a well-formed figure which she has not lost even in her old age. Her feet and hands were exquisitely fashioned. Her features were regular and refined—a delicate aquiline nose, a rather long and pointed chin, a firm mouth, and a high, broad forehead. Her most striking feature was her big, grey eyes. Deep-set and overhung by dark lashes, they had the gift of emotional expression. "When she was angry," says an old neighbor, "they became fairly black." All her life, those eyes have had such an effect upon their be-holders that they may justly be called an important factor in her career. Her skin was clear red and white, and her hair was wavy brown."[610]

Many young men were interested in her because of her beauty and her family's improved social position. In 1843, she accepted the marriage proposal of George Glover; his sister was married to Mary's

---

[609] Ibid., 40-45.
[610] Ibid., 52.

eldest brother, and Glover also physically resembled her brother George. Mary was in love—following the usual romantic conventions of the day—but her father found George's character suspect and did not like him. George was involved in a variety of business ventures that depended on slave labor, but he did not tell this to his young bride. She moved down to Charleston, SC, where she seems to have enjoyed a happy life and became pregnant. George, though, was stricken ill and died after just two weeks.

After giving birth to a son in September, Mary found herself in the extremely difficult position of being a young widow with a child. Her husband died without leaving much money, and she didn't have her own source of income. She first attempted journalism as a source of income but was too isolated in New Hampshire from major urban centers, and so she started a school for preschoolers, but it soon failed because of financial pressures; very few independent schools were sustainable in those days, and widows were seldom employed by other schools. She now had few options, and for seven years, from 1844-1853, she lived near poverty, dependent on her relatives.[611]

Mary was now almost constantly ill. In 1849, her beloved mother died. While her death deeply affected Mary, her father's quick remarriage to a widow may have hit her even harder. She saw how easily and quickly her gifted and dutiful mother had been replaced. She struggled on as a widow, but the problem of caring for her boy now overwhelmed her, so she placed him in the care of their family nurse. Unbeknownst to Mary, the nurse's husband would treat him cruelly.

She desperately needed a husband for support. Because of her severe dental problems, she went to see a dentist, Daniel Patterson, who soon declared his love for her and became her second husband. Patterson was both handsome, clean, and orderly—something that was very important to Mary who remembers not being able to sleep as a child unless her shoes were straightened.[612]

---

[611] Ibid., 69-79.
[612] Ibid., 85-101.

But Patterson turned out to be a poor provider and a philanderer; still, the two seemed to have genuinely cared for one another. The couple was soon mired in poverty. Mary now began to exhibit symptoms that were very much like hysteria; she may well have turned her emotions inward—as many women did—which, in turn, presented themselves as back pain and indigestion. In one remarkable story showing the possibly psycho-somatic nature of her illnesses, Mary jumped out of her bed—despite being 'sick'—to protect her husband who was being assaulted by a father and his axe-wielding son.[613] Stories like this caused snickering among townspeople who saw Mary's illness as faked and were unsympathetic to any woman who did not work as hard as they did. Others, though, remembered her having a powerful presence and great kindness which attracted children.[614]

Mary Baker Eddy.

The couple moved from one set of rooms to another, town to town, but still their financial situation did not improve. When her niece

---

[613] Ibid., 107.
[614] Robert Peel, *Mary Baker Eddy: The Years of Discovery 1821-1875*, (Boston, MA: The Christian Science Publishing Society, 1966) 122.

passed away, she was unable to join her family in mourning. She also could not repay a debt that she owed to her sister who then suffered as a result. Worst of all, her husband refused to allow her son George to visit her because he was concerned that the boy's wild behavior would make Mary's health worse.[615] George's surrogate family then moved to Minnesota, taking him far from his troubled mother. This was a final blow, and she began a slow turning away from the world.[616]

During the late 1850s, she spent much time going over the homeopathic materials belonging to her husband. When she saw several patients use homeopathic remedies, Mary began to consider a 'mental' approach to illness[617] and took her first steps towards an entirely new life in the person of Dr. Phineas P. Quimby.

Phineas Quimby, a charismatic clockmaker with a lively mind but little formal education, became interested in various new 'sciences' of healing: mesmerism, a form of hypnotism with clairvoyance; spiritualism, in which he acted as a medium; and 'rubbing', a form of laying on of hands and manipulation.[618] Mary came to him exasperated by current medicine and open to new ways of treating her persistent ailments. Quimby had come to believe in a 'mind' orientation towards healing in which mind meant 'spiritual'.[619]

Mary had tremendous faith in Quimby, and after her first visit to him in 1862, she felt better. One of the later accusations against Mary was that she accepted the use of mesmerism from Quimby, but in her later writings, she repudiated both the popular mesmerism and spiritualism of the day, and there is no evidence that these formed any part of her own approaches to treatment. Though she always remained grateful to Quimby and stayed under the spell of his powerful personality for several years—even if only through letter writing—her good

---

[615] Ibid., 116.
[616] Ibid., 118.
[617] Ibid., 136.
[618] Ibid., 164.
[619] Ibid., 153.

health did not last. She also developed some distinctively different ideas from him. To Mary, God was at the center: "…that God is the only healer and healing principle, and that Principle is divine not human."[620]

The God of the Bible seemed different to her from Quimby's concept of 'mind' and 'thought'. To Mary, God, was transcendent and not merely part of the body's 'energy'. God was not 'in man', rather, she asked, "Is not our comforter always from outside and above ourselves?"[621] She came to rely on a God beyond human comprehension whereas, for Quimby, God was present, and 'thought' was to be used by man for his own healing. She would always remember Quimby fondly, but his system did not allow sufficiently for the healing power of a transcendent God's grace.[622]

Another frequent accusation against Mary was that her ideas expressed later in her life were plagiarized from Quimby, but he did not write down his theories and practices; it was his assistant who did so. The relationship between Mary and Quimby was very dialogical which helped both of them develop their ideas further.[623]

Since Mary's husband was still unable to provide for her, she had to rely on her sister's generosity to supplement her meager income. She was coming into her own ideas. In early 1864, she gave a well-received public talk regarding the metaphysical dimensions of healing.[624] In these months she began to think that there must be a 'science' of Christianity:

> "…when I found that Quimbyism was too short, and would not answer the cry of the human heart for succor, for real

---

[620] Ibid., 205.

[621] Ibid., 170.

[622] Ibid., 159-160.

[623] The assistant's name was Sarah Ware (Gill, 138-146).

[624] Peel, 178.

aid, I went, being driven thence by my extremity, to the Bible, and there I discovered Christian Science."[625]

God was revealing Himself through his holy laws even in this increasingly scientific age, and knowledge of these laws was an eternal science.[626]

In the small town of Warren, Massachusetts, Mary gave two more public lectures to counter the view that she was a spiritualist. The most important event of those two months in Warren was her successful treatment of a patient's ills because it gave her confidence in her own skills. She moved in again with her husband who was by now a known philanderer and an embarrassment to her. She became socially active as the presiding officer of the local temperance organization by which she gained valuable administrative experience. Then personal loss struck again. In the fall of 1865, her father, the towering figure of her childhood, passed away; he left most of his estate to his grandson and one dollar to Mary. A few months later, Quimby, who was playing such a large role in her new life, died as well.[627]

Her life now turned the corner. On Thursday evening of February 1st, 1866, Mary slipped on the ice, badly injuring herself. During the next few days, the doctor visited her at her bedside. He was very concerned about her condition. Helpless in bed that Sunday afternoon, she asked that a Bible be brought to her, and she read from it. Soon, she felt flooded with the presence of Jesus and rose out of her bed. The doctor came the next day and to his amazement—and concern—she was up and about.[628] She remembered later:

"That short experience included a glimpse of the great fact that I have since tried to make plain to others, namely, Life

---

[625] Ibid., 183.
[626] Ibid., 179.
[627] Ibid., 184-192.
[628] Ibid., 195-7.

in and of Spirit; this Life being the sole reality of existence."[629]

Later, she called this the beginning of Christian Science: "It was in Massachusetts, in February, 1866,…that I discovered the Science of divine metaphysical healing which I afterwards named Christian Science."[630] Mary was now convinced that healing could happen when an individual was open to it as it flowed from God through the Bible.[631]

A new life had begun for her.

By the end of 1866, she was sure of her own ideas. She divorced her husband. Age forty-five, poor, but certain of her powerful vision, she concentrated on her theological writing. Her first work was a commentary on the Book of Genesis. In her interpretation of the phrase, "In the beginning," from Genesis meant God and Spirit. Man was in the image of God, wholly good.[632]

Mary continued to live as a poor wanderer; from 1866 to 1870, she moved nine times. She gathered a group of students around her to whom she imparted her theology and healing. In Lynn, MA, she built a successful practice with the help of a talented student. Some students were loyal to her, others took the knowledge they had acquired from her and went off on their own, and some even turned against her, leveling criticisms that her healing was essentially 'mesmerism'. This kind of criticism by students who had been her close friends was personally painful to her,[633] but her group of students continued to grow because she had a great deal of personal charisma, and her influence spread.[634]

---

[629] Ibid., 197.
[630] Gill, 162.
[631] Ibid, 168.
[632] Peel, 205-207.
[633] Gill, 203.
[634] Ibid, 172.

The foundational text of Mary's Christian Science, *Science and Health*, was published in 1875. This text went through numerous revisions until 1907, when it reached the mature form and was read in Christian Science churches everywhere. The original book was an audacious attempt for the time—by a woman no less—to deal with major theological questions. Mary was also not a person with a classical education, and therefore, it took great courage for her to put her ideas out in public in a printed form. The flow of her ideas was decidedly non-linear and suffered from a disorganization which was corrected in later revisions.[635]

The first edition of *Science and Health* began with Mary going to great lengths to distinguish Christian Science from Spiritualism. She reinterpreted the origins of the world in Genesis and the Virgin birth of Jesus and presented a new way of looking at Jesus's life, death, and resurrection. She then explained her very particular ideas on prayer, atonement, marriage, and physiology and closed with her views on healing.

The natural state of human beings was wellness. Sickness could be eliminated by following the laws and examples of Jesus. The soul was more powerful than the body and could rule it:[636]

> "When we possess a true sense of our oneness with God, and learn we are spirit alone, and not matter, we shall have no such opinins as these, but will triumph over all sickness, sin, and death, thus proving our God-being."[637]

By following in the footsteps of Christ and living by the holy law we, too, could perform the miracles attributed to Jesus which, from this point of view, were demonstrations that Spirit ruled over matter. Such teachings were shocking to her fellow Christians. The many rewrites to

---

[635] Ibid., 217.
[636] Ibid., 222.
[637] Ibid., 221.

come tried to make them more palatable for a public possibly unready for a naked expression of her thoughts.[638]

The next years were ones of intense activity with the publication of *Science and Health,* the acquisition of her first home, the founding of the Christian Science Association, and her marriage to Mr. Asa Eddy. She engaged in ill-advised lawsuits—encouraged by a student—and suffered betrayals by former students. Still, the movement grew, and in 1879, the Association formed the Church of Christ, Scientist. She became its pastor in 1881. The construction of a Mother Church was completed in Boston by 1894.[639] Though there were many attacks on Mary Baker Eddy and the movement, both from within and without, the most important attack was a series of articles put out by the 'yellow journalist' Joseph Pulitzer that hammered away at some of the criticisms and rumors which had always followed Eddy and included, among others that she had taken her teachings from Quimby, that she had known more men in her life than was appropriate, and that she had been a hysteric as a child. She was also ridiculed by prominent Americans such as Mark Twain, who described Eddy as a, "sordid and ignorant old purloiner of that gospel."[640]

Mary Baker Eddy's extraordinarily rocky ride from a sickly farm girl to being the only female founder of a major Christian denomination, as well as a deep theological thinker, charismatic teacher, administrator and leader, was bound to attract much criticism. While such attacks from men could be expected, her main challenge in later years came from another unorthodox belief system, spiritualism.

3.

During her career as a religious leader, Eddy argued forcefully against spiritualism in her effort to distinguish it from her teachings. Spiritual-

---

[638] Ibid., 222.

[639] Ibid., xxxi-xxxxv.

[640] Mark Twain, *Autobiography of Mark Twain, Volume 1: The Complete and Authoritative Edition* (NY, NY: Harper Collins 1990) 136.

ism had spread very rapidly. Eddy accused most spiritualist mediums of being frauds, and that spiritualist beliefs lessened personal moral responsibility by allowing for continued contact after death. She asked why a soul, once freed from the struggles of this world, would want to keep in such close touch, like a butterfly wanting to remain a caterpillar.[641] The practical reason she spent so many pages attempting to refute spiritualism may have been, in part, because spiritualism had become enormously popular in the United States, and Christian Science, in a sense, was its 'competitor'. Strange as it may have appeared and spontaneously as it may have arisen, spiritualism hit a nerve among many thousands of Americans and brought women into public-speaking roles in substantial numbers for the first time.

From its beginnings in 1848 when the Fox girls were thought to be communicating with the spirit world, spiritualism spread rapidly. This movement had no formal organization—no 'church' nor clergy; rather, it spread through public presentations during which a medium spoke in a 'trance' state like an empty vessel through which the spirit world communicated to the audience. Most mediums were women; people tended to trust the communications of younger women who were seen as more innocent than older women. In fact, medium-ship advantaged all the qualities which were more valued in women of the 19th century such as passivity, emotionality, and physical weakness. The very qualities which made women dependent in society made them religious leaders in the spiritualist movement. Female mediums saw themselves as having been chosen for this role *because* of their passivity and meekness.[642] They were helpless before the spiritual power which moved through them. One such medium recalled:

> "…that I, a woman and moreover, "*a lady by birth*," and *English*, above all, that I would go out, like "strong minded woman," and hector the world, on public platform! Oh,

---

641 Gill, 220-1.
642 Braude, *Radical Spirits*, 82.

shocking! I vowed rebellion—to give up Spirits, Spiritualism, and America; to return to England and live "a feminine existence" once again. With these magnanimous resolves upon me *one week, the next* saw me on a public platform, fairly before the world as a trance speaker."[643]

To most people, women standing up to speak in public with little preparation was itself evidence that they were being controlled from the spirit world, and in some sense, 'unconscious'. As one reporter observed:

"...lady trance speakers have never been able, nor even attempted, as far as we know, to give such lectures in the normal state."[644]

An experienced trance speaker, Lizzie Doten, wrote of the spiritual connection women had:

"Woman does not need to cultivate her intellect in order to perceive spiritual truths. Let her live, only, true to her Divine nature and her spiritual perceptions." "Make a home in your heart for God and His angels shall come, and all that is needed for spiritual perception and development comes in with that inspiration...But God does not wait for this [education]. He has made woman a religious teacher...."[645]

Young, innocent, and untrained girls like Cora Hatch and Fanny Burbank, who were trance speakers when still teenagers, were evidence for many people of the existence of a capacity in women to make a direct connection with the spirit world through their unconscious.[646]

By the late 1850s, trance mediums quickly outnumbered all other speakers. In early 1860, a spiritualist paper listed twenty-three women

---

[643] Ibid, 84.
[644] Ibid., 85.
[645] Ibid., 85-6.
[646] Ibid., 86-87.

speakers, and by the end of the year, the list had doubled; by comparison, in the whole pre-Civil War period there had been roughly twenty-
five female reform speakers.[647]

Mrs. Bushnell spoke in a trance in several states in 1850, soon after
the beginning of the movement. Mrs. Herrick gave radical trance
lectures in Chicago in the early 1850s. Mrs. Britt did this every
Sunday in St. Louis. By the mid-1850s, weekly trance lectures in
spiritualist meetings took place in many cities, and some women had
permanent positions doing this such as Cora Hatch in Buffalo, NY,
Achsa Sprague in South Reading, VT, and Charlotte Beebe in Milwaukee, WI. A female speaker as well-known as Antoinette Brown
Blackwell could not secure a regular speaking position in one city
while the medium, Ms. Gibson, sold out a concert hall in Augusta,
Maine, for six nights in a row.[648]

Trance speaking provided a transitional phase from women having to
be silent in public life to women lecturing and preaching openly. The
trance state itself helped women overcome their normal fears of public
speaking. Believing themselves to be spiritually guided, trance mediums felt a special calm come over them whereas many reform speakers
continued to feel great trepidation. Even as fervent a reformer as Susan
B. Anthony hesitated about speaking in public.[649] Also, women, being
the 'weaker' vessel, were not supposed to speak loudly, so just being
heard could be an issue; as one female reformer who opposed public
speaking by women herself noted: "…ladies did not come there to
screech; they came to behave like ladies and to speak like ladies."[650]

Whether people believed the content of the trance talks or not,
simply seeing women speaking publicly went a long way towards
making audiences more comfortable with conceiving of women in a
public role. One very skeptical male reporter noted that the trance

---

[647] Ibid., 90-92.
[648] Ibid., 92.
[649] Ibid., 96-7.
[650] Ibid., 97.

speaker was eloquent and moving and that he'd "...never heard so beautiful and touching an exhortation."[651]

Spiritualism affected the rise of the women's rights movement. The two groups shared many leaders in common and flowed through the same social networks—initially that of the Quakers. Both movements challenged standard beliefs and practices among Americans. The most radical members of the women's movement tended to be spiritualists.[652]

Elizabeth Lowe Watson was an example of a woman who was very active locally in the spiritualist movement and a supporter of the struggle for women's rights. Born in Ohio, she grew up to become a travelling speaker and wrote inspirational poems and essays. Her husband and she gave generously of their personal wealth and were constantly engaged in humanitarian efforts. As their health declined and they experienced financial reversal, the couple moved to California where Elizabeth became the regular pastor of the First Spiritual Union of San Francisco. Soon, she was a regular speaker at the Golden Gate Religious and Philosophical Society of San Francisco where she drew increasingly large and devoted audiences. She made two lengthy trips, one to Australia and another to the East Coast, and on both trips spoke extensively and was much sought after. After the turn of the century, she served for two years as the President of the California Equal Suffrage Association.[653] She understood spiritualism to mean that the spirit world existed within and around the world of nature.[654]

---

[651] Ibid., 95.

[652] Ibid., 60.

[653] Julia Schlesinger, "J. J. Morse," *Psypioneer Journal,* Volume 8, No 10 (October 2012): f. 23, 342; Mae Silver, "Elizabeth Lowe Watson," *DigitalArchive@*Foundsf, accessed October 26, 2013, http://www.foundsf.org/index.php?title=Elizabeth_Lowe_Watson.

[654] Elizabeth Lowe Watson, *Song and Sermon* (The Thicks Judd Company: San Fransisco, CA, 1905), 148.

Through wisdom both the individual and the infinite were linked.[655] She saw a 'new woman' coming:

> "The Coming Woman": Yes! She is swiftly coming, and behold! within her hands/She bears a precious passport to all Life's Treasure-lands; / A Title Deed of Self-hood and full freedom to pursue / All the highways and byways to the Beautiful and True."[656]

In keeping with the reforming spirit that change was possible, she wrote of progress: "The evils under which humanity groans are not a necessity. Ignorance and selfishness are curable."[657]

Spiritualism tended to encourage a very individualistic stance in its rejection of many gender roles including those taught in mainstream churches. This emphasis on individualism tended to attract like-minded people such as radical abolitionists and ardent proponents of other reform efforts like the temperance, Indian rights, and anti-capital punishment movements. The more radical reformers tended to be very 'religious', but they rejected the church's association with things which they deemed evil such as slavery. Spiritualism provided such people with some form of spiritual life without the dogmas and institutions of established churches. The fast growing network of spiritualists was able to marshal large groups of reform-minded individuals from different causes. One large gathering in Rhode Island stated that, "all departments of human improvement and practical reform come legitimately within the scope of a broad Spiritualism."[658] The Spiritualists joined themselves to various reform movements because, "spiritual growth and welfare depends on [one's] physical health and surroundings."[659] There were many famous reformers like William Lloyd Garrison, the

---

[655] Watson 23.
[656] Ibid., 25.
[657] Ibid., 48.
[658] Braude, *Radical Spirits*, 69.
[659] Ibid., 69.

Grimke sisters, and Thomas Wentworth Higginson, among others, who believed in spiritualism but did not identify themselves as such.[660]

Though often overlooked in the historical record, spiritualists contributed significantly to the efforts to gain the right to vote for women with their iconoclastic beliefs and practices and their fearlessness. Although not all women's rights activists were spiritualists, all female spiritualists were women's rights activists.

4.

The women's rights advocates were originally a movement within other reform movements such as abolitionism.[661] Their push to make women's suffrage the ultimate goal brought down on them the opprobrium of society, other reformers, and, most painfully, other women.

After the Civil War, most female reformers were asked to concentrate on gaining complete rights for the men newly freed from slavery and to set aside the women's rights agenda. The spiritualist women, though, continued to push for women's rights after the Civil War with female mediums speaking out consistently on this topic. At a large spiritualist convention in Chicago, 1865, women's rights continued to be in the forefront. The first speaker advocated for woman's suffrage and the second speaker spoke in favor of easier clothing for women to protect their health—the current state of formal dress being not only uncomfortable but damaging to a woman's body. Using the spiritualist network, women's rights advocates lectured and published newspapers and books, ran organizations, and held conventions for several decades. Though spiritualists were mostly left out of the historical record—possibly due to the unusual nature of their beliefs—spiritualism

---

[660] Ibid., 60-73.

[661] Robert H. Abzug, *Cosmos Crumbling: American reform and the religious imagination* (Oxford U. Press: Oxford, UK, 1994), 184.

created a huge audience for those who doggedly pushed for the advancement of women's rights.[662]

For those reformers, the 1850s had begun as a promising decade. Elizabeth Cady Stanton saw a change after the Seneca Falls Convention of 1848:

> "Now you seldom take up a paper that has not something about woman; but the tone is changing—ridicule is giving way to reason. Our papers begin to see that this is no subject for mirth, but one for serious consideration...We have every reason to look hopefully into the future."[663]

The movement did not have a formal organization as most prominent reformers thought this would create division and stifle their creative initiative. The main organizing vehicles were the local, regional, and national conventions which brought like-minded people together to discuss the challenges facing women and what actions to take. The blueprint was the first National Women's Rights Convention held in Worcester, Massachusetts, on October 23rd and 24th, 1850. Paula Wright Davis, the wife of a successful merchant who supported her activities, organized the Convention. Her husband's early death left her a wealthy widow, so she studied physiology and then went on the lecture circuit where she shocked audiences by using life-size mannequins from Europe to demonstrate her points. For the Convention, she invited prominent reformers in this field: Lucretia Mott; Lucy Stone; William Ellery Channing, one of the most influential Unitarian ministers and theologians of the time; William A. Alcott, an educational reformer and physician who wrote over one hundred books; Wendell Phillips, an abolitionist who also worked for Indian causes; Harriot Hunt, a female physician who was the first to

---

[662] Braude, *Radical Spirits*, 79-81.
[663] McMillen, *Seneca Falls*, 104.

apply to Harvard Medical School but was denied entrance;[664] Stephen Foster, the famous songwriter who wrote "O, Susanna" but died young with thirty-seven cents to his name and his wife, Abbey;[665] William Lloyd Garrison; Sojourner Truth; Ernestine Rose, a Prussian born Jewish woman who became an atheist and abolitionist and was an important intellectual force in the women's movement;[666] and Frederick Douglass, among others.[667] Around one-thousand people—the majority of them men—filled Worcester's Brinley Hall, and heard Davis open the convention by framing the importance of the drive for equal rights:

> "…the emancipation of a class, the redemption of half the world, and a conforming re-organization of all social, political, and industrial interests and institutions."[668]

Davis also encouraged everyone to maintain a civil and courteous tone, but this was soon ignored by Abbey Foster, an avid abolitionist, who was used to confrontation. Over the next two days, a variety of related issues were raised: access to higher education, greater employment opportunities for women, reorganizing duties in the home, and opening trades and profession to women. The convention also passed a resolution regarding slave women stating that these women were "the most grossly wronged and foully outraged of all women"[669] and were due all the rights given to other people.[670]

---

[664] Harriot Hunt, *Glances and Glimpses; Or, Fifty Years' Social, Including Twenty Years' Professional Life* (Boston: J.P. Jewett and Company, 1856).

[665] W. Tomaschewski, "The Last Chapter," *Stephen Collins Foster,* accessed August 4 2012.
http://www.stephen-foster-songs.de/end.htm.

[666] Yuri Suhl, *Ernestine L. Rose: Women's Rights Pioneer* (New York: Biblio Press, 1990).

[667] McMillen, *Seneca Falls,* 105-108.

[668] Ibid., 108.

[669] Ibid.

[670] Ibid.

This was the first large public appearance for the gifted orator Lucy Stone. She arrived exhausted; she had travelled a long distance to nurse her brother who soon died of cholera in front of her, then she settled his estate, left with her very pregnant sister-in-law who gave birth prematurely to a still born child, and while Lucy was nursing her back to health, she contracted typhoid fever, causing her to drift in and out of consciousness for days. She survived and made it to the Convention. The huge success of the gathering buoyed her spirits as it did for all the attendees who felt keenly the success of their event and the importance of their cause.[671]

A few months after the convention, Elizabeth Cady Stanton, who had not been able to attend because of her advanced pregnancy, met the woman with whom she made history: Susan B. Anthony. The two women were very different and complemented each other well. Stanton was passionate and exuberant while Anthony was tireless and self-disciplined. Their working relationship was a prime moving factor in raising the status of women to full citizenship.[672]

Anthony (1820-1906), the second of eight children, developed early on an orientation towards social justice from growing up in a family with firm Quaker beliefs. In the Quaker Meeting House, she experienced both men and women speaking out in public, but once out in the larger world, she saw that equality between the genders did not exist. Her father sent her to Quaker schools for her education. After her father's mill failed, the family moved to a farm in Rochester which became a hub of abolitionism; Frederick Douglass was a regular guest there. She went into teaching to help her family financially and by the time she met Stanton, she was working for social causes, chiefly abolitionism and temperance. During her life as a reformer, Anthony was often reviled and ridiculed in the press. She turned her attention to the cause of women's suffrage after being denied speaking time at a temperance convention because she was a woman and became a

---

[671] Ibid., 109.
[672] Ibid.

confirmed supporter after reading the words that Lucy Stone had spoken at the 1850 Convention:[673]

> "We want to be something more than the appendages of Society; we want that Woman should be the coequal and help-meet of Man in all the interest and perils and enjoyments of human life. We want that she should attain to the development of her nature and womanhood; we want that when she dies, it may not be written on her gravestone that she was the "relict" of somebody."[674]

The working partnership of Anthony and Stanton stretched out over half a century. Soon after meeting they founded the Women's New York State Temperance Society in 1852 and then the New York State Woman's Rights Committee. Despite being publicly ridiculed early on, Anthony was very active in speaking and organizing public petition drives. In one memorable moment, she showed up to vote for President in the elections of 1872. She was subsequently arrested, tried, and fined $100—which she never paid—but the trial brought her and her message to greater prominence.[675]

Until the outbreak of the Civil War in 1860, women's rights activists held annual meetings in different cities such as Syracuse, Cincinnati, Cleveland, Worcester, and New York City, to bring publicity for this issue to different parts of the country and to reach the media. A frequent topic was the opening of higher education to women. This view countered the idea that intellectual life was for men and was fundamentally 'unwomanly'. Controversial topics were brought up as well. In 1850, prostitution was discussed; it came to be the sole focus

---

[673] Elinor Rice Hays, *Morning Star: A Biography of Lucy Stone 1818–1893,* (NY, NY: Harcourt, Brace & World, 1961).

[674] Andrea Moore Kerr, Lucy Stone: Speaking Out for Equality (Rutgers, NJ: Rutgers University Press, 1992), 60.

[675] Linder, Soug, "The Trial of Susan B. Anthony for Illegal Voting," *University of Missouri-Kansas City, accessed May 5, 2013,* http://law2.umkc.edu/faculty/projects/ftrials/anthony/sbaaccount.html

of an entire reform movement. In 1858, birth control, a taboo subject, was brought up by Stephen Pearl Andrews.[676] At these conventions, there were also speeches on more abstract topics such as the idea of separate spheres for the activity of men and women and how men and were different or similar.

Because of their efforts at inclusiveness, the conventions could get unruly. The two day convention in 1853 in New York City was announced in the paper with the heading, "Strong-minded Women are Getting up their Pluck." From the platform Garrison described those who opposed women's rights as "malignant, desperate, and satanic." By the time Lucy Stone stood to speak, there was so much shouting and booing that the meeting broke down in chaos. The second day began civilly but then descended into shouting as arguments broke out over the correct interpretation of the Bible's teachings on women. The 1860 convention was the most divisive due to disagreements between the female leaders. Stanton, attending her first national women's rights convention, wanted to raise issues regarding the marriage laws in New York State that disadvantaged women. Others told her privately not to bring up marriage issues because the more religious women in attendance upheld marriage values. Stanton, who did not speak often in public, preferred to shock audiences because this generated controversy, and, therefore, press coverage. So when it was her time to speak, Stanton spoke fervently against the subjugation of women in marriage and asserted the need for freer

---

[676] Andrews, who was an abolitionist from New Hampshire and almost killed in Texas for speaking against slavery, was a leader among the spiritualists, and a radical individualist, brought up this incendiary topic. A brilliant linguist, he had invented his own language and was said to be able to write thirty-two languages by the time of his passing. He believed in the absolute sovereignty of the individual so advocating for a woman's rights to determine their own pregnancies was a natural fit for him (Jeff Riggenbach, "Stephen Pearl Andrews's Fleeting Contribution to Anarchist Thought," *Miles Institute*, accessed November 12, 2013, mises.org/daily/5161/Stephen-Pearl-Andrewss-Fleeting-Contribution-to-Anarchist-Thought).

divorce laws. Many of the more religious women, such as Antoinette Brown Blackwell, spoke just as strongly against these propositions, arguing that marriage should be strengthened by elevating both men and women.[677]

Throughout the decade of the 1850s, women such as Lucy Stone and Susan B. Anthony travelled the lecture circuit expounding on the needs for women's rights. Stone was especially gifted. An editor hostile to women's rights heard her speak at the Syracuse Convention of 1855 and was so taken by her talk that he said, "Whether we like it or not, little woman, God made you an orator!" But life on the road for these women was very arduous in every way. They faced hostile crowds and could be pelted with eggs, rotten fruit, and stones. Overland travel could be brutal; Anthony rode through a New York winter night on an open sleigh which got stuck in fifteen foot drifts. 'Sleeping accommodations' often meant sharing rooms with strangers in beds which had fleas. Most women lecturers became ill and exhausted.[678]

Newspapers varied in their coverage of these conventions and lectures. Stanton was friends with Horace Greely, the editor of the influential *New York Tribune*, and, so, he reported women's rights events in positive terms. On the other hand, the *New York Herald* described the Worcester convention as a "motley mingling of abolitionists, socialists, and infidels of all sexes and colors."[679] and gave the titles of "Hens Convention" and "Insurrection in Petticoats" to the second annual meeting.[680] Anthony was a popular target. *The Utica Evening Telegraph* wrote of her speech and appearance:

> "We were inexpressibly disgused with the impudence and impiety evidenced n her lecture. Personally repulsive, she

---

677 McMillen, *Seneca Falls*, 111-119.
678 Ibid., 120-1.
679 Ibid., 125.
680 Ibid.

seems to be laboring under feelings of strong hatred towards male men, the effect we presume, of jealousy and neglect."[681]

The only real political power the women came through petition drives. There were many such drives throughout the 1850s usually coinciding with state constitutional conventions during which laws were framed. Stanton oversaw a petition drive for the right to vote in upstate New York after the Worcester Convention and had her husband, then a legislator himself, submit the petition with all the signatures. The legislators ridiculed it. During the winter of 1854-5, Anthony travelled alone through fifty-four counties collecting signatures for a petition demanding fairer marriage property laws.[682]

Petitions, though, did not result in much change despite the extensive efforts made by their organizers. Some women resorted to different forms of civil disobedience. Stone refused to pay her property taxes in 1857 because, she wrote, she had no say in the government. The city government did not agree and sold all of her household goods at auction, which a sympathetic neighbor bought and gave back to her.

Clothing was also a very visible way to protest. An upper or middle class woman's clothing could weigh up to twelve pounds and include very restrictive corsets and undergarments, tight lacing, and hoop skirts. This could affect a woman's internal organs and her overall health. Women such as Catherine Beecher and Sarah Grimke campaigned against such styles, pointing out that men did not have to carry the same weight. Amelia Bloomer's newspaper *The Lily* advocated for the wearing of loose fitting pantaloons which became known as 'bloomers'. Stanton and Stone adopted the new style. Other women's rights activists felt that the focus on clothes—and the shock it could cause—detracted from more important issues. The public was, in fact, shocked and disliked what was seen as a 'loss of femininity'. Before the bloomer ran its course, it was ridiculed in publications and

---

[681] Ibid., 126.
[682] Ibid., 127.

among the general population and was not fully supported by reformers, though a Dress Reform Association was eventually founded.[683]

As the equal rights movement spread, opposition became more active. Ministers were generally unsupportive of the drive for the right to vote. One minister wrote an article typical of the mainstream view titled, "The Woman Question," in which he expressed sympathy for women's economic situations and offered that they should receive more education to better their minds which could translate into more economic opportunity and better pay. But a woman, he wrote, should not go beyond her sphere into public life by speaking from platforms or pulpits or engaging in the world of politics. Her most important work was to keep a harmonious household and marital happiness both of which could be harmed by any kind of ambition.[684]

What was more surprising to reformers was the opposition and indifference from other women. Anthony wrote: "Woman is the greatest enemy of her own sex. She spurns the betrayed but feels flattered by the betrayer."[685]

Many female reformers thought that women were so downtrodden that they didn't even realize it. It may also have been the case that many average women had daily cares which precluded attendance at anything—much less conventions—and had little time or education to read radical papers.[686]

Relationships between reformers began to fray as differences and jealousies surfaced. Paulina Davis thought Lucretia Mott was past her prime, while others found Davis overbearing. Douglass gave a lengthy criticism in public of Lucy Stone because she lectured in a whites-only building. He also had a falling out with William Lloyd Garrison, and some women found his interpersonal manners too rough. Stanton did not think that Amelia Bloomer was a true reformer and so undermined

---

[683] Ibid., 128-133.
[684] Ibid., 136.
[685] Ibid., 138.
[686] Ibid., 138-9.

her. These types of conflicts were compounded by personal struggles and losses in the lives of the reformers. Motherhood affected the female reformers as well, especially Stanton, who bore seven children and both loved motherhood and the full household and missed her public life.[687]

During the 1850s, the cause of women's rights made discernible advances. About twenty-four states expanded the property rights of women in marriage. Michigan and Kentucky allowed women to vote in school board elections. In some states, divorce laws were liberalized. A medical college for women was founded in Philadelphia, and design schools for women were opened in Boston and Philadelphia.[688]

But the 1850s was also a decade of increasing turmoil and violence throughout the United States as the country careened into a Civil War. With its outbreak in April of 1861, the work for the advancement of women took a back seat to the needs of the conflict. Northern women threw themselves into relief work; the Women's Central Association, the largest women's relief organization, was founded. With so many men away at the front, women in the North and in the South filled in for jobs they had never done—or had never been previously permitted to do—before, becoming factory workers, clerks, scribes, and even spies and soldiers. But the most important new line of work into which women entered in large numbers was nursing. Previously, this work had been considered too rough for women, but now, in places where female nurses worked, mortality dropped by fifty percent due to the concerns of women for cleanliness, ventilation, and nutrition. Dorothea Dix, famous for her reform on behalf of prisoners and the mentally ill, supervised the Union Army's entire nursing corps. Another profession into which women entered in unprecedented numbers was teaching. In addition to filling vacancies in schools throughout the north, women from the north also ventured south to educate newly freed slaves; this began in the Sea Islands of Georgia

---

[687] Ibid., 140-144.
[688] Ibid., 148.

which were held by Union troops. Families of reformers were also affected by the war. Two of Stanton's sons, one of Sojourner Truth's grandsons, two of Douglass' sons, and Thomas Higginson all went to war for the Union army.[689]

After the end of the Civil War, in April 1865, the work of abolitionists now focused on gaining basic freedoms for the men newly freed from slavery, and so, the fight for equal rights for women was put second. Stanton consistently spoke and wrote against this view, believing that the hour had come to implement both reforms together. She saw subjugation to black men as being no different than domination of women by white men but many reformers and members of Lincoln's Republican Party disagreed and saw suffrage and rights for the newly freedmen as the central issue. Some reformers were also discouraged by the indifference of many women towards the struggle for women's rights.[690]

The Congress was now debating changes to the Constitution and including the word 'male' in the proposed amendment. Stanton, Stone, and Anthony wrote a passionate appeal against passage of the amendment to the Congress as it excluded all women. The 11th Annual Women's Rights Convention met in May 1866, at the same time as the New York legislature was re-writing its State Constitution. The Convention decided to found an organization dedicated solely to the agenda of 'universal suffrage' called the American Equal Rights Association. Even so, divisions arose again on the issue of priorities and even whether there should be any priorities at all.[691]

The Congress passed the Fourteenth Amendment enfranchising black men but not women. Stanton and others were very discouraged by this and lost hope in the political parties. In protest, Stanton ran for public office in New York State in 1866 on the platform *"free speech, free press, free man and free trade"* saying that educated, propertied

---

[689] Ibid., 149-153.
[690] Ibid., 161-2.
[691] Ibid., 162-3.

women were far better for the nation than uneducated, landless black men in the South. She garnered twenty-four votes out of twenty-thousand cast but continued to speak out, accusing men of being responsible for the nation's ills. A writer and editor, George Curtis, wrote that women's suffrage would not drag women down into the dirty world of politics; rather, it would lift men out of it. There was more promise of success in Massachusetts and Kansas, but these efforts also failed to get women the right to vote. After Kansas, Stone said, "the Negroes are all against us."[692] Sojourner Truth spoke twice at AERA conventions:

> "There is a great stir about colored men getting their rights, but not a word about the colored women, and if colored men get their rights, and not colored women get theirs there will be a bad time about it."[693]

She pointed out what may have been obvious about women's enfranchisement: "I know that it is hard for one who has held the reins for so long to give up."[694]

In the late 1860s, divisions deepened between the women's rights reformers. The Thirteenth Amendment abolishing slavery and the Fourteenth Amendment enfranchising black men had been passed, and now the Fifteenth Amendment, stating the right to vote could not be abridged by any state on the basis of race, came up. Stanton and Anthony argued against supporting the amendment because it did not include women. Stone, Douglass, and others supported it with Douglass arguing against Stanton pointing out that the suffering of slaves had been enormous. He was asked if black women had not suffered as well, and he answered that their suffering had been based on race not gender and that with the vote, black men would be better able to protect black women. Anthony argued against him saying that women

---

[692] Ibid., 166.
[693] Ibid., 167.
[694] Ibid.

could not just stand aside while black men got the right to vote but not women. As the argument continued, Douglass saw the convention as being about women's rights not universal equal rights.[695] In a sense, both sides brought their own biases: Stanton and Anthony in favor of educated women, whom they saw as the better citizens because of their education, and Douglass with his bias towards the suffering of male slaves. Anthony and Stanton withdrew from the AERA and formed the National Women's Suffrage Association. Angered at not having been invited to join, Stone and Henry Blackwell founded the American Woman Suffrage Association which supported women's rights and the passage of the Fifteenth Amendment. The two organizations had different approaches—the AWSA sought to gain suffrage for women at the state level and admitted all members, while the NWSA lobbied for a Constitutional Amendment guaranteeing woman's suffrage and admitted only woman members. In addition to this rivalry, there continued to be opposition to the very concepts of equal rights for women; many ministers still spoke of it as un-Biblical, un-feminine and un-natural. The only real success for these reformers in the late 1860s was securing suffrage in the Western territories of Wyoming and Utah; in these frontier areas, women tended to have greater equality because of the interdependence between men and women necessary for survival, and, in these new territories, it was much easier legislatively for such laws to pass.[696]

The road to guaranteeing the right to vote for women would be a long one. Anthony and Stanton first proposed such an amendment to the Constitution in 1878. It was defeated in the Congress in 1887 and in 1915 by a smaller margin, while activists worked to gain such voting rights at the state level.

American women would have to wait for decades for this amendment to be incorporated into the country's legal framework. This long struggle for women's suffrage culminated in victory with the passing of

---

[695] Ibid., 173.
[696] Ibid., 177-184.

a Constitutional Amendment guaranteeing women the right to vote in 1920, seventy-two years after the Seneca Falls convention.

The Amendment read: "The right of citizens of the United States to vote shall not be denied or abridged by the United States or by any state on account of sex. Congress shall have power to enforce this article by appropriate legislation."

Originally the Amendment had been called the "Anthony amendment" but Susan B. Anthony did not live to see the legal fruition of her life's work. Neither did Stanton. She passed away in 1906, four years after her long-time sister in the trenches.

EPILOGUE

In January, 1930, an American Baha'i journalist, Martha Root, stepped into the room of the home in Qazvin in which Tahirih had been born and knelt down and kissed the floor over which the great mystic had walked. At that moment, Martha Root was a pilgrim enthralled with the figure of Tahirih.[697]

The attempt to wipe away the traces of Tahirih by destroying her personal records after her execution had failed.

Descendants from Tahirih's family watched this woman from the west paying deep homage to their relative.[698] The owner of the hotel where Martha Root was staying had reprimanded one of Tahirih's relatives by saying that the family should be ashamed for not having done more with her memory while an American had come from so far to pay homage to her. This rebuke resulted in the relative—a Muslim—bringing the American pilgrim to Tahirih's family's home which still retained its appearance as a beautiful old palace with delicate lattice work. Martha Root was shown the women's quarters in which Tahirih was born and the "quaint" library on the second floor where she had become a young scholar. The relative met Martha Root later and confessed: "I have known for twenty years that I should be a Baha'i, but I have never had the courage to do it."[699]

The memory of Tahirih travelled east and west through the arteries of the Baha'i Faith,[700] the fruition of the Bab's revelation. Jinab-i-Baha, who had guided the Babi community through the Conference of Badasht and its break with the Islamic past, was Baha'u'llah, the manifestation of God for whom the Bab had been preparing the way. The Bab had been the first Divine outpouring, and Baha'u'llah, the

---

[697] Root, *Táhirih the pure*, 49.
[698] Mabel R. Garis, *Martha Root: Lioness at the Threshold* (Wilmette IL: Bahá'í Publishing Trust, 1983), 341.
[699] Ibid.
[700] Her great grandson, Varta, became a Baha'i (Hoseini, *Hadrat-i-Tahirih*, 164).

second. The Babis became Baha'is, and the Baha'i Faith spread beyond the borders of Persia, out of the Islamic world, and all the way to the West, where it was discovered by thousands including Martha Root, who came to know about this great apostle of the Bab.

In the great Baha'i chronicle, *Dawnbreakers*, and the foundational history of the Baha'i Faith, *God Passes By*, Tahirih was memorialized as a woman who completely renounced the world for reunion with God through her love of the Bab. Her awareness of God's presence in the world compelled her into action whatever the social costs to herself. She set aside with no hesitation the restrictions on public teaching and social muteness placed on women. In the West, this is the aspect of Tahirih which was brought to the fore. She was cast as a champion of women's rights as understood by the new century's context of the struggle for women's suffrage in the West. In the Indian subcontinent, it was her poetry, expressive of her courage, that continued to speak throughout the decades, while in Persia, her verses—those which had not been expunged by persecution—lived on in song. All over the world, Tahirih's life and sacrifice continue to inspire the Baha'i faithful towards renunciation, and through that, the finding of a new power beyond gender.

So even by the time trees had grown out of the ground in which Tahirih's body had been placed decades earlier before Martha Root's visit and completely unbeknownst to her relatives, her resurrection had already begun.

APPENDIX A:
TAHIRIH IN THE WEST AND THE EAST

Tahirih had been a passionate apostle and witness for the Bab's faith—a religion which along with its successor, the Baha'i Faith—was characterized as heretical by the Shi'a clerical establishment and severely persecuted throughout the country. Baha'is were often shunned, their children humiliated, their businesses plundered, and their homes targeted. Being a Baha'i in late 19th century Persia could also be fatal. So to identify oneself as a believer was an act of faith expressed in courage. In such an atmosphere, there was little chance that a Babi poet would be publicly celebrated or that family members would want to promote a relative whose heretical beliefs might endanger the whole family. Some of her poems, nevertheless, survived in anthologies of women poets, and her most famous poem became part of the standard vocal repertoire.[701]

Tahirih's name travelled westward almost immediately after her execution.

Sir Justin Sheil, a British general and diplomat who served as Queen Victoria's representative to the court of the King of Persia, sent the first known mention of the execution of Tahirih in this dispatch dated August 22nd, 1852:

> "Among those who have suffered death was a young woman, the daughter of a Teacher of the Law in Mazanderan of great celebrity who has been three years in confinement in Tehran. She was venerated as a prophetess by the Babees, and her designation among them was 'Koorat ool ain' – 'Pupil of the eye.' She has been strangled by the Shah's order. The Sedr Azim has opposed some of these acts, but the Shah's anger

---

[701] Prof. Dominic Brookshaw, September 15th, 2013.

and vindictiveness have not allowed him to pay attention to advice."[702]

The next day, Prince Dolgorukov, the Russian ambassador to Persia sent this dispatch:

> "…For a long time there has been imprisoned in Tihran under the surveillance of Mahmud Khan, Chief of Police, a Babi woman (Tahirih). In spite of this she apparently found means daily to gather around herself many members of her sect. She was strangled in a garden in the presence of Ajudan-Bashi…."[703]

Russia, more than any other foreign country, was involved in the internal affairs of Persia because of their long common border and its competition with England over Persia's resources. Prince Dolgorukov, who came from a Russian noble family that had almost become Czars, became the subject of a slanderous hoax meant to discredit Russia. A fictional memoir supposedly written by him was published which claimed that he was collaborating with the Bab to overthrow the Qajar dynasty. There was no basis to this claim as these were not the aims of the Bab. Prince Dolgorukov knew little about him, and he was not in Persia during the years indicated by the memoir.[704]

Soon her execution was the subject of a whole newspaper article in the October 13th, 1852, edition of the *Times of London* titled "*How they punish treason in Persia*":

> "We mentioned a few days since the attempt against the Shah of Persia. We now learn that Hajee Suleiman Khan, ac-

---

[702] Moojan Momen, *The Babi and Baha'i Religions, 1844-1944, Some Contemporary Western Accounts* (Oxford, UK: George Ronald, 1981), 135.

[703] Ibid., 143.

[704] Masumian, Adib, "Debunking the Myths: Conspiracy Theories on the Genesis and Mission of the Bahá'í Faith," *Academia,* accessed October 3, 2013, http://www.academia.edu/343383/Debunking_the_Myths_Conspiracy_Theories _on_the_Genesis_and_Mission_of_the_Bahai_Faith.

cused as the instigator of the crime, was seized, his body carefully drilled with a knife in parts which would not at the
moment cause death: pieces of lighted candles were then introduced into the holes, and, thus illuminated, carried in
procession through the bazaar, and finally conveyed to the
town gates, and there cleft in twain like a fat ram. The Kur-
ret-il-Ain, better known as Bab's Lieutenant, or the fair
Prophetess of Kazoeen [Qazvin], who since the late religions
outbreak had been kept a close prisoner at the capital, has
been executed with some dozen others. His Majesty, received
three slug wounds in the shoulders, but all of a very slight
nature."[705]

In the coming two and a half decades, there were several important
first mentions of Tahirih in the West.

The first woman to publish a mention of Tahirih was in Lady Mary
Sheil's, "Glimpses of Life and Manners in Persia." published in 1856:

"There was still another victim. This was a young woman,
the daughter of a moolla in Mazenderan, who, as well as her
father, had adopted the tenets of the Bab. The Babees venerated her as a prophetess; and she was styled Khooret-ool-eyn,
which Arabic words are said to mean, Pupil of the eye. After
the Babee insurrection had been subdued in the above province, she was brought to Tehran and imprisoned, but was
well treated. When these executions took place she was
strangled. This was a cruel and useless deed."[706]

A British diplomat, Robert Grant Watson, wrote a history of Persia
covering the first half of the 19th century, *A History of Persia,* which

---

[705] The Times, October 13, 1852, cited in Momen, *The Babi and Bahá'í
Religions,* 132.
[706] Lady Mary Sheil, Glimpses of life and manners in Persia, quoted in Farzaneh
Milani, *Veils and Words, The emerging voices of Iranian women writers* (Syracuse,
NY: Syracuse University Press, 1992), 97.

was published in 1866. In this book, Watson made a brief mention of Tahirih, "...the daughter of a celebrated teacher of the law, and who was considered by the Babis to be a prophetess...."[707]

The first book about the history of the Bab and his followers in a Western language was *The Báb and the Bábis: Religious and Political Unrest in Persia in 1848-1852*, written in Russian by Aleksandr Kazem-Bek,[708] and published in 1865. Kazem-Bek was a philologist who straddled the Russian and Persian worlds; he was born in Persia, died in St. Petersburg and was of Azerbaijani origin. He wrote his first book—-on the subject of Arabic grammar—at age 17 and later converted to Christianity.[709]

In 1865, an Austrian doctor, Dr Jakob Polak, claimed to have been present at her execution—a claim which has never been verified:

> "I was witness to the execution of Qurret el ayn, who was executed by the war minister and his adjutants; the beautiful woman endured her slow death with superhuman strength."[710]

The book which introduced the Bab to a broad generation of European intellectuals was *"Religions et philosophies dans l'Asie central"* (Religions and philosophies of Central Asia), by Joseph Arthur, Compte de Gobineau (1816-1882), published in 1865. Gobineau was a French writer and diplomat who had been posted in Persia during the time of the Bab. He wrote an account of his impressions and understanding of the religious beliefs of the people in that part of the world which contained the first extensive account of the Babi religion

---

[707] Robert Grant Watson, *A History of Persia* (London, UK: Smith, Elder and Co., 1866), 409.

[708] Jan T. Jasion, "*Tahirih on the Russian stage*," Sabir Afaqi, Ed., *Tahirih in History* (LA, CA: Kalimat Press, LA, 2004), 232.

[709] Momen, *The Babi and Baha'i Religions*, 26-7; "Alexander Kazembek (Russian Orientalist)," *World Public Library*, accessed 9 October 2013, http://netlibrary.net/articles/Alexander_Kazembek_(Russian_orientalist).

[710] Ibid., 144.

and early history of the faith. He had come into possession of the only manuscript of a history of the Babi faith which had been written by Haji Mirza Jani, a Babi who was killed during the persecutions of 1852. Gobineau wrote a description of Tahirih which conveys the degree of her talent and capacity and the high regard in which she was held:

> "Not only did she have a rare command of Arabic, but she became outstanding in her understanding of the interpretation of the Qur'an, the Islamic traditions (hadiths), and great Islamic thinkers. In Qazvin, she came to be regarded as a prodigy."[711]
>
> "...she was not content with passive belief; she spoke publically about the teachings of her master; she stood up not only against polygamy but also against the use of the veil, and showed her face in public places to the great shock and scandal of her family and all sincere Muslims, but also to the applause of the numerous people who shared her enthusiasm and whose public preaching greatly added to the circle of believers."[712]
>
> "...she consecrated herself fully to her Apostleship of the Bab to which he had given all the rights and entrusted her with many responsibilities. Her knowledge of theology became immense...I never heard any Muslim put in doubt the virtue of such a unique person."[713]

Gobineau imagines a scene at Badasht at which Tahirih is seated cross-legged on a throne built for her from which she preaches that the time had come to spread the Bab's religion all over the earth, and also that women must work along with men in making their contribution. According to Gobineau's Persian sources, Tahirih's speech was simple

---

[711] Gobineau, *Religions and Philosophies*, 168.
[712] Ibid.
[713] Ibid., 169.

yet very effective in moving the hearts of people. He describes simple country people at Badasht as being transformed after hearing her speak.[714]

Gobineau's book was reviewed and cited many times. The *Journal des Savants* in France published a review of Gobineau's book which included a whole paragraph on Tahirih, stressing how she stood up for the women of the Orient and called on them to rise up out of the seclusion in which they had been kept.[715] In August of 1868, *Le Temps* of Paris published a series of three articles with two paragraphs on Tahirih which made the point that the very presence of a woman of this capacity showed that the Bab's faith was intent on real social change.[716]

Some very prominent French thinkers and scholars also used Gobineau in their descriptions of the Babi movement and Tahirih. Joseph Ernest Renan, an eminent French religious thinker and political philosopher, made mention of the Babis over several pages in his book, *Les Apotres* ('The Apostles'),[717] dwelling on the physical cruelty they suffered and their single-mindedness of purpose which he describes as a characteristic of people from 'that part of the world'.[718]

A second French scholar, André-Ursule Casse de Bellecombe, wrote an entire article on Tahirih—for whom he used the title 'Qurratu'l-Ayn'—in the historical journal of the Institute of France, "*L'Investigateur*," in 1870.[719] Bellecombe served as the Director the Institut Historique of France. He wrote on a very wide variety of subjects—Italian, Chinese, Mexican, and Central American History, Tahirih and the Bab, and the Amazon—he even wrote a four volume

---

[714] Ibid., 182.

[715] Momen, *The Babi and Baha'i Religions*, 23-24; Adolphe Franck, "Deuxième et Dernier Article," *Le Journal des Savants,* December (1865): 776-777.

[716] Ibid., 24; Michel Nicolas, "Le Babysme," *Le Temps* August 14, 19, 20 (1868): 3, 3, 3.

[717] Momen, *The Babi and Baha'i Religions*, 22-3.

[718] Joseph Renan, *Les Apotres* (Paris, France: Michel Levy Freres, 1866), 377.

[719] Momen, *The Babi and Baha'i Religions*, 27.

history of the world which included the history of science. He was in constant contact with the most prominent literary and scientific minds of the day in France. A humble and learned man, he believed in the value of the diversity of races.[720] In this article, he described the Bab as a "poor cloth merchant" with a very ascetical and mystical orientation who attracted thousands of followers and promoted the advancement of women, the unity of all Muslims, and religious tolerance. He praised Tahirih's courage in standing up to doubters and social conventions while remaining unafraid in the face of physical threats. He accused the Shi'a clerics of trying to discredit her through the use of their own fanciful interpretations of Islamic Doctrine. According to Bellecombe, Tahirih taught the equality of men and women, marriage rights for women, the prohibition against divorce, and unity between a husband and wife. She was accused, he wrote, of encouraging a communal ownership of property, but she actually taught love and unity between the Babis as they awaited the coming Kingdom; until then, the Babis could follow the Shari'a Law or their own conscience. Bellecombe defends her by writing that the difference between Tahirih's teaching and the accusations of communalism would be like comparing the sharing between the early apostles of Christ to socialism.[721] By way of summary, he calls Tahirih the emancipator of Muslim women and compared her to women in the West who advanced the cause of woman; specifically he mentioned Elisabeth Blackwell, the first woman in the United States to receive a medical degree—which was in 1849—and Amelia Bloomer, the passionate

---

[720] "Dictionnaire biographie de Lot-et-Garonne," *C.H.G.H.47,* accessed October 1, 2013.
genealogie-en-47.fr/Articles/Dossiers/Dictionnaire_biographique_01.html.
[721] Andre-Ursule de Bellecombe, *"La belle Kourret ou l'Hain reformatrice persanne,"* L'Investigateur Tome X, 1870 (L'Institut Historique de France: Paris, France, 1870): 161.

advocate for the 'bloomer', and to the demand for political rights by English and French women.[722]

A third French scholar, Clement Huart, wrote a short book, "*La Religion du Bab*," in 1889, which included Tahirih.[723] Huart began learning Arabic at the age of fourteen and went on to study the languages and literatures of the Arabic, Turkish, and Persian worlds. In addition, he had an excellent knowledge of English, Italian, and German.[724] In this book, Huart praises Tahirih's great knowledge and her independent spirit, citing her going about unveiled. Because of his great linguistic talents, Huart devotes many pages to his own translations from Persian and Arabic into French of passages from the Bab's Writings and explicates some of his teachings.[725]

England's *Contemporary Review*, published a whole article, "*Story of the Bab*," in December of 1885,[726] with a description of Tahirih based on Gobineau "as a woman who, had she been born in Europe, would have ranked with our most honored heroines of this or any age" and who had a courage "as indomitable as that of her master."[727]

Kazem-Bek and Gobineau's works became the main source for knowledge of the Babi faith in the West.

Marie von Najmájer, an Austrian writer and activist for the advancement of women, wrote the first literary work or poem to use Tahirih as a character,[728] "*Gurret-ül-Eyn. (A picture from the Persian*

---

[722] "Elizabeth Blackwell Counterslip 1821-Schottland 1910," *Art Directory,* accessed November 4, 2013, www.elizabeth-blackwell.com/.

[723] Momen, *The Babi and Baha'i Religions*, 40.

[724] Jean Calmard, "HUART, CLÉMENT," in the Encyclopaedia Iranica, edited by Ehsan Yarshater, accessed October 23, 2013, www.iranicaonline.org/articles/huart-clment.

[725] Clement Huart, La Religion du Bab (Ernest Leroux Editeur: Paris, France 1889).

[726] Momen, *The Babi and Baha'i Religions*, 25.

[727] Mary Wilson, "*Story of the Bab,*" The Library, Jan-April 1886, v. 7 (NY, NY: John B. Alden Publisher 1886), 813.

[728] Momen, *The Bábi and Bahá'i Religions*, 47.

modern times in 6 Songs)," published in 1874.[729] She used Kazem-Bek and Gobineau for her basic information. Many decades later, Marianna Hainisch, mother of a President of Austria, heard of Tahirih from Martha Root, and professed: "I shall try to do for the women of Austria what Tahirih gave her life to do for the women of Persia."[730]

In December, 1880, Michele Lessona, a prominent Italian scientist specializing in amphibians, who had translated Darwin and went on to influence generations of Italian scientists,[731] organized two conferences on the Babi movement. The proceedings were published as a book, *I Babi*, in 1881.[732] He went to Persia on behalf of the King of Italy in 1862, to be a physician for the delegation going to establish relations between the two Kingdoms. There in Tabriz he met Daud Khan who told him all about the Bab. He tried to visit the places associated with the Bab and met often with Gobineau who was then the French Ambassador. Most of his information on the Babi faith came from these two sources, especially Gobineau. He found it difficult, though, to get any first-hand information about the Babis:

> "...In Persia, it is impossible to speak of the Babis or to learn something of their affairs. The terror which this name awakens is such that no one dares to speak, or even think, of it."[733]

---

[729] Marie von Najmájer, "*Gurret-ül-Eyn. (A picture from the Persian modern times in 6 Songs),*" Originalausg. ersch Vienna 1874 Photomechan Nachdr. d Originalausg, ext, erg and with biography, FWD and hist demolition. [With portraits. fig u]). - Vienna: National Spiritual Assembly of Bahá'ís in Austria, 1981. ANL-1202994 B. Neu Mag.

[730] Marzieh Gail, "*With Martha.*" in Root, *Táhirih the pure,* 6.

[731] Momen, The Babi and Baha'i Religions, 27; Ugo R. Giachery, "An Italian Scientist Extols the Bab." The Bahá'í World, Vol 12, 1950-1952 (Wilmette, IL: Bahá'í Publishing Trust 1956), 900.

[732] Julio Savi. "Italy: History of the Baha'i Faith," Bahá'í Library Online, accessed October 2, 2013.
http://bahai-library.com/savi_encyclopedia_italy.

[733] Giachery, "*An Italian Scientist Extols the Bab,*" 902.

Another Italian, Belgian-born Carla Serrana, travelled through Persia and wrote a travelogue, *"Men and objects in Persia,"* which was published in 1883[734] and then translated into nine languages. Her account included a chapter, "Formation of the Babi sect," based entirely on information from Gobineau in which she described Tahirih as an extraordinary talent.[735] Serrana was the first European woman to travel to the Caucasus through which she travelled alone in her fifties. When she returned, she was invited to speak at conferences in Rome about her travels, but she declined because, "women in Italy don't speak in public." In 1873, she was sent by a newspaper to Vienna, and this began a trip east which lasted six years. Unlike other European travelers who came before her, Serrana was particularly attentive to the daily life of the country people whom she met.[736]

One of the most learned expositions of the Bab's teachings, his life, and the history of his followers was written by Edward Sell, an Anglican churchman who was a missionary in India for years, authored over fifty scholarly works and could read Persian, Arabic and Hindi, among other languages.[737] Though he was able to read the sources directly, he did make use of the histories by Kazem-Bek and Gobineau. He wrote three treatises about the Babis/Baha'is: "The Babis," in 1896,[738] "The Bab and the Babis," a missionary view, in 1901,[739] and "Bahaism," an

---

[734] Momen, *The Babi and Baha'i Religions*, 28.

[735] Carla Serena, *Hommes et choses en Perse* (Paris, France: Charpentier et Cᵒ, 1883).

[736] Monica Di Barbora, "Carla Serena," *Encyclopedia delle donne*, accessed October 29, 2013,
http://www.enciclopediadelledonne.it/biografie/carla-serena/.

[737] C. E. Buckland, *Dictionary of Indian Biography* (London: Swan Sonnenschein & Co. Lim., 1906), 382.

[738] Edward Sell, "The Babis," *The Church Missionary Intelligencer* 47:21 (1896): 324-335.

[739] Edward Sell, "The Bab and the Babis," in *Essays on Islam* (London: Simpkin, Marshall, Hamilton, Kent &. Co., 1901) 46-98.

early book-length overview for a missionary audience, in 1912.[740] His
pieces contained lengthy explanations of the Islamic context of Babi
history, theological details and issues, the connection between
Shaykhis and Babis and the history of the Babi faith itself. He was able
to include direct quotations from the Bab's scripture because of his
knowledge of Persian. His praise of Tahirih was reinforced by his
ability to read her in the original Persian:

> "Some of her poems breathe the spirit of Ṣúfísm and show
> how deeply her mind was imbued with mystic lore. This is
> far more apparent in the original than in any translation of
> them. The following lines are from a translation by Mr.
> Browne."[741]

Another insightful and generally well-informed account of the Bab's
life which included the story of Tahirih was, "The Reconciliation of
races and religions," a compilation of talks given by Prof. Thomas
Kelly Cheyne, an English Christian minister, Biblical scholar, and
Oxford Professor, and published in 1914. Possibly as a result of his
study, he became a Baha'i.[742] He wrote in his chapter on Tahirih that
she had an exalted position:

> "Indeed, the only difference in human beings is that some
> realize more, and some less, or even not at all, the fact of the
> divine spark in their composition. Ḳurratu'l 'Ayn certainly
> did realize her divinity."[743]

He gives a generally accurate account of the story of her life in broad
strokes, noting the close association of Tahirih with Baha'u'llah. The

---

[740] Edward Sell, *"Bahaism,"* (London, UK: Christian Literature Society for India,
1912).
[741] Sell, *"The Bab and the Babis,"* 66.
[742] Momen, *The Babi and Baha'i Religions,* 52.
[743] Thomas Kelly Cheyne, D.D. *The Reconciliation of Races and Religions.* PDF e-
book.
http://www.gutenberg.org/cache/epub/7995/pg7995.html.

unveiling of her face was a "...bold act of Ḳurratu'l 'Ayn which shook the foundations of a literal belief in Islamic doctrines among the Persians."

He finished this chapter by recounting an interesting episode about suffragettes from Turkey who were banished to Akka:

"The poetess (i.e. Tahirih) was a true Bahaite. More than this; the harvest sown in Islamic lands by Ḳurratu'l 'Ayn is now beginning to appear. A letter addressed to the *Christian Commonwealth* last June informs us that forty Turkish suffragettes are being deported from Constantinople to Akka (so long the prison of Baha-'ullah): "'During the last few years suffrage ideas have been spreading quietly behind in the harems. The men were ignorant of it; everybody was ignorant of it; and now suddenly the floodgate is opened and the men of Constantinople have thought it necessary to resort to drastic measures. Suffrage clubs have been organized, intelligent memorials incorporating the women's demands have been drafted and circulated; women's journals and magazines have sprung up, publishing excellent articles; and public meetings were held. Then one day the members of these clubs—four hundred of them—*cast away their veils.* The staid, fossilized class of society were shocked, the good Mussulmans were alarmed, and the Government forced into action. *These four hundred liberty-loving women were divided into several groups. One group composed of forty have been exiled to Akka, and will arrive in a few days.* (italics added here) Everybody is talking about it, and it is really surprising to see how numerous are those in favour of removing the veils from the faces of the women. Many men with whom I have talked think the custom not only archaic, but thought-stifling. The Turkish authorities, thinking to extinguish this light of liberty, have greatly added to its flame, and their high-handed action has materially assisted the creation of a wider public

opinion and a better understanding of this crucial problem."[744]

While the exact sources to verify this story of Turkish women suffragettes in Akka have not been found, there was, in 1913, a great rise in
activism for the advancement of women in Turkey. There were many
women's associations founded there during the late Ottoman pe-
riod/early 1900s. The first women's organization, *Cemiyet-i İmdadiye*,
was founded in 1908, by Fatma Aliye, to provide winter clothing for
the soldiers on the frontier by selling handcrafts. Another organization
founded that same year to help orphaned girls and boys was opened to
women regardless of their religion.[745] The Union and Progress Voca-
tional School for Girls and its many branch offices were begun.[746]
Political parties set up charity unions for women and field offices to
engage women in political support; one even had the slogan, "in order
to free the country from collapse, it is essential to mind girls firstly."[747]
There was a proliferation of associations to defend the rights of
women, to open hospitals and schools, to assert the rights of women
without disregarding traditional values,[748] to participate in working life
and begin businesses for women,[749] to found a university for women,
to advocate for women's suffrage, and to publish women's periodicals
which called for a Constitutional form of government.[750] At the core of
these associations were two ideas: the importance of educating women
because it was, "the keystone of social progress,"[751] and crucial to the

---

[744] Ibid.
[745] Aygül, Ceren, *Change in the status of turkish women during the ottoman
modernization and self-evaluation of women in kadinlar dünyasi of 1913*, Ankara,
Turkey: Middle East Technical University, Dept. of History 2010, 51,
http://etd.lib.metu.edu.tr/upload/12612331/index.pdf.
[746] Ibid., 52.
[747] Ibid., 54.
[748] Ibid., 56.
[749] Ibid., 55, 57-8.
[750] Ibid., 57-8.
[751] Ibid., 84.

development of Turkey as a modern nation,[752] and the assertion and defense of the rights of women within the family[753] and in public life.

One year after the publication of Gobineau's book, the first account of the religion of the Bab appeared in North America, "A New Religion," in *The Nation* June, 1866.[754] Wendell Phillips Garrison, son of the most famous white abolitionist, William Lloyd Garrison, was the literary editor of *The Nation*. In this account, the Bab was described as "addicted to religious thought and novel ideas," as having "great physical beauty, great simplicity of manners, and sweetness of character," and that he "resolved upon the destruction of Islam."[755] His account followed the basic outline of the life of the Bab but most of the details related to him were not accurate. Tahirih was described as an apostle who was one of, "the most striking apparitions to shed lustre on Babism." She had "extraordinary beauty," "eloquence," and "purity of manners," and she "preached the abolition of veiling and polygamy."[756] The end of the article contains some musings regarding the "oriental" nature of the Bab's teachings as being progressive by Persian standards:

> "The re-birth in this system of the mystical fancies and many of the puerile superstitions of Oriental superstitions of Oriental antiquity, in combination with some of the most modern and most advanced ideas of the Western mind, is a very curious spectacle."[757]

He wonders whether Babis will join the growing nationalist movement and call for an armed uprising or become obsolete. There is no mention of the role of the Bab's role as forerunner of Baha'u'llah."[758]

---

[752] Ibid., 87.

[753] Ibid., 71-2.

[754] Momen, *The Bábí and Bahá'í Religions*, 24.

[755] Wendell Phillips Garrison, ed., "A New Religion." *The Nation*, (1866): 793.

[756] Ibid, 794.

[757] Ibid., 795.

[758] Ibid., 795.

Numerous newspaper accounts of the Bab and Tahirih appeared in American newspapers: *The Methodist Quarterly Review*, July, 1866, included a paragraph in, "Foreign Intelligence... France"; William Hepworth Dixon published a travel book in 1867, with a history and commentary which mentions the Bab and Babis twice; Evans, E.P. wrote, "Bab and Babism," for *Hours at Home*, in January, 1869; Edwin Bliss also wrote a similarly titled article, "Bab and Babism," for the *Missionary Herald*, May, 1869; "A New Religion," appeared in the July 17, 1869, issue of *All the Year Round*; the *Brooklyn Eagle*, and *The Hawaiian Gazette*, carried stories on the new religion in their August and September, 1869, issues respectively; Robert Arbuthnot wrote a lengthy history of Faith titled, *"The Bab and Babeeism,"* which included some of its theology, teachings and a paragraph on Tahirih, for the August, 1869, issue of *Contemporary Review*; the August, 1869, issue of *Saturday Review of Politics, Literature, Science and Art*, published an article, "Reviews: The Philosophical Year and the Bábys," which mentioned Gobineau's version of her martyrdom; the article, "The Bábys," in *The Church Missionary Intelligencer*, June, 1872, included a long introduction that showed how Muhammad got his teachings on the progressive nature and continuity of religion from Christianity and Judaism and how the Bab's teachings were also influenced by Christianity, and it described Tahirih as eloquent and beautiful.[759]

Another lengthy summary of the Babi Faith, "Babysme," appeared in the 1868 version of the French Encyclopedia, *L'Annuaire encyclopédique*. The entry attempted to explain the Bab's teachings such as the common divine origin of all religions, the brotherhood of man, the new social laws, though it also described the Bab as a "hypochondriac" for his religious intensity. A substantial paragraph on Tahirih gave some of her biographical details, emphasized her physical beauty— saying her charms and seductiveness helped the Bab's faith as "only a woman could do," and stating that she was called 'Solace of the Eyes'

---

[759] Momen, *The Bábí and Bahá'í Religions*, 24-5.

because of her beauty, which was inaccurate. She was one of the pillars of the new faith with the courage to break with the past.[760]

One of the more unusual mentions of Tahirih was made during a series of lectures by William Rossetti, brother of the famous 19th-century English poet, Christina Rossetti, which was published in *The Dublin University Magazine*, March, 1878. He was lecturing on the poem, "The Revolt of Islam," by Percy Bysshe Shelley. The poem has no actual basis in Islam nor does it seek to depict it, but its male character is a spiritual reformer seeking to reestablish virtue. He is aided by his influential female companion. Rossetti wrote of the connection between the poem and the story of the Bab:

> "…the very singular and striking resemblance which the in-vented story of the "Revolt of Islam," written in 1817, bears to some historical events of much more recent date in Persia. I refer to the career of the sect named the Babys, founded by a young man, a native of Shiraz—Mirza-Ali-Muhamad, who in 1843, was a student in a theological school."[761]

Rossetti writes that Tahirih had an "almost magical influence over large masses of the population."[762] To Rossetti, Shelley's characters seem to prefigure both the lives of the Bab and Tahirih and the great changes of the 19th century following the French Revolution. Shelley wrote that the poem:

---

[760] A. Bonneau, "Babysme," *L'Annuaire encyclopédique VIII* (Paris: Bureau de L'Encyclopedie,
1869), 255. Several of these sources were found from the following page:
"Travelers and Scholars on the Bábí/Baha'i Faiths," in the *Bahaikipedia*, accessed September 10, 2013,
https://bahaikipedia.org/Travelers_and_Scholars_on_the_Bábí/Baha'i_Faiths.
The list on this encyclopedia page was compiled from lists by Collins, McEoin, and Momen,
[761] William Michael Rossetti, "Shelley's Life and Writings, Two Lectures," *The University, A Literary and Philosophical Review* vol. 1 (1878): 264.
[762] Ibid..

"...is, in fact, a tale illustrative of such a revolution as might
be supposed to take place in an European nation, acted upon
by the opinions of what has been called (erroneously, as I
think) the modern philosophy, and contending with ancient
notions and the supposed advantage derived from them to
those who support them. It is a Revolution of this kind that
is the beau idéal, as it were, of the French Revolution, but
produced by the influence of individual genius and out of
general knowledge."[763]

Knowledge of Tahirih's life and love for her poetry went east and
south to the Indian subcontinent where her memory has been celebrated ever since. The first mention of Tahirih made on the Indian
subcontinent was in 1870. A steady stream of Babi and Baha'i teachers
came to India to spread the new teachings, including one of the Bab's
Letters of the Living, Shaykh Sa'id-i Hindi, who hailed from the city
of Multan, a center of Islamic mystical practice.[764]

Sa'id-i-Hindi, who, like Tahirih, had been part of the Shaykhi school
and then became a follower of the Bab, was sent to the Indian subcontinent to announce the good news of the advent of the Bab. He
reached Multan—in today's Pakistan—in 1844, where he carried out
his mission to his fellow countrymen. One of those who converted to
the new faith was Basir-i-Hindi, a blind man of the Multan area who
had great spiritual and intellectual qualities.[765]

Members of the Bab's family, also, had settled in India. The Bab had
worked in his uncle Siyyid Ali's cloth trade, and business contacts had
been made in India. The family business had offices in Shiraz,
Bushihr, and Bombay (Mumbai). It was probably in 1870 that, Haji
Siyyid Mahmood Afnan and Haji Siyyid Mirza Mahdi Afnan, established in Bombay a business by the name of "Haji Siyyid Mirza

---

[763] Filiz Turhan, *The Other Empire: British Romantic Writings about the Ottoman Empire* (New York: Routledge, 2003), 82.
[764] Afaqi, "Qurratu'l-'Ayn Tahirih in Urdu literature," *Tahirih in History*, 29.
[765] Mazandarani, *Zuhur'ul-Haqq*, vol. 3, 454.

Mahmood Afnan & Co.," and, later, a printing press, the Nasiri Printing Press, to publish the Babi and Baha'i holy writings. These maternal relatives and other followers could spread the new teachings from Bombay to the rest of India and Burma, and it became the first major center of Baha'i activity in the Indian subcontinent.[766]

The first written mention of Tahirih in India came thirty-seven years after her execution, in a compilation of Persian poetry edited by 'Abdulghafur Nassakh, and published in Calcutta. The first researcher to write about her from an academic perspective was Prof. M Hidayat Hossein who was the secretary of the Royal Asiatic Society in Calcutta.[767]

In 1902, a Baha'i came to Lahore to spread the Baha'i teachings. In the neighborhood in which he was staying, he met and befriended one of the most influential Indians of the early 20th century, Muhammad Iqbal.[768] Iqbal was a much admired poet who wrote in both Urdu and Persian and a philosopher-activist who laid the intellectual groundwork for the formation of a separate Muslim state to be carved out of northwestern India. As a Muslim Indian, he was concerned that the Muslim population of India would be at the mercy of the Hindu majority and so proposed a two-state solution. Educated in England, he was eventually knighted. In death he was memorialized as one of the founders of Pakistan with his birthday becoming a national holiday and many institutions named after him.

In 1930, Iqbal met Martha Root twice. In the intervening years since he had first heard of Tahirih, a booklet about her had appeared in Urdu, and, in 1930, a collection of some of her poems was published in Karachi which was then presented to Iqbal at his first meeting with Martha Root. At their second meeting in June of 1930, Iqbal spoke with reverence to Martha Root and expressed his deep interest in the

---

[766] Ibid.
[767] Afaqi, "Qurratu'l-'Ayn Tahirih in Urdu Literature." 29.
[768] Ibid., 29-30.

figure of Tahirih. He said that he was including the Persian mystic in his long poem about the spiritual journey.[769]

On his journey through the skies, Iqbal meets three important holy figures, one of whom is Tahirih. In the first section of the "Song of Tahira," he is deeply moved by their spiritual ardor, and it appeals to his own inner longings:

> "If ever confronting face to face my glance should alight on you
> I will describe to you my sorrow for you in the minutest detail
> That I may behold your cheek, like the zephyr I have visited
> house by house, door by door, lane by lane, street by street.
> Through separation from you my heart's blood is flowing
> From my eyes
> river by river, sea by sea, fountain by fountain, stream by stream,
> My sorrowful heart wove your love into the fabric of my soul
> thread by thread, thrum by thrum, warp by warp, woof by woof.
> Tahira repaired to her own heart, and saw none but you
> page by page, fold by fold, veil by veil, curtain by curtain.
> The ardour and passion of these anguished lovers
> cast fresh commotions into my soul;
> ancient problems reared their heads
> and made assault upon my mind.
> The ocean of my thought was wholly agitated;
> its shore was devastated by the might of the tempest.
> Rumi said, "Do not lose any time,
> you who desire the resolution of every knot;
> for long you have been a prisoner in your own thoughts,
> now pour this tumult out of your breast!'"[770]

In another section of "Song of Tahira," he marvels at how spiritual passion can bring new life into being and break through the old ways.

---

[769] Ibid., 30-31.
[770] Ibid., 47-8.

Iqbal was a poet and thinker who was very interested in the relationship between sacrifice and progress:[771]

> "From the sin of a frenzied servant of God
> new creatures come into being;
> unbounded passion rends veils apart,
> removes from the vision the old and the stale,
> and in the end meets its portion in rope and gallows
> neither turns back living from the Beloved's street
> Behold Love's glory in city and fields,
> lest you suppose it has passed away from the world;
> it lies concealed in the breast of its own time—
> how could it be contained in such a closet as this?"[772]

Martha Root continued with her journey meeting other known leaders and writers who may have included the Nobel Prize winner for Literature, Rabindranath Tagore.[773] She wrote it seemed that many people could recite verses from Tahirih. On her third trip through India in 1936-7, she brought with her the short biography of Tahirih which she had written. Using information from her 1930 trip to Iran where she met Tahirih's family, she was able to begin a short biography, *Tahirih, The Pure*. In early March, 1938, she stayed at the home of the first Baha'i of Hindu background, and while she looked out over the ocean, she finished this book.[774] Then she had 3,000 copies of it printed in Karachi and mailed many to prominent Indians as well as giving them away to those whom she met. The book was soon being

---

[771] Ibid., 31.

[772] Ibid., 48-9.

[773] According to Mabel R. Garis, (*Martha Root: Lioness at the Threshold*, Wilmette IL: Bahá'í Publishing Trust, 1983), 453), the two were supposed to have met at the Second Indian Cultural Conference in Calcutta, December, 1937, but he took ill and there is no further mention of the meeting. According to Sabir Afaqi, ("Qurratu'l-'Ayn Tahirih in Urdu literature." *Tahirih in History* (LA, CA: Kalimat Press, 2004), 31; Tagore was one of the distinguished people whom she met.

[774] The first Bahá'í of Hindu background was N.R. Vakil (Garis, *Martha Root*, 458).

translated into Persian, Czech, Urdu, and Japanese.[775] In Urdu, it went through at least three editions, being reprinted for the third time in Karachi, in 1974.[776] Martha Root had hoped that Tahirih and the Baha'i teachings would become better known this way and wrote that she hoped friends would speak about Tahirih in all possible venues so that Tahirih would go on a, "...teaching tour around the world...."[777]

In the following decades of the 20th century, there were over one-hundred authors, most working in Urdu, who made mention of Tahirih, translated her poems, included them in compilations, wrote books, short stories and articles about her, and held symposiums in celebration of her life.

A number of these were due to her having been one of the subjects of poems and essays by Iqbal. At the University of Punjab—the oldest university in a majority Muslim area of the Indian subcontinent[778]— two dissertations and a paper on Iqbal's thought included Tahirih. Prof. Jagannath Azad, a prolific writer who wrote over seventy works and who was also an expert in the writings of Iqbal, travelled to the United States from India and wrote a book about his travels, *In the land of Columbus*, in which he remembered:

> "When I reached the Mashriqu'l-Adhkar (Baha'i Temple) of Chicago, I was charmed by the atmosphere and freshness of its gardens. My friend Iftekhar Nasim chanted for me the poem of Qurratu'l-Ayn Tahirih "Gar bat u Uftadam Nazar..." and I lose myself in its melody and felt the same feeling that she cherished for the founder of the Baha'i Faith."[779]

---

[775] Garis, *Martha Root*, 462, 464.

[776] Afaqi, "Qurratu'l-'Ayn Tahirih in Urdu literature," 32.

[777] Garis, *Martha Root*, 464.

[778] "University of the Punjab," *University of the Punjab*, accessed November 1, 2013. http://pu.edu.pk/page.

[779] Prof. Jagannath Azad cited in Afaqi, "*Qurratu'l-'Ayn Tahirih in Urdu literature*," 36.

An entire book published in Peshawar, *Iqbal Aur Qurratu'l-Ayn*, by another scholar, Dr. Syed Chiragh Hussain Shah, was devoted to the relationship between Iqbal and Tahirih.[780]

Independent of the connection with Iqbal, much was written in the Indian subcontinent about Tahirih's poetry. She was one of the poets included in the 1905 compilation by Prof. Mohammad Ishaque, published in Calcutta, titled, *Four Eminent Poetesses of Iran*. Abr Ahsani Ginnauri Badayuni, a Baha'i poet who had a very wide circle of influence among poets wrote a piece on Tahirih for the *Baha'i Magazine*, published in Lahore. A famous poet writing in Urdu, Ra'is Amrahvi, who had founded an institute for self-improvement in Karachi, wrote poems regularly for a daily paper, and one of these was in a style imitating a poem by Tahirih which was re-published in a compilation.[781] Over the decades, many other poets imitated her work as well as reprinting and compiling it, so much so that a renowned critic and journalist, Dr. Mohammad Ali Si, asserted in a Karachi newspaper article: "There would seldom be any poet of the Urdu language who would not have said a poem following the style of Tahirih."[782]

Her work was also studied. At a 1933 academic conference in Lahore, Prof. M. Hidayat Hossein, a Muslim professor from Calcutta presented a paper on, "The female martyr of the Babi Faith". Her worthiness to be studied was confirmed by her inclusion in an Urdu Encyclopedia of Islam published in 1964, which included a summary of her life, and another Urdu encyclopedia in 1984, in which the compilers noted: "To summarize, she was matchless in the art of poetry."[783]

Tahirih was also the subject of short stories. A story bearing her home name, "Zarrin Taj," written by Prof. Aziz Ahmad, a much

---

[780] Afaqi, "*Qurratu'l-'Ayn Tahirih in Urdu literature*," 34.

[781] Ibid., 32-34.

[782] Ibid., 38-9.

[783] Ibid., 35-6.

respected writer whose short stories were especially notable, was published in a monthly literary magazine in Lahore. It was given a dramatic reading on Radio Pakistan in Rawalpindi, in 1963.[784] Sheikh Manzoor Elahi, another well-respected short story writer produced a piece titled, "Qurratu'l-Ayn," which appeared in print in Lahore in 1965.[785]

Book length works about Tahirih also appeared such as a short biography put out by the Baha'is of Lahore in 1974, and Jamilah Hashmi, a novelist who imagined her storied life in his work, *Chihra bachihrah rubaru*. An English-language, fictionalized rendering of Tahirih's life by Clara A. Edge was translated into Urdu, published in a monthly journal in its entirety in 1998, and sold to its readership and in bookshops, creating a much greater awareness of her.[786]

Back in the West, in 1885, a convert to the Unitarian ministry, John Tunis,[787] made extraordinary use of Tahirih as a symbol in his article, "Woman in the Ministry: An Appeal to Fact," in *Unity*, May 9, 1885.[788] He wanted to advance the view that women should be permitted to preach in churches and wanted to base his argument on reason and fact; his model for his argument was Tahirih:

> "It is needful to repeat again and again, that the right and fitness of a woman to preach, depends solely on an appeal to fact. Moreover, the fact must be a fact from our own century…a woman who must remain the crown of her sex in the present age. It is on this woman…renamed with the beautiful name of "Consolation of the Eyes" that I propose to base

---

[784] Ibid., 37.

[785] Ibid., 33.

[786] Ibid., 35, 40-1.

[787] "History of First Parish of Norwell Unitarian Universalist," *First Parish Norwell History,*
accessed November 26, 2013, www.firstparishnorwell.org/history.htm#tunis

[788] Tunis, John. "Woman in the Ministry: An Appeal to Fact." *Unity*, Vol XV, No 6, (1885):92-94.

an appeal to fact in the question, ought women to preach?"[789]

Tunis praised the power of Tahirih's faith:

"A passive sympathy was too little for her ardent spirit...She threw off the veil, she denounced polygamy and...began openly to preach and make converts...The uncle, the father, the husband, ransacked their erudite brains for arguments to reduce her to the old state of subordination. In vain, she answered by the unanswerable argument of faith wearied of the old commonplace. In the end, she left her home and consecrated herself to the Apostolic mission which the new religion conferred on her."[790]

Tunis told how Tahirih had courageously called for emancipation of women from age old customs:

"She began of telling of her great truth, that the time had come for the new religion of the Bab to cover all the surface of the earth, and that in obedience to this new faith God must be worshipped henceforth in the spirit and in truth...Therefore it was high time that woman should rouse herself, should share the toil of her father, her husband, should brave equally with them the dangers. It was no longer time for them to be shut up in the inner women's courts, waiting in listless indolence while men wrought for them...let them be companions of the men, follow them, die with them, even on the field of battle."[791]

He concluded by holding Tahirih up as a model and a challenge for Western peoples:

---

[789] Ibid., 92.
[790] Ibid., 93.
[791] Ibid., 93.

"Such is my appeal to fact. The question of the propriety of
women in the ministry is a pressing one...the real value of
our consideration of this Eastern woman is that we remain in
the neighborhood of the question."[792]

Jane Dieulafoy, a French archaeologist who considered herself an
absolute equal to men, wrote about Tahirih. She was best known for
her excavations of Susa, a settlement in southeastern Iran dating back
millennia, with her husband.[793] Dieulafoy's 1887 book, *La Perse, La
Chaldee et La Susiane*, included a short mention of Tahirih. While
Dieulafoy asserted the rights of all women, she opposed divorce as
harmful to women and remained loyal to her husband. She worked for
greater participation by women in the war effort of World War I.[794]

E.G. Browne was one of the most important scholars to first bridge
the distance between the Western and Persian worlds. Though he
came from a wealthy family of shipbuilders and was put on a track to
become a doctor, the outbreak of the Russo-Turkish war aroused a
lifelong interest in the near East because he sympathized with the
underdog Turks.[795] Browne had a humanistic outlook on life with
concerns for human liberty, internationalism, constitutional government, and the brotherhood of man. He may have become attracted to
the story and teachings of the Bab and Baha'u'llah, because these were
similar to his own views. He read about Babism in Gobineau's book
and came to admire the Bab's high-minded morals, courageous
behavior and universal teachings. By 1887 he had become deeply
interested in Persian language, culture, and history, and so he under-
took a year-long trip through Persia in 1887-8. A main reason for this

---

[792] Ibid., 94.
[793] Momen, *The Babi and Baha'i Religions*, 499; "Jane Henriette Magre
Dieulafoy," in the *Encyclopaedia Iranica*, edited by Ehsan Yarshater, accessed
October 19, 2013.
www.iranicaonline.org/articles/dieulafoy-1.
[794] Ibid., 28.
[795] Ibid., 34.

trip was to research Babi origins by meeting believers and finding original manuscripts. By this time, though, most Babis had become Baha'is.[796]

One of the results of this trip was the travel book, *A Year Amongst the Persians,* in which Browne described Persian society with both great learning and sympathy. He described the Baha'i gatherings:

> "The memory of those assemblies can never fade from my mind; the recollection of those faces and those tones no time can efface. I have gazed with awe on the workings of a mighty Spirit, and I marvel whereunto it tends."[797]

Though it took several attempts to find a publisher, and although it did not receive much attention during Browne's life, *A Year Among the Persians* came be seen as a classic of English travel literature.[798]

Another important piece of work from this trip was Browne's translation of a history of the Babi and Baha'i Faiths, *A Traveller's Narrative,* written by the son of the prophet founder of the Baha'i Faith, 'Abdu'l-Baha. He had acquired the text in the original Persian while in Palestine and then translated and annotated it.[799] He praised and made this definitive assessment of Tahirih:

> "the appearance of such a woman as Qurratu'l-'Ayn is in any country and any age a rare phenomenon, but in such a country as Persia it is a prodigy—nay, almost a miracle. Alike in virtue of her marvelous beauty, her rare intellectual gifts, her fervid eloquence, her fearless devotion and her glorious mar-

---

[796] Moojan Momen, "Browne, Edward Granville," *Baha'i Library Online,* (1995), http://bahai-library.com/momen_encyclopedia_browne.

[797] Nicholas James Bridgewater, "*A Year Amongst the Persians,*" accessed September 10, 2013, librivox.org/a-year-amongst-the-persians-by-edward-granville-brown/.

[798] G. Michael Wickens, "Browne's Life and Academic Career," in the *Encyclopaedia Iranica,* edited by Ehsan Yarshater, accessed November 24, 2013, http://www.iranicaonline.org/articles/browne-edward-granville.

[799] Momen, "Browne, Edward Granville".

tyrdom, she stands forth incomparable and immortal amidst her country-women. Had the Bábí religion no other claim to greatness, this were sufficient—that it produced a heroine like Qurratu'l-'Ayn."[800]

Browne wrote several well-informed articles in the 1890s about the new religion for the *Journal of the Royal Asiatic Society of Great Britain*. In one he describes the difficulty of finding information and documents related to Tahirih, echoing Lessona's earlier and similar complaint:

> "Anxious as I was to obtain some of her poems, I only met with a very limited amount of success. None of the Babis at Shiraz whom I conversed with had any in their possession, and they said that Kazvin and Hamadan, where Kurratu'l-Ayn had preached, and Teheran, where she had suffered martyrdom, would be the most likely places to obtain them. However, at Yazd, I saw copies of two short poems (ghazals) attributed to her authorship...I wrote to one of my friends at Shiraz, and asked his opinion on their authenticity. He replied that one of them...was not by Kurratu'l-'Ayn, but by a Sufi poet called Suhbat, of Lar...it must be borne in mind that the odium which attaches to the name of Babi amongst Persian Muhamadans would render impossible the recitation by them of verses confessedly composed by her. If, therefore, she were actually the authoress of poems, the grace and beauty of which compelled an involuntary admiration even from her enemies, it would seem extremely probable that they should seek to justify their right to admire them by attributing them to some other writer, and this view is supported by an assertion which I have heard made by a learned Persian with whom I was acquainted in Teheran, and who,

---

[800] E.G Browne, Tr., Abdu'l-Bahá, *A Traveller's Narrative* (Cambridge, UK: Cambridge University Press 1891), 309.

though not actually a Babi, did not lack a certain amount of sympathy for those who were such, to the effect that many poems written by Kurratu'l-'Ayn were amongst the favorite songs of the people, who were for the most part unaware of their authorship. Open allusions to the Bab had, of course, been cut out or altered, so that no one could tell the source from whence they came."[801]

In later years, Browne channeled his energy towards working for the Constitutional movement in Persia and assembling his massive compilations on the history of Persian literature, which included some of the writings of the Bab and Baha'u'llah. His interest in the study of the Babi and Baha'i Faiths receded in part because of attacks by fellow academics that he was wasting his great talent and knowledge on an obscure Persian religious movement.[802]

Another important book about Persia written by a Westerner, *Persia and the Persian Question*, was published in 1892. Its author, Lord Curzon, would travel widely throughout his life, going so far as Korea, and eventually serve as Viceroy of India. In this book, he wrote an excellent and insightful summary of the Babi movement,803 including this passage about Tahirih:

"Beauty and the female sex also lent their consecration to the new creed, and the heroism of the lovely but ill-fated poetess of Kazvin, Zerin Taj (Crown of Gold), or Kurrat-el-Ain (Solace of the Eyes), who, throwing off the veil, carried the

---

[801] Edward Granville Browne, "Art. XII.—The Bábís of Persia. II. Their Literature and Doctrines." *Journal of the Royal Asiatic Society of Great Britain* v. 21, Issue 4 (October, 1889): 54-6.
[802] Momen, "Browne, Edward Granville".
[803] Momen, *The Babi and Baha'i Religions*, 45-7.

missionary torch far and wide, is one of the most affecting episodes in modern history."[804]

In a *New York Times* review of an article written by Coutts Trotter for the *Scottish Review*, April 1892 edition, "A New religion." Tahirih was described as the Bab's "most effective recruit" and that her "influence" was "much assisted by her beauty." She had such "unconventional behavior" like her "ardor of speaking" that "her veil would sometimes fall off."[805]

Sir Francis Edward Younghusband (1863-1942), an English explorer, diplomat, and military man who made extensive expeditions throughout China, India, and Tibet's remote and mountainous regions, came to the United States in 1893 to give a presentation at the world religious conference in 1893.[806] In a later book, he described Tahirih as "Almost the most remarkable figure in the whole movement...." who "...was known for her virtue, piety" and that, for her faith, "...she gave up wealth, child, name and position for her Master's service."[807]

A British journalist, Sir Ignatius Valentine Chirol, wrote a book on British interests in the Middle East, *The Middle Eastern Question*, published in 1903.[808] In his retelling of the story of the Bab, he praised Tahirih as standing in contrast to orthodoxy's dim view of women:

---

[804] George Curzon, *Persia and the Persian question*, (London UK: Longmans, Green and Co, 1892), 497.

[805] "A New Religion," *New York Times* (New York: NY), June 5, 1892.

[806] "Sir Francis Younghusband (1863-1942)." *Baha'i Tributes*, accessed June 25, 2013,
https://bahaitributes.wordpress.com/category/bab/.;
"Sir Francis Younghusband, British Army Officer," *Encyclopaedia Britannica*, accessed June 25, 2013,
http://www.britannica.com/biography/Francis-Edward-Younghusband.

[807] Sir Francis Younghusband, *The Gleam* (London, UK: John Murray 1923), 202-3.

[808] Momen, *The Babi and Baha'i Religions*, 57-8.

"Socially one of the most interesting features of Babiism…is the raising of women to a much higher plane than she is usually admitted to in the East. The Bab himself had no more devoted a disciple than the beautiful and gifted lady, known as Kurrat-el-Ain, the "Consolation of the Eyes," who, having shared all the dangers of the first apostolic missions in the north, challenged and suffered death with virile fortitude, as one of the Seven Martyrs of Teheran. No memory is more deeply venerated or kindles greater enthusiasm than hers, and the influence which she wielded in her lifetime still ensures to her sex. That women, whom orthodox Islam barely credits with the possession of a soul, are freely admitted to the meetings of Babis, gives their enemies, the Mullas, ample occasion to blaspheme. But they have never produced a tittle of evidence in support of the vague charges of immorality they are wont to bring against the followers of the new creed. Communism and socialism are also often imputed to them, and some of them appear to have borrowed from the West the terminology of advanced democracy. Probably Babiism is still in a state of flux, and represents, apart from its doctrinal aspects, an association of many heterogeneous elements loosely bound together by a common spirit of revolt against the scandalous depravity of the Court, the corruption of the ruling classes, and the intolerance and greed of the orthodox clergy."809

The next year, 1904, Tahirih was the subject of a play put on in Saint Petersburg, Russia. Written by Isabella Grinesvkaya, the pen name of the Jewish writer Berta Friedberg, who may have heard of the story of the Bab from the great Russian novelist, Ivan Turgenev, who—according to Benjamin Jowett—a distinguished Oxford professor, often spoke of the Bab.810 She was a member of the Philosophic society, the Oriental Society, and the Bibliographical Society, as well as

---

809 "Ignatius Valentine Chirol (1852-1929)," accessed June 25, 2015, https://bahaitributes.wordpress.com/category/bab/.

810 Jan T. Jasion and Sabir Afaqi, editors, "Tahirih on the Russian stage," *Tahirih in History* (LA, CA: Kalimat Press, LA, 2004), 232.

literary groups and unions. The play, "The Bab," was published in 1903, and was performed in one of the principal theaters of St. Petersburg in 1904. Leo Tolstoy, the great Russian novelist, read it. He wrote the author expressing his admiration for the Baha'i teachings, and the letter was published in a newspaper. Her play was the first introduction of the Bab and Baha'u'llah to Russians—she wrote a play on Baha'u'llah as well. She thought that the Faith had disappeared until after her play appeared in 1903, and she received a letter from a Baha'i in Baku, Azerbaijan, requesting a copy of it. The subsequent correspondence showed her that there were active Baha'is in the world.[811] She eventually became a Baha'i after moving to Constantinople[812] which had a large Baha'i community.[813]

The five-act play is a fanciful account of certain events from the life of the Bab as seen through the eyes of Tahirih. It opens after Tahirih's mother has died, and Tahirih is looking for the Bab who, in this play, is her childhood friend with whom she has a deep relationship; her father, though, wants her to stay away from him. The Bab re-appears in a scene in the bazaar before a crowd in which he proclaims himself to be the Bab, a 'new man', and speaks forcefully on the position of women in the Qur'an. In the scene of his execution, Tahirih and he say to each other that they are already together in the spiritual worlds; the Bab appears Christ-like. In the final scene, Tahirih rallies women to raise up their positions in society, and they all remove their veils.

While not historical in any sense, Grinesvkaya's play was celebrated in the press as a source of spiritual inspiration. A second edition was

[811] Martha L. Root, "Russia's cultural contribution to the Bahá'í Faith," *Bahá'í World VI* (Wilmette, IL: Bahá'í Publishing Trust 1937), 708.

[812] John Walbridge, "Chapter Four - The Baha'i Faith in Turkey," *Occasional Papers in Shaykhi, Babi and Baha'i Studies,* accessed 21, 2013, www.h-net.org/~bahai/bhpapers.htm.

[813] William P. Collins and Jan T. Jasion, "Lev Tolstoi and the Bábí and Bahá'í Faiths a Bibliography," *Journal of Bahá'í Studies* Vol. 3, number 3 (1991), http://bahai-library.com/pdf/c/collins_jasion_lev_tolstoy.pdf.

published in 1916 and put onstage again in 1917 with many foreign dignitaries in attendance, including the Ambassador of China.[814]

On the other side of Europe in France, in 1905, the first full-length history of the Bab was published, *Siyyid Ali Muhammad dit le Bab,* by the French Consular official who served in Persia, A.L.M. Nicolas. Nicolas first came to know about the Bab because his father's diplomatic service in Tihran overlapped with that of Gobineau. His father and Gobineau had gotten into a dispute over the nature of a manuscript acquired by the former. Nicolas found in his father's papers a critique of Gobineau's book on the religions of Central Asia, so he decided to research the subjects in the book, and, in this way, came into contact with the writings of the Bab.[815] As he worked on understanding the Bab's text, *The Seven Proofs,* he became so moved that he became a believer:

> "My reflections on the strange book [The Seven Proofs by the Báb] that I had translated, filled me with a kind of intoxication and I became, little by little, profoundly and uniquely a Bábí. The more I immersed myself in these reflections, the more I admired the greatness of the genius of him who, born in Shíraz, had dreamt of uplifting the Muslim world...."[816]

Nicolas wrote a thorough account based on Persian sources and observation of the history of the Bab and the Babi movement as well as translated three of the Bab's major works. One appreciation by a later scholar stated:

> "No European scholar has contributed so much to our knowledge of the life and teachings of the Bab as Nicolas.

---

[814] Martha L. Root, *Russia's cultural contribution,* 708.
[815] Momen, *The Babi and Bahá'í Religions,* 36-40.
[816] Ibid., 37.

His study of the life of the Bab and his translations...remain
of unsurpassed value."[817]

In his book, Nicolas devoted many pages to Tahirih. He pointed out
that Tahirih had responded immediately to the Bab's teachings and
did not allow petty literal interpretations of the Qur'an to interfere.[818]
The whole of chapter twelve describes Tahirih's execution. She is
described as having attracted many women to the Bab by telling them
of the liberty promised in the new Revelation and then having been
subject to seven interviews about her beliefs and teachings by two
prominent Mullas.[819] She criticized the clerics for their literal interpretation of prophecy. The clerics declared her a heretic and left. Nicolas
tells the story of her martyrdom in which, after sunset, the streets were
emptied, and she was taken to the Il-Khani gardens, and there, one of
the captain's soldiers was ordered to strangle her.

In 1910, a second play on the Bab was put on, this time, in the
English speaking world by Laura Barney, *God's Heroes*. Laura Barney
was the daughter of a socially prominent artist in Washington DC,
was educated by private tutors, and attended a boarding school in
France founded to educate girls. She continued her studies in Paris
where she first heard about the Baha'i Faith and became a believer; she
married the first Frenchman to convert to the Baha'i Faith, Hippolyte
Dreyfus. She went on to use her wealth to finance the travels of Baha'i
teachers and to make repeated visits to Palestine, where she compiled a
long set of answers given by 'Abdu'l-Baha to questions on the Baha'i
teachings later published as a book, *Some Answered Questions*, which
became one of the most important sources for the explication of Baha'i

---

[817] Ibid., 36.
[818] Nicolas, *Seyyed Ali Mohammed dit le Bab*, 210-1.
[819] Ibid., 446.

teaching. She went on to be very active in international affairs using her rare skill of fluency in Persian.[820]

Laura Barney wrote *God's Heroes* in Paris, 1909. During these first decades, Paris attracted a number of very talented artists. For poets, the city gave them an opportunity to have their far more experimental work published; and for artists, the city had many potential art dealers and, as one artist put it, "If I was going to starve, I might as well starve where the food was good...."[821] As this bustling collective was breaking the molds of the past, it also advocated lifestyles free of conventional morality. Hearing that a known actress wanted to bring Tahirih to the stage, Barney feared that such a presentation might not reflect the dignity of a saintly figure like Tahirih. She, therefore, decided to write this play, knowing that if other writers knew she was tackling the subject, they would, out of professional courtesy, not attempt to write about it themselves. In this way, the figure of Tahirih and the story of the Bab would be spared the indignities of an inappropriate stage play.[822]

The first act opens with Tahirih giving an exposition on the continuity of Divine revelation and followed by her arguments against her husband and a dream in which she predicts seeing a man's mouth filled with blood; the act finishes with the murder of her father-in-law in an alley. In the second act, the emancipation of women is the focus beginning with a female character observing that a woman's life has two masters—men and death; the claims of the Bab are then discussed, including those related to women. Babis gather together at the Conference of Badasht, and the Qur'anic Revelation is once again the topic of debate with the Qur'an being characterized as having been for a

---

[820] Mona Khademi, "A Glimpse into the Life of Laura Clifford-Barney," *Irfan Colloquia,* accessed November 11, 2013, http://irfancolloquia.org/pdf/lights10_khademi.pdf.

[821] Perry Miller Adato, dir.. *Paris: The Luminous Years.* PBS, December 15, 2010, video, 31 sec., http://video.pbs.org/video/1691415260/.

[822] Khademi, *"Life of Laura Clifford-Barney,"* 85.

"wilder" people who had not been informed by the teachings of the "Nazarine" and that converts must now be won through love and not force. The Babis also disagree on the finality of the Qur'an and discuss the constancy of the inner reality of religion while its forms change, and Tahirih asserts the existence of a new revelation marking the Day of Judgment. They discuss the fuller teachings of Baha'u'llah and the Houses of Justice, described as 'councils'. The act ends with Tahirih appearing unveiled, shocking the men. Act IV centers on marriage with Tahirih receiving proclamations of love from the Kalantar's son, dispensing love advice to a young woman and presenting the teachings of the Bab to women who have come for a wedding. In the final act, she challenges the Mullas who, at first, are impressed by her courage and knowledge but then demand that she recant her faith, which she refuses. Later the son of the Kalantar bursts in to rescue her but is too late, as soldiers emerge with her lifeless body. He weeps for her while the Mullas go off to pray.

A few years after the publishing of this play, Charlotte Despard, an English women's rights advocate who served the poor in Dublin, wrote several substantial pieces on Tahirih.[823] She was the editor of a weekly newspaper in England, *The Vote*, which had as its mission statement:

> "To secure for Women the Parliamentary vote as it is or may be granted to men; to use the power thus obtained to establish equality of rights and opportunities between the sexes, and to promote the social and industrial well-being of the community."[824]

In three editions of *The Vote* during September and October of 1911, she wrote a biographical account of Tahirih. In her account,

---

[823] Selena M. Crosson, "Shaping Women's Role in Early Baha'i Culture 1898-1940," (A thesis submitted to the Department of History, University of Saskatchewan, Canada, June, 2013), 59.
[824] Charlotte Despard, "An Eastern Prophet's Message." *The Vote* Vol. VII, n. 168 (January 10, 1913): 181.

entitled, "A woman apostle in Persia," she re-imagines Tahirih as a rebel against the religious subjugation of women. Despard imagines Tahirih as saying:

> "I have always rebelled," so her thoughts ran. "I have felt it was an ill thing to be a woman, and worse to rail against the decree of Allah in making woman subject. And I have fought against my free mind as evil in a woman."[825]

She characterized the Bab as a prophet of peace who empowered women:

> "The Master we follow teaches peace and tolerance...the Master is right. Women must go out; women must preach the gospel of peace."[826]
> "His voice was very calm and sweet, and yet there was that in it which inflamed the soul. That the world changed; that customs and conventions and ideas, good for one generation were as cruel fetters for another; that every man and every woman—how she, Quarratu'l' Ain, and her sister trembled behind their curtain! –had a right to freedom; that all religions were good, and that brotherly love and toleration would hold families and nations together...."[827]

Charlotte Despard's description of Tahirih is really a description of herself: a peace activist, a pacifist, a suffragette, an advocate for purity, and a deeply spiritual person. What she knew of Tahirih's life must have resonated deeply with her own concerns for improving the standing of women in her society and advancing the cause of peace in the pre-World War I years. She no doubt was thinking of her own life's work when she attributed these words to Baha'u'llah as he commands Tahirih to tear off her veil:

---

[825] Charlotte Despard, "A woman apostle in Persia." *The Vote* Vol. IV, no. 101 (September 30, 1911): 280-1.
[826] Ibid.
[827] Ibid.

"Not for thyself, my daughter, for the iron will enter into thy soul; but for the sake of the others—of the women who are in prison and who dare not move until one shall show them the way."[828]

'Abdu'l-Baha spoke to the Women's Freedom League on January 2nd, 1913, on, "The Equality of Women," in which he spoke of Tahirih, the first time anyone had done so publicly in England. A version of his talk appeared in the Friday, January 10th, 1913, edition of *The Vote*:

"Amongst the women of our time there is Qu'urat'ul Ain, the daughter of a Mohammedan priest; at the time of the appearance of the Bab she showed such tremendous courage and power, that all who heard her were astonished. She threw aside her veil, despite the immemorial custom of the Persians, and although it is considered impolite to speak with men, this heroic woman carried on controversies with the wisest men, and in every meeting she vanquished them. The Persian government took her prisoner, she was stoned in the streets, anathematized, exiled from town to town, threatened with death, but she never failed in her determination to work for the freedom of her sisters. She bore persecution and suffering with the greatest heroism; even in prison she gained converts. To a Persian Minister, in whose house she was imprisoned, she said: "You may kill me as soon as you like, but you cannot stop the emancipation of women." At last the end of her tragic life came; she was carried into a garden and strangled. She put on, however, the choicest robes as if she were going to join a bridal party. With such magnanimity and courage she gave her life, startling and thrilling all who saw her. She was truly a great heroine. To-day in Persia among the Baha'is, there are women who also show unflinching courage, and are endowed with great poetic insight;

---

[828] Despard, "A woman apostle in Persia," 291.

they are most eloquent, and speak before large gatherings of people."[829]

Another English woman, Elizabeth Maud Constance, had a great interest in the woman's suffrage movement which she explored in her 1911 novel, *No Surrender*. She met the son of Baha'u'llah during his visit to England and wrote an article about him.[830] Another of her articles, "The first Persian Feminist," was published in *The Fortnightly Review*. In the article, she describes Tahirih as a "martyr" for the "great Awakening" of women to their terrible plights. She singles out Tahirih as one who, "no name deserves to stand higher," that she had a "quality of mind that refused to be bent and moulded by external circumstances," that, "the spiritual force of her personality," was able to break down the barriers of her "barred window," the "high walls" of her garden, the "impassable barriers of religion and custom." She was transformed by the new spiritual message that there was "one universal brotherhood" and "one centre" to all religions which was God, and the "equality of the sexes." This new belief, "stirred her soul," and she "shook off the old bonds." She goes on to write a short bio of Tahirih emphasizing her independence born of her firm belief that God was calling her. The account is mostly accurate, though she relates that Tahirih was eventually put in prison, and there, even, "hardened criminals," who were sent to her cell to torture her, came out saying they could never do such a thing to a saint.[831]

A defining description—from a Baha'i perspective—of Tahirih and account of her life was given in the Baha'i chronicle, *The Dawnbreakers*, by Nabil-i-Zarandi, a follower of the Bab and Baha'u'llah, and was translated into English and then published in 1932. Nabil characterizes Tahirih by her union with God and the Bab, her intuitive spiritual

---

[829] Despard, "An Eastern Prophet's Message," 181.

[830] Constance Elizabeth Maud, "Abdul Baha (Servant of the Glory)," *The Fortnightly Review* vol. 97, April (1912).

[831] Maud, Constance Elizabeth Maud, "The First Persian Feminist," *The Fortnightly Review* No. DLVIII, June (1913): 1175-1182.

knowledge, her courage and her faithfulness. God had "…kindled the light in Táhirih, a light that was destined to shed its radiance upon the whole of Persia."[832] Almost immediately she "…perceived the dawning light of the promised Revelation breaking upon the city of Shíráz, and was prompted to pen her message and plead her fidelity to Him who was the Revealer of that light."[833] The depth of her conviction gave her great focus: "The innate fearlessness and the strength of her character were reinforced a hundredfold by her immovable conviction of the ultimate victory of the Cause she had embraced…."[834] and "…few could escape the contagion of her belief."[835] In the dramatic rendering of the end of Tahirih's life, she appeared ready for martyrdom, "…fully adorned, dressed in a gown of snow-white silk. Her room was redolent with the choicest perfume…."[836] She tells the wife of the Kalantar, "I am preparing to meet my Beloved,"[837] and that, now, she would be re-united with God: "This day I intend to fast—a fast which I shall not break until I am brought face to face with my Beloved."[838]

---

[832] Zarandi, *The Dawn-Breakers*, 191.
[833] Ibid., 192.
[834] Ibid.
[835] Ibid.
[836] Ibid., 455.
[837] Ibid.
[838] Nabíl-i-A'zam, *The Dawn-Breakers*, 455-6.

APPENDIX B:
EDUCATION OF WOMEN AND GIRLS IN PERSIA

By the beginning 20th century, modernism and the Baha'i Faith impacted Persia in one area in particular that Tahirih would have much appreciated: education. The efforts to educate the people of Persia, including its women, were well underway despite the deep concerns regarding its overall effect.

Persian men and many women had the same concerns regarding the education of girls: too much schooling would make them unmarriage-able or poor spouses. The experience of a Persian noblewoman, the daughter of the Persian Ambassador to the Ottoman Court, reflects this concern:

> "...she...learned French and Istanbul Turkish like an expert; she was also total versed in the Persian language and knew the arts and crafts of Istanbul ladies...She had pulled herself out of the world of women and reached the level of learned men. She was a learned person and did not bother looking after her husband and trying to please him. She paid little attention to her husband and was not attached to him. Because of these tendencies, the relationship between her and her husband went cold. They didn't get along."[839]

In the late 19th century, the education of girls became part of the general debate on education. A Persian general[840] who was a tutor to a prince and an advocate of women's education wrote:

> "Teach your children, sons and daughters, science and obedience."[841]

---

[839] Afsaneh Najmabadi, *Women with Mustaches and Men without* Beards (U. of California Press: Berkeley CA, 2005), 181.
[840] Mirza Taqi Khan Kashani (Najmabadi, *Women with Moustaches*, 189).
[841] Ibid., 189.

Another prominent Persian man[842] who took an interest in education asserted:

> "…the more we work for education and learning of women, the more we would serve the uplifting, progress and perfection of our nation."[843]

Comparisons were made with Europe and even India, bemoaning the advances made in those places to educate women.[844] Women's education came to national attention in 1900 with the publication of a book, *The Liberation of Women*, which pointed out that thinkers in Europe advocated for women's rights including education.[845] The author[846] contended that:

> "…the evidence of history confirms and demonstrates that the status of women is inseparably tied to the status of the nation."[847]

A female school principal challenged Persian women:

> "At least we should follow our Asian sisters, the Japanese…in pursuit of sciences and industries. It must be emphasized that educating women is more important than educating men, since the education of men is dependent on education of women…Therefore, you respected women must seriously and with great effort seek sciences and spread knowledge…so that liberty, equality and fraternity could be established in our homeland and we too could acquire that civilization and life that the Europeans have."[848]

---

[842] Mahumad Afshar (Ibid., 189).

[843] Ibid.

[844] Ibid., 191.

[845] Ibid., 193.

[846] Qasim Amin (Ibid., 193).

[847] Ibid.

[848] Ibid., 194.

Women's roles were changing, and they were becoming much more the household managers than simply dependents on the male head of household. Educating women was primarily to make women more effective as household managers and mothers, similar to the American concept of the 'Republican mother'—the mother who raised the future of the nation.[849] A female student wrote at graduation:

> "Because of the duties of a woman to mother and educate humanity, the harms of ignorance are a hundredfold worse for them and the advantages of learning a thousand times greater. A learned woman will keep her house clean and orderly, thus making her spouse happy. A learned woman will educate her child according to rules of health and hygiene and wisdom...A learned woman will protect her family relationship and will prevent discord and difference which is the greatest cause of destruction of family and nation...."[850]

Women raised the male citizenry; a woman had to govern the home with all the skill that a man had to administer the lands and country.[851]

Westward looking intellectuals who saw the positive results of European schools in Persia supported female education as integral to the overall development of the nation. Conservative clerics were opposed to modern schools, and even more, to educating girls. When a school for girls was opened in Tihran in 1903-4, clerics issued a formal decree calling it "against the principles of Shi'i Islam."[852] Three years later, a similar school was begun only to be threatened by locals with the destruction of the building, so the Ministry of Education advised the school founder to close the school for its own protection.[853] Opening

---

[849] Ibid.
[850] Ibid., 194-5.
[851] Ibid., 196-7.
[852] Soli Shahvar, *The Forgotten Schools: The Baha'is and Modern Education in Iran, 1899-1934* (NY, NY: IB Tauris and Co Ltd, 2009), 56.
[853] Ibid.

schools for girls became possible in 1909 when a coup overthrew the conservative elements in government. The second school for girls to be opened by a Persian—all others had previously been foreign schools— was opened by a Baha'i.[854]

By the time of the new Constitutional government in 1911, initiatives were underway for the establishment of schools for girls as well as modern schools. In 1917-8, the first ten state schools were started and secondary schools started a few years later. The purpose of state schools was to raise good citizens. Private schools proliferated and expanded beyond elementary education.[855]

Baha'is built the first modern Baha'i school in 1899—the Baha'i Boys' School, the Tarbiyat School, in Tihran. Building schools was a natural extension of the social mission of the Baha'i religion because of its emphasis on the importance of education; over the next thirty-five years more than forty more Baha'i schools were built. The Constitutional Period gave them a big material boost; a wave of school-building went over Persia in the 1910s. Like the state schools whose curriculum they followed,[856] Baha'i schools taught citizenship, but what was distinctive about them was the inculcation of a piety based on the Baha'i Writings which reinforced what the students experienced at home. The Ministry of Education may well have allowed such Baha'i schools to be started out of its support for reform and modernization. There were also a number of Baha'is in senior positions in the country to help support and protect them.[857]

Baha'i schools were supervised by the Baha'i National Spiritual Assembly and greatly aided by Americans who offered professional service as teachers, administrators and developers of curricula. While

---

The two schools here were the Parvarish Girls' School in Tihran founded by Tuba Rushdiyyih and the Dushizihgan begun by Bibi Khanum Vaziruv Astarabadi.

[854] Munirih Ayadi, founder of the Ta'yidiyyih-yi Dushizigan-i-Vatan (Ibid., 57).

[855] Najmabadi, *Women with Mustaches*, 200-1.

[856] Shahvar, *The Forgotten Schools*, 60.

[857] Ibid., 63-65.

these schools were local, they were connected to the wider world through assistance from 'Abdu'l-Baha, the son of the founder of the Baha'i Faith, the Baha'is in the United States, and the sizable Persian diaspora, which was spread over much of the world. Baha'is all over the world saw these schools in Iran as an expression of the highest values of their faith being put into action to help society. For years, there was an active correspondence between American Baha'i women and the Persian educational efforts.[858] The American women took a particular interest in the situation of their counterparts in Persia and lent much expertise to the Baha'is in Iran.[859]

By 1913 the Tarbiyat Baha'i School for girls was educating four percent of the girls going to school in Tihran. 'Abdu'l-Baha actively recruited teachers and aid—in the form of textbooks and much-valued paper—and the Baha'is in Iran provided most of the financing. The Tarbiyat School began in a private home, and after overcoming financial and administrative struggles, grew to the point where it and other Baha'i schools came to be recognized by the ministry of education for their excellence. Their graduates had a far greater rate of passing national exams than students from other schools; they were also distinguished by having higher moral standards of behavior. In the 1920s one minister reflected the continuing religious prejudice when he bemoaned the fact that these excellent schools were run by Baha'is.[860]

Baha'i schools opened up in at least ten more locations throughout the country. This brought modern education to areas of Persia that had never had it. In these more rural areas, the population also tended to associate 'Baha'ism' erroneously with the Constitutional reform movement and encroaching modernism, so mobs vented their anger at these schools. Because the Baha'i schools were based on spiritual

---

[858] Kaveh Hemmat, "Bahá'í Schools in Iran" (presentation, Iranian Constitutional Revolution Centennial Conference, Oxford, U.K., 2006), 3
[859] Ibid., 7-8.
[860] Ibid., 2-4.

teachings and were private, corporal punishment was not used and a greater degree of care and kindness was shown by teachers for students. This gave the schools a positive atmosphere. In addition, the school grounds and facilities were maintained with great care, bringing beauty to the educational experience of the students.[861]

At the Baha'i schools, Persian girls were taught a rigorous curriculum that included science, basic hygiene, math, Persian literature, Arabic, the Qur'an, grammar, and even sewing. These schools were also among the first to have actual 'physical' education. Girls enjoyed reading women's magazines which came from the United States. In the mornings, the girls stood in the yard while one prayed aloud. At these schools, girls were given opportunities for growth which they could get nowhere else in Persia. Even so, like in America, most girls were destined to work as wives and mothers, so the Baha'i schools also taught home-making skills such as health care and sewing.[862]

The Ministry of Education ranked the two Tarbiyat schools at or near the top of all the schools in the country, and as a result, its graduates had an opportunity for great professional advancement. The Tarbiyat School for Girls also came to be valued by reformers as promoting the emancipation of Persian women.[863] The two Baha'i schools in Hamadan boasted a library of four-thousand books, a substantial number at that time, and the Baha'i school in Yazd saw the first girls ever to graduate from a sixth-grade, and the Baha'i boys' school reached one-hundred percent pass rate in the nationwide exams.[864] More and more Muslim, Zoroastrian, and Jewish families sent their children to these schools because of their reputation, until something like six and a half percent of the total school population in the country attended a Baha'i school; prominent families even sent

---

[861] Ibid., 4-6.
[862] Ibid., 11.
[863] Shahvar, *The Forgotten Schools*, 95.
[864] Ibid., 88.

their children to them despite the anti-Baha'i feeling among many people and clerics.[865]

The opposition to Baha'i schools was always most vigorous from the clerics who opposed modernization, westernization—which included female education—and local clerics who lost paying students for their own schools to the Baha'i schools. The cleric who ran the Ministry of Education in Kashan and referred to himself as the "light" was able to get the Baha'i school closed down based on rumors. Then 'Abdu'l-Baha intervened at a higher level, and it was re-opened, showing the high regard in which he was held in certain sections of Persian society.[866] Such regular harassments by the clergy went on for decades as a part of the larger struggle between reform and traditionalism. Opposition was mitigated by the Baha'is who were in high positions, by the respect with which people held 'Abdu'l-Baha even in high governmental circles in Persia, by the excellence of the schools—and the related drive for reform—and by the fact that the Baha'i schools did not teach the Baha'i religion; rather, this was done at Friday schools.[867]

With the next dynasty, the Pahlavis, Reza Shah's increasing authoritarian drive to have complete control over the state may have led ultimately to the closing down of Baha'i schools. Just as the Shah sought to impose his will in all areas of Persian administration, the Baha'is of Iran were becoming more organized and established, having elected a national governing body for the first time in 1934. In addition, Shoghi Effendi, the head of the Baha'i Faith, encouraged all Baha'i institutions and individuals to obey their conscience in matters of faith while obeying their respective governments. Baha'i schools, following his guidance, were closed on Baha'i Holy Days in obedience to Baha'i law. The Shah, who worked incessantly, had an office across from the courtyard of the Tarbiyat School. He enjoyed hearing the prayers sung in the courtyard. One day all was quiet. He asked why

---

[865] Ibid., 93-96.
[866] Ibid., 99.
[867] Ibid., 106.

there were no prayers being sung and his assistants told him it was a Baha'i Holy Day. This conflict between a need for an absolutist kind of national unity on the part of the Shah, the establishment of the Baha'i institutions in Persia, and persistent opposition may well have condemned the Baha'i schools to closure.[868]

---

[868] Ibid., 108-116.

APPENDIX C:
TRANSLATION

Most of the translations in this book were done by two distinguished professors from UCLA, Prof. Amin Banani and Prof. Jascha Kessler.

Prof. Banani was the founder of the Iranian Studies Program at UCLA having been invited to UCLA by Prof. Gustave von Grunebaum for this purpose. He taught history and Persian literature and helped launch the western world's first Bachelor of Arts program in Iranian studies. His many publications include: *The Modernization of Iran; Islam and Its Cultural Divergence; Iran Faces the Seventies;* and *Individualism and Conformity in Classical Islam.* He also edited and contributed to *The Epic of Kings* among many other works.

Prof. Kessler also taught at UCLA, as a Professor of English and Modern Literature which included poetry, fiction, and playwriting. He has published eight books of his poetry and fiction. His most recent titles include *Siren Songs & Classical Illusions: 60 Fables, Revised with a Preface* (McPherson & Company, 2013) and *King Solomon's Seal: 75+ fables* (Xlibris, 2013). A distinguished translator, he has completed six volumes of translations of poetry and fiction from Hungarian, Persian, and Bulgarian, several of which have won major prizes including the Finnish Literary Translation Center Award and the Translation Award from the National Translation Center (Marlboro Press) for his 1989 translation of Sándor Rákos' *Catullan Games.* His other awards and grants for writing including an NEA Fellowship, two Senior Fulbright Awards, and a Rockefeller Fellowship. He had collaborated previously with Prof. Amin Banani on a translation of the works of the Persian poet Forough Farrokhzad, *Bride of Acacias: the Poetry of Forugh Farrokhzad.*

Prof. Kessler described his effort to bring Tahirih alive in our world while retaining aspects of the original context of her life:

> "My decision was therefore to carry over into our vernacular in both form and content, deliberately risking an exotic,

sometimes anachronistic, effect. I see nothing to be gained by removing her altogether from the forms of her nineteenth-century Persian world, which most assuredly would have occurred in any free-verse translation. Tahirih, it should be remembered, was first and foremost writing *poems*. She was writing song, meditation, prayer, exordium, ecstatic outpouring—in *formal* verses. In short, she crafted her utterance. And that is why I have tried to show her as a poet, not as the purveyor of a passionate and esoteric religiosity, although the work obviously and naturally contains material wholly expressive of just that.

If the reader can believe that it is Tahirih who is speaking in these poems, Tahirih as she stands in the Persian, then I have succeeded in my aim to represent her—again, as *she* is, and not as she would look garbed in the casual American dress of fashion today. Underlying my judgment that in practice this was the best course to follow lies a premise I hope is shared by my collaborator, Amin Banani, who proposed the project and prepared the texts for me, as well as by those of Tahirih's co-religionists unable to read her work except in this Englishing. The premise cannot be over-emphasized. Her poetry remains rooted absolutely in her time and place—and her tradition. She is seen best by her own light."[869]

Prof. Kessler goes on to explain the actual steps taken to go from the Persian to the English:

"…the lines of her poems were marked for me by Amin Banani as to meter, and set down in Persian written in the Roman alphabet. The lines were paralleled through metaphrase into English lines, that is, they followed the original word order and syntax. The act of "translating" the Persian takes

---

[869] Banani and Kessler, 36-7.

place in the next step, in which I seek to paraphrase those texts into what is, I hope, poetry in our language."[870]

Here is an example of these steps, the first being writing and arranging the original lines in Persian spelled out in Roman letters:

"Agar be bád daham zoff-e anbar ásá rá
Aseer-e khish konam áhuán-e sahrá rá"[871]

This line comes out like this in a literal English translation:

"if / to / wind / I give / hair of / amber / scent
Captive of / mine/ I would make / deer of / wilderness"[872]

Then the final step is to take this literal version and turn it into poetry in the English language which attempts to convey the emotions expressed in the original Persian:

"Just let the wind untie my perfumed hair,
My net would capture every wild gazelle.
Just let me paint my flashing eyes with black,
And I would turn the day as dark as hell."[873]

---

[870] Ibid., 38.
[871] Ibid., 41.
[872] Ibid.
[873] Ibid.

BIBLIOGRAPHY

"A New Religion." *New York Times* (New York: NY), June 5, 1892.

'Abdu'l-Baha. *Memorials of the Faithful.* Wilmette, IL: Baha'i publishing Trust, 1971.

—*A Traveller's Narrative.* Translated by E.G Browne. Cambridge: Cambridge University Press, 1891.

Abzug, Robert H.. Cosmos Crumbling: American reform and the religious imagination. Oxford: Oxford U. Press, 1994.

Adato, Perry Miller dir.. *Paris: The Luminous Years.* PBS, December 15, 2010, video. 31 sec. Accessed November 1, 2013. http://video.pbs.org/video/1691415260/.

Afaqi, Sabir. "Qurratu'l-'Ayn Tahirih in Urdu literature." In *Tahirih in History*, edited by Safir Afaqi, 23-44. Los Angeles: Kalimat Press, 2004.

Ahlstrom, Sydney E.. A Religious History of the American People. New Haven: Yale U. Press, 2004.

al-Saltanah, Muhammad Hasan Khan I'timad. "Khayrat-i hisan." *Women's Worlds in Qajar Iran.* Accessed November 7, 2103. http://www.qajarwomen.org/en/items/901D4.html.

"Alexander Kazembek (Russian Orientalist)," World Public Library, accessed 9 October 2013. http://netlibrary.net/articles/Alexander_Kazembek_(Russian_orientalist).

Amanat, Abbas. Resurrection and Renewal, the making of the Babi Movement in Iran, 1844-1850..Ithaca, NY: Cornell U. Press, 1989.

—"Qurrat al-'Ayn: The Remover of the Veil." In *Tahirih in history: Perspectives on Qurrat al-'Ayn from East and West,* edited by Sabir Afaqi, 113-158. Los Angeles: Kalimat Press, 2004.

—*Pivot of the Universe.* London: I. B. Tauris, 2008.

Amanat, Mehrdad. Jewish Identities in Iran: Resistance and Conversion to Islam and the Baha'i Faith. New York: I.B. Taurus, 2011.

"Amherst's History." *Amherst College.* Accessed September 9, 2013. https://www.amherst.edu/amherst-story/history.

Arjomand, Said Amir. "Islam in Iran VI., the Concept of Mahdi in Sunni Islam." In the *Encyclopaedia Iranica,* edited by Ehsan Yarshater, XIV (Fasc. 2) (2007): 134–136. Accessed June 7, 2013.
http://www.iranicaonline.org/pages/editors.

Arnold, Mathew. *Essays on Criticism.* Oxford: MacMillan and Cº, 1875.

Avarih, Jinab-i-. *Star of the West* vol. 14, No 12 (1924): 359-360.

Aygül, Ceren. *Change in the status of turkish women during the ottoman modernization and self-evaluation of women in kadinlar dünyasi of 1913.* Ankara, Turkey: Middle East Technical University, Dept. of History 2010. Accessed November 3, 2013.
http://etd.lib.metu.edu.tr/upload/12612331/index.pdf.

The Bab. *'Qayyum al-asmā.'* ms. dated 1261, in Afnan Library, Tonbridge, UK.

—*Selections from the Writings of the Bab.* Haifa, Israel: Bahá'í World Centre, 1982.

Baghdadi, Muhammad Mustafa. Ar-Risalah al-Amriyyah. (Treatise on the Cause). Appended to Ahmad Suhrab. Ar-Risalah at-Tis` `Ashariyyih. Cairo: Matba`at as-Sa`adah, 1919/1338. Digitally republished, East Lansing, Mi.: H-Bahai, 1998.

Baha'u'llah. *Epistle to the Son of the Wolf.* Wilmette IL: Baha'i Publishing Trust, 1988.

—*Kitab Iqan.* Wilmette IL: Baha'i Publishing Trust, 1989.

—*Epistle to the Son of the Wolf.* Wilmette IL: Baha'i Publishing Trust, 1988.

Balyuzi, H. M.. *The Bab.* Oxford: George Ronald, 1973.

—Bahá'u'lláh: The King of Glory. Oxford: George Ronald, 1980.

—*Khadijih Bagum.* Oxford: George Ronald, 1981.

Banani, Amin and Jascha Kessler. *A portrait in poetry.* Edited by Anthony Lee. Los Angeles: Kalimat Press, 2004.

—*Táheréh: A Persian Mystical Poet.* Santa Monica, CA: Unpublished manuscript, 1991.

Baumann, Roland M.. "Constructing Black Education at Oberlin College." *Ohio University Press.* Accessed September 10, 2013. ohioswallow.com/book/Constructing+Black+Education+at+Oberlin+College.

Bausani, Alessandro. *Religion in Iran.* New York: Bibliotheica Persica Press, 2000.

de Bellecombe, Andre-Ursule. "La belle Kourret ou l'Hain reformatrice persanne." *L'Investigateur* Tome X (1870).

Bednarowski, Mary Farrell. "Outside the mainstream: Women's Religion and Women Religious Leaders in Nineteenth-Century America." *Journal of the American Academy of Religion* XLV111/2 (1980): 207-231.

Bernhard, Virginia, and Fox-Genovese, editors. *The Birth of American Feminism: The Seneca Falls Woman's Convention of 1848.* St. James, NY: Brandywine Press, 1995.

The Bible: New International Version. Biblica Inc, 2011.

Birkett, Dea. *Spinsters Abroad: Victorian Lady Explorers.* Oxford: Basil Blackwell, 1989.

Bogdanov, L.. "The Home and Life in Persia." *Islamic Culture* 5 (1931): 407-21; 6 (1932): 290- 306, 468-85.

Bolden, Tonya. "Biographies." *Digital Schomburg African American Women Writers of the 19th Century.* Accessed November 1, 2013. ohioswallow.com/book/Constructing+Black+Education+at+Oberlin+College.

Bonneau, A.. "Babysme." *L'Annuaire encyclopédique VIII.* Paris: Bureau de L'Encyclopedie (1869): 255.

Braude, Ann. *Radical Spirits.* Boston: Beacon Press, 1989.

—*Sisters and Saints: Women and American Religion.* Oxford: Oxford University Press, 2008.

—*Women and American Religion.* Oxford: Oxford U. Press, 2000.

Brekus, Catherine A.. *Strangers and Pilgrims: Female preaching in America, 1740-1845.* Chapel Hill, NC: U. Of North Carolina Press, 1998.

"Bridal Traditions." Oklahoma Woman *(Oklahoma City: ProQuest).* Accessed November 9, 2013. http://search.proquest.com/docview/196655798.

Bridgewater, Nicholas James. *"A Year Amongst the Persians."* Accessed September 10, 2013. librivox.org/a-year-amongst-the-persians-by-edward-granville-brown/.

Brown, Olympia. *Acquaintances, Old and New.* Milwaukee: S.E. Tate, 1911.

—"Brown, Olympia, 1835-1926. Papers, ca. 1849-1963: A Finding Aid." *Harvard Library OASIS.* Accessed October 9, 2013. oasis.lib.harvard.edu//oasis/deliver/deepLink?_collection=oasis&uniqueId=sch00054.

—"Biography." Olympia Brown Papers, ca.1849-1963; item description, dates. A-69, folder #. Schlesinger Library, Radcliffe Institute, Harvard University, Cambridge, Mass. http://oasis.lib.harvard.edu/oasis/deliver/~sch00054.

Browne, Edward Granville. "Art. XII.—The Bábís of Persia. II. Their Literature and Doctrines." *Journal of the Royal Asiatic Society of Great Britain* v. 21, Issue 4, (October, 1889): 881-1009.

Buckland, C. E.. Dictionary of Indian Biography. London: Swan Sonnenschein & Co. Lim., 1906.

Cahill, Susan, editor. *Wise Women, Over 2000 years of spiritual writing by women.* New York: WW Norton and Co, 1996.

Calmard, Jean. "HUART, CLÉMENT." In the *Encyclopaedia Iranica,* edited by Ehsan Yarshater. Accessed October 23, 2013. www.iranicaonline.org/articles/huart-clment.

—"Jane Henriette Magre Dieulafoy." In the *Encyclopaedia Iranica,* edited by Ehsan Yarshater. Accessed October 19, 2013. www.iranicaonline.org/articles/dieulafoy-1.

"Catherine Beecher." *An American Family: The Beecher Tradition.* Accessed November 4, 2013. http://www.baruch.cuny.edu/library/alumni/online_exhibits/digital/2001/beecher/catherinc.htm.

Cazden, Elizabeth. *Antoinette Brown Blackwell, A Biography.* Old Westbury, NY: The Feminist Press, 1983.

"Childbirth and birth control in the 19th century." *Kate Chopin.* Accessed 20, 2013. http://www.loyno.edu/~kchopin/new/women/bcabortion.html.

Cheyne, Thomas Kelly D.Litt., D.D. *The Reconciliation of Races and Religions.* PDF e-book. http://www.gutenberg.org/cache/epub/7995/pg7995.html.

Chodas, Paul W., and Zdenek Sekanina. "A New Orbit Determination for Bright Sungrazing Comet of 1843." *The Astrophysical Journal* 687 (2008): 1415–1422.

Cobb, Stanwood. *The Worldwide Influence of Qurratu'i-Ayn.* Wilmette, IL: Baha'i Publishing Trust, 1980.

Cole, Juan. "ii. Browne on Babism and Bahaism." In the *Encylcopedia Iranonica*, edited by Ehsan Yarshater, (1989): 483-488. Accessed June 7, 2013.
www.iranicaonline.org/articles/browne-edward-granville.

Cole, Juan, and Moojan Momen. "Mafia, Mob and Shiism in Iraq: The Rebellion of Ottoman Karbala 1824-1843." Past & Present No 112 (1986): 112-143.

Collins, William P., and Jan T. Jasion. "Lev Tolstoi and the Bábí and Bahá'í Faiths A Bibliography." Journal of Bahá'í Studies Vol. 3, number 3 (1991): 1-9.
http://bahai-library.com/pdf/c/collins_jasion_lev_tolstoy.pdf.

Cote, Charlotte. *Olympia Brown: The Battle for Equality*. Racine, WI: Mother Courage Press, 1988.

Cott, Nancy F.. *The Bonds of Womanhood*. New Haven: Yale University Press, 1977.

Crosson, Selena M.. "Shaping Women's Role in Early Baha'i Culture 1898-1940." A thesis submitted to the Department of History, University of Saskatchewan, Canada, June, 2013.

Curzon, George. *Persia and the Persian Question*. London: Longmans, Green and Co., 1892.

Dabashi, Hamid. *Shi'ism, A Religion of Protest*. Cambridge, MA: Harvard University Press, 2011.

de Bellecombe, Andre-Ursule. "La belle Kourret ou l'Hain reformatrice persanne." *L'Investigateur*, Tome X, (1870): 161

DeMause, L., editor. *The history of childhood*. New York: Harper & Row, 1974.

Despard, Charlotte. "A woman apostle in Persia." The Vote vol. IV, Nos. 101-103 (1911); "A woman apostle in Persia." The Vote Vol. IV, n. 102 (1911); "An Eastern Prophet's Message," The Vote vol. VII, n. 168 (1913).

Di Barbora, Monica. "Carla Serena." *Encyclopedia delle donne.* Accessed October 29, 2013.
http://www.enciclopediadelledonne.it/biografie/carla-serena/.

Diba, Layla S.. "CLOTHING x. In the Safavid and Qajar periods." In the *Encyclopaedia Iranica,* edited by Ehsan Yarshater. Accessed October 4, 2013.
http://www.iranicaonline.org/articles/clothing-x.

"Dictionnaire biographie de Lot-et-Garonne." *C.H.G.H.47.* Accessed October 1, 2013.
genealogie-en-47.fr/Articles/Dossiers/Dictionnaire_biographique_01.html.

Douglas, Ann. *The Feminization, of American Culture.* New York: Farrar, Strauss, and Giroux, 1977.

Dureka, Derek. "Elaw, Zilpha." Pennsylvania Center for the book. Accessed June 20, 2013.
http://pabook2.libraries.psu.edu/palitmap/bios/Elaw_Zilpha.html.

Eastwick, Edward B.. *Journal of a Diplomat's Three Years Residence in Persia Vol I.* London: Kessinger Publishing, LLC, 2007.

Edge, Clara. *Tahirih.* self-published, 1964.

The Editors. "Letters of the Living (*Huruf-i-Hayy).*" In the *Baha'i Encyclopedia Project,* edited by L. Bucknell, B. Fisher, F. Kazemzadeh, T. Lawson, H. Moayyad, G. Morrison, S. Quinn, M. Schweitz, R. Stockman, W. van den Hoonaard Accessed June 6, 2015.
http://www.bahai-encyclopedia-project. org/.

The Editors of Encyclopaedia Britannica. "Sir Francis Younghusband, British army officer." *Encyclopaedia Britannica.* Accessed June 25, 2013.
http://www.britannica.com/biography/Francis-Edward-Younghusband.

Shoghi Effendi. *God Passes By.* Wilmette, IL: Bahá'í Publishing Trust, 1979.

—*Citadel of Faith.* Wilmette, IL: US Bahá'í Publishing Trust, 1980.

—*The Dispensation of Baha'u'llah.* Wilmette, IL: Bahá'í Publishing Trust, 1983.

"Eliza C. Allen (1803-1848)." *Portraits of American Women in Religion.* Accessed September 24, 2013.
http://www.librarycompany.org/women/portraits_religion/allen.htm.

"Elizabeth Blackwell Counterslip 1821-Schottland 1910." *Art Directory.* Accessed November 4, 2013.
www.elizabeth-blackwell.com.

Ellis, J. "The Growth of the United States During the 19th Century." *The Free Resource.* Accessed September 23, 2013.
http://www.thefreeresource.com/american-history-the-growth-of-the-united-states-during-the-19th-century/.

Eskandari-Qajar, Prof. Manoutchehr M. "Mahd-e-Olia." *Portraits of Qajar Women.* Accessed October 24, 2013.
http://www.qajarpages.org/mahdeolia.html.

Fathi, Asghar. "*Women and the Family in Iran.*" Boston, MA: Brill Publishing, 1997.

Ferrier, Joseph P.. "Situation de la Perse en 1851." *Revue Orientale et Algeriennce* vol 1, Paris (1852): 141-59.

Fisher, William Bayne; Avery, Peter; Hambly, Gavin and Melville, C. P., editors. *The Cambridge History of Iran: From Nadir Shah to the Islamic Republic.* Cambridge, UK: Cambridge U. Press, 1991.

Flinders, Carol Lee. *Enduring Grace, Living portraits of seven women mystics.* San Fransisco, CA: Harper, 1993.

Floor, W. and W. Kleiss. "BATHHOUSES." In the *Encyclopaedia Iranica,* edited by Ehsan Yarshater. Accessed October 1, 2013.
http://www.iranicaonline.org/articles/bathhouses#pt1.

Francis, Richard. *Ann the Word: The Story of Ann Lee, Female Messiah, Mother of the Shakers.* New York: Arcade Publishing, 2000.

Franck, Adolphe. "Deuxième et Dernier Article." *Le Journal des Savants.* December (1865): 776-777.

Gail, Marzieh. "Stanza from Tahirih." *The journal of Baha'i Studies,* vol.7, (1980).

—"The White Silk Dress." In *Baha'i World,* v. 9, 814-21. Wilmette, IL: Baha'i Publishing Trust, 1980.

—*The Sheltering Branch.* Oxford: George Ronald, 1959.

—*Dawn over Mount Hira.* Oxford: George Ronald, 1976.

Garis, Mabel R.. *Martha Root: Lioness at the Threshold.* Wilmette IL: Baha'i Publishing Trust, 1983.

Garrison, Wendell Phillips. "A New Religion." *The Nation* (1866).

Giachery, Ugo R.. "An Italian Scientist Extols the Bab." In *The Baha'i World,* v. 12, 1950-1952, Wilmette, IL: Baha'i Publishing Trust, 1956.

Gill, Gillian. *Mary Baker Eddy.* Cambridge: MS: Perscus Books, 1998.

de Gobineau, Artur. *Religions and Philosophies of Central Asia.* Paris: Didier and Co, 1865.

—*Essai sur l'inegalite des Races Humaines.* Paris: Librairie de Firmin Didot Freres, 1853.

Grove, Cornelius N. Ed.D. "Evolving Notions of Child-Rearing in Pre-Civil War America." *The Aptitude Myth.* Accessed November 11, 2013.
http://www.theaptitudemyth.info/Recall-11.pdf.

"Growth of Cities." *The First Measured Century.* Accessed November 1, 2103.
http://www.pbs.org/fmc/timeline/ecities.htm.

Haeri, Shahla. "MOTʻA." In the *Encyclopaedia Iranica,* edited by Ehsan Yarshater. Accessed October 26, 2013.
http://www.iranicaonline.org/articles/mota.

Hakimian, Hassan. "ECONOMY viii. IN THE QAJAR PERIOD." In the *Encyclopaedia Iranica,* edited by Ehsan Yarshater. Accessed September 21, 2013.
http://www.iranicaonline.org/articles/economy-viii-in-the-qajar-period.

Hareven, T.. "Review essay: origins of the "modern family" in the United States." *Journal of Social History 17* (1983-4): 339-344.

Harper, Ida Husted. *The Life and Work of Susan B. Anthony.* Indianapolis, IN: Bowen-Merrill Company, 1898.

"Harriet Beecher Stowe's Life Introduction." *Harriet Beecher Stowe Center.* Accessed October 2, 2013.
www.harrietbeecherstowecenter.org/hbs/.

Hartman, Dorothy W.. "Women's Roles in the Late 19th Century." *Conner Prairie.* Accessed September 24, 2013.
http://www.connerprairie.org/Learn-And-Do/Indiana-History/America-1860-1900/Lives- Of-Women.aspx.

Hatcher, John, and Hemmat, Amrollah. *Adam's Wish, Unknown Poetry of Tahirih.* Oxford: George Ronald, 2008.

—*The Poetry of Tahirih.* Oxford: George Ronald, 2002.

Hawes, J., and Hiner, N., Editors. *American childhood, a research guide and historical handbook.* Westport CT: Greenwood Press, 1985.

Hays, Elinor Rice. *Morning Star: A Biography of Lucy Stone 1818–1893.* New York: Harcourt, Brace & World, 1961.

Hemmat, Kaveh. "Bahá'í Schools in Iran." Presentation, Iranian Constitutional Revolution Centennial Conference, Oxford, 2006.

"Here Comes the Bride: A History of the American Wedding." *Random History and Word Origins for the Curious Minds.* Accessed 1, 2013.
http://www.randomhistory.com/1-50/009wedding.html.

Heschel, Susannah. *The Aryan Jesus: Christian theologians and the Bible in Nazi Germany.* Princeton: Princeton University Press, 2008.

"History." *Mount Holyoke*. Accessed October 28, 2013.
www.mtholyoke.edu/about/history.

"History of First Parish of Norwell Unitarian Universalist." *First Parish Norwell History*. Accessed November 26, 2013.
www.firstparishnorwell.org/history.htm#tunis.

Homa Irani Behbahani, Ph.D; Fakhri Khosravi, M.Sc.. "Iranian Garden: A Place of Coexistence: City-Nature-Landscape Case study: Tehran Gardens in 19th Century." *Academia*. Accessed October 1, 2013.
https://www.academia.edu/710119/Iranian_Garden_A_Place_of_Coexistence_City-Nature landscape_Case_study_Tehran_Gardens_in_19th_Century.

Htoo, Naw Diana. "Persian Dress through the Ages." *Iran Dokht*. Accessed November 22, 2013.
http://www.irandokht.com/editorial/index4.php?area=per&sectionID=3&editorialID=958.

Huart, Clement. *La Religion du Bab*. Paris, France: Ernest Leroux Editeur, 1889.

Hume-Griffith, M. E.. *Behind the Veil in Persia and Turkish Arabia*. Philadelphia: J.B. Lippincott and Co., 1909.

Hunt, Harriot. *Glances and Glimpses; Or, Fifty Years' Social, Including Twenty Years' Professional Life*. Boston: J.P. Jewett and Company, 1856.

Hoseini, Nosratollah Mohammad. *Hadrat-i-Tahirih*. Dundas, Ontario, Canada: Association for Baha'i Studies in Persian, 2000.

"Ignatius Valentine Chirol (1852-1929)." Accessed June 25, 2015.
https://bahaitributes.wordpress.com/category/bab/.

Ishaque, M.. *Four Eminent Poetesses of Iran*. The Rian Society: Calcutta, 1950.

Ishraq-Khavari, Abdu'l-Hamid. *Kitab Muhadhirat*. Germany: Baha'i -Verlag, 142BE/1987.

Jasion, Jan T. "Tahirih on the Russian stage." In *Tahirih in History*, edited by Sabir Afaqi, 231-8. Los Angeles: Kalimat Press, LA, 2004.

Johnston, Ted. "Trends in American Child Rearing Practices to 1950." *Generation Ministries*. Accessed October 1, 2013. http://www.generationsministries.org/uploads/2/5/2/7/25278738/child_rearing_prac tices _history.pdf.

Keniston, K., and the Carnegie Council on Children. *All our children: the American family under pressure*. New York: Harcourt, Brace Jovanovich, 1977.

Kerr, Andrea Moore. *Lucy Stone: Speaking Out for Equality*. Rutgers. NJ: Rutgers University Press, 1992.

Khademi, Mona. "A Glimpse into the Life of Laura Clifford-Barney. " *Irfan Colloquia*. Accessed November 11, 2013. http://irfancolloquia.org/pdf/lights10_khademi.pdf.

Khan, Sadat A.. "Unveiling the Veil: Garment of Modesty – In different ages and cultures." *New Age Islam*. Accessed October 20, 2013. http://www.newageislam.com/islam,-women-and-feminism/unveiling-the-veil--garment-of-modesty-in-different-ages-and-cultures/d/4363.

Kidd, Thomas S.. "Daniel Rogers' Egalitarian Great Awakening." *Medieval Christianity*. Accessed November 2, 2013. https://medievalchristianityd.wikispaces.com/file/view/DANIEL+ROGERS+EGALITA RIAN+GREAT+AWAKENING.pdf

Knight, George R.. *Millenial Fever and the End of the World*. Boise, Idaho: Pacific Press Pub. Association, 1993.

Kriwaczek, Paul. *In Search of Zarathustra*. New York: Vintage Books, 2002.

Lambert, Tim. "Children in the 19th Century." *A World History Encyclopedia*. Accessed September 24, 2013. http://www.localhistories.org/19thcenturychildren.html.

Lasser, Carol. "American National Biography Online: Stone, Lucy." *American National Biography Online.* Accessed September 24, 2014.
http://www.anb.org/articles/15/15-00663.html.

Lawson, Dr. Todd. "The Authority of the Feminine and Fatima's Place in an Early Work by the Bab." *OJBS: Online Journal of Baha'i Studies Volume 1 (2007)I*: 137-170. Accessed September 5, 2013.
http://oj.bahaistudies.net/OJBS_1_Lawson_Fatima.pdf.

Lepard, Brian. *In the Glory of the Father.* Wilmette, IL: Bahá'í Publishing Trust, 2008.

Linder, Soug. "The Trial of Susan B. Anthony for Illegal Voting." *University of Missouri-Kansas City.* Accessed May 5, 2013.
http://law2.umkc.edu/faculty/projects/ftrials/anthony/sbaaccount.html.

Lindley, Susan Hill. *You Have Stept Out of Your Place.* Louisville: Westminster John Knox Press, 1996.

Lloyd, Ivan. *Tahirih, A poetic vision.* Eloy, AZ: Desert Rose Publishing, 1999.

Lockridge ,Kenneth A.. *Literacy in Colonial New England.* New York: Norton, 1974.

Ma'ani, Baharieh Rouhani. *Leaves Of The Twin Divine Trees.* London: George Ronald Pub Ltd, 2008.

Mabro, Judy. *Veiled Half-Truths: Western Travellers' Perceptions of Middle Eastern Women.* London: I.B. Tauris, 1991.

MacEoin, Denis. *From Shaykhism to Babism: a study in charismatic renewal in Shī'ī Islam.* Indiana University: King's College, 1979.

—"*Barağānī, Moḥammad-Taqī.*"In the *Encyclopaedia Iranica,* edited by Ehsan Yarshater. Accessed September 24, 2013.
http://www.iranicaonline.org/articles/baragani-molla-mohammad-taqi-qazvini-sahid-e-ale-an-important-shiite-alem-of-qazvin-d.

Mahdavi, Shireen. "*The Qajar-Period Household.*" In the *Encyclopaedia Iranica,* edited by Ehsan Yarshater. Accessed November 11, 2013. http://www.iranicaonline.org/articles/qajars-period-household.

Maneck, Susan Stiles. "Táhirih: A Religious Paradigm of Womanhood." *Journal of Bahá'í Studies* Vol. 2, number 2 (1989). Accessed July 3, 2013. https://bahai-studies.ca/wp-content/uploads/2014/05/2.2-Maneck.pdf.

Masumian, Adib. "Debunking the Myths: Conspiracy Theories on the Genesis and Mission of the Bahá'í Faith." Academia. Accessed October 3, 2013. http://www.academia.edu/343383/Debunking_the_Myths_Conspiracy_Theories_on _the_Genesis_and_Mission_of_the_Bahai_Faith.

—"A Brief History Of Women's Movements In Iran 1850 – 2000." *Iran Chamber.* Accessed September 23, 2013. http://www.iranchamber.com/society/articles/history_women_movements.php.

Maud, Constance Elizabeth. "Abdul Baha (Servant of the Glory)." *The Fortnightly Review,* vol. 97, April (1912);

—"The First Persian Feminist." *The Fortnightly Review* No. DLVIII, June (1913): 1175-1182.

Mázandaráni, Mírzá Asadu'lláh Fádil-i. *Zuhúr al-Haqq, Volumes 1–4.* Tihrán, Iran: Bahá'í Publishing Trust, 1973.

McLoughlin, William G.. *Revivals, Awakenings, and Reform.* Chicago: U. of Chicago Press, 1978.

McMillen, Sally. *Seneca Falls and the Origins of the Women's Rights Movement.* Oxford: Oxford University Press, 2008.

Milani, Farzaneh. *Veils and Words, The emerging voices of Iranian women writers.* Syracuse, NY: Syracuse University Press, 1992.

Momen, Moojan. The Babi and Baha'i Religions, 1844-1944, Some Contemporary Western Accounts. Oxford: George Ronald, 1981.

—Browne, Edward Granville." *Baha'i Library Online* (1995). Accessed
    June 1, 2013.
    http://bahai-library.com/momen_encyclopedia_browne

—"The Social Basis of the Babi Upheavals in Iran (1848-1853): A
    Preliminary Analysis." *Int. J. Middle East Studies* 15 (1983): 157-
    183. Momen, Moojan. "Mulla `Ali Bastami, Letter of the
    Living." *Wendy and Moojan Momen*. Accessed August 1, 2013.
    http://www.momen.org/relstud/alibast.htm.

—"Usuli, Akhbari, Shaykhi, Babi: The Tribulations of a Qazvin
    family." *Iranian Studies* volume 36, # 3 (2003): 317-337.

—"WOMEN iv. in the works of the Bab and in the Babi Movement."
    In *Iranica Online* edited by Ehsan Yarshater, (2011). Accessed
    July 23 2013.
    http://www.iranicaonline.org/articles/women-babi.

Najmabadi, Afsaneh. *Women with Mustaches and Men without Beards*.
    Berkeley: U. of California Press, 2005.

—"Education XXV. Women's Education in the Qajar Period." in
    Encyclopaedia Iranica, edited by Ehsan Yarshater. Accessed
    October 18, 2013.
    http://www.iranicaonline.org/articles/education-xxv- womens-education-in-the-
    qajar-period.

Najmájer, Marie von. *"Gurret-ül-Eyn. (A picture from the Persian
    modern times in 6 Songs)."* Originalausg. ersch Vienna 1874
    Photomechan Nachdr. d Originalausg, ext, erg and with
    biography, FWD and hist demolition. [With portraits. fig u]). -
    Vienna: National Spiritual Assembly of Baha'is d in Austria,
    1981. ANL-1202994 B. Neu Mag.

Nakhjavani, Bahiyyih. *La femme qui lisait trop*. France: Actes Sud,
    2007.

Nichol, Francis D.. *Ellen White and Her Critics*. Hagerstown, MD:
    Review and Herald,1951.

Nicolas, A. L. M. *Seyyed Ali Mohammed dit le Bab*. Paris: Dujarric and Cie, Editeurs, 1905.

Nicolas, Michel. "Le Babysme." *Le Temps* August 14, 19, 20 (1868): 3, 3, 3.

Noble, Laurie Varter. "Olympia Brown." *Dictionary of Unitarian and Universalist Biography*. Unitarian Universalist History and Heritage Society. Accessed May 5, 2013. http://uudb.org/articles/olympiabrown.html.

Not For Ourselves Alone – The Story of Elizabeth Cady Stanton & Susan B. Anthony. Directed by Paul Barnes and Ken Burns. 1999. USA: Florentine Films, WETA.

"Oberlin College and Conservatory." *About Oberlin*. Accessed October 1, 2013. http://new.oberlin.edu/about/.

Older, Julia. *Tahirih Unveiled, Turning Point*. Cincinnati: Word Tech Communications, 2007.

Painter, Nell Irvin, editor. *The Narrative of Sojourner Truth*. New York: Penguin Books, 1998.

Peel, Robert. *Mary Baker Eddy: The Years of Discovery 1821-1875*. Boston, MA: The Christian Science Publishing Society, 1966.

—*Mary Baker Eddy: The Years of Trial*. Boston: The Christian Science Publishing Society, 1971.

Price, Massoume. "Iranian Birthdays and Rituals of Birth: A Brief History." *Culture of Iran*. Accessed September 21, 2013. www.cultureofiran.com/iranian_birthday.html.

—"Iranian Marriage Ceremony, Its History & Symbolism." *Iran Chamber Society*. Accessed September 21, 2013.

Rafati, Vahid. *The Development of Shaykhi Thought in Shi'i Islam*. UCLA: PhD Dissertation, unpublished, 1979.

Renan, Joseph. *Les Apotres.* Paris: Michel Levy Freres, 1866.

"Report of the Woman's Rights Convention." *Women's Rights.* Accessed January 1, 2014.
http://www.nps.gov/wori/historyculture/report-of-the-womans-rights-convention.htm.

Riggenbach, Jeff. "Stephen Pearl Andrews's Fleeting Contribution to Anarchist Thought." Miles Institute. Accessed November 12, 2013.
mises.org/daily/5161/Stephen-Pearl-Andrewss-Fleeting-Contribution-to-Anarchist-Thought.

Root, Martha. *Táhirih, the Pure.* Los Angeles: Kalimat Press, 1981.

—"Russia's cultural contribution to the Baha'i Faith." In *Baha'i World VI,* 707-28. Wilmette, IL: Baha'i Publishing Trust, 1937.

—"Tahirih, The Pure, Iran's Greatest Woman." *Bahá'í Library Online.* Accessed October 1, 2013.
http://bahai-library.com/martharoot_tahirih_pure_1938.

Rossetti, William Michael. "Shelley's Life and Writings, Two Lectures." *The University, A Literary and Philosophic Review* vol. 1 (1878): 264.

Rowe, David L.. *God's Strange Work, William Miller and the end of the world.* Grand Rapids, MI: Wm. B. Eerdman's Publishing Company, 2008.

Ruhe, David S.. Robe of Light, the Prophetic Years of the Supreme Prophet Baha'u'llah 1917-1852. Oxford UK: George Ronald, 1994.

Saiedi, Nader. *Gate of the Heart: Understanding the Writings of the Báb.* Waterloo, Ontario: Wilfrid Laurier University Press, 2008.

Samandar, Shaykh Kazim. "Biography of Tahirih." In *Four historical narratives about Tahirih,* edited by A.Q. Afnan. Third Conference of Alt and Culture. Landegg, Switzerland: Landegg University, September, 1991.

Savi, Julio. "Italy: History of the Baha'i Faith." *Bahá'í Library Online.* Accessed October 2, 2013. http://bahai-library.com/savi_encyclopedia_italy.

Silver, Mae. "Elizabeth Lowe Watson." *DigitalArchive@*Foundsf. Accessed October 26, 2013. http://www.foundsf.org/index.php?title=Elizabeth_Lowe_Watson.

Ruhe-Schoen, Janet. *Rejoice in my gladness, the Life of Tahirih.* Wilmette, IL: Baha'i Publishing Trust, 2011.

Schlesinger, Julia. "J. J. Morse." *Psypioneer Journal* Vol. 8, No 10 (2012): f. 23, 342.

Schwartz, Benjamin, editor. *Letters from Persia written by Charles and Edward Burgess, 1828-1855.* New York: The New York Public Library, 1942.

Sell, Edward. "The Babis." *The Church Missionary Intelligencer* 47:21 (1896): 324-335.

—"The Bab and the Babis." In *Essays on Islam,* 46-98. London: Simpkin, Marshall, Hamilton, Kent &. Co., 1901.

—*Bahaism.* London: Christian Literature Society for India, 1912.

Serena, Carla. *Hommes et choses en Perse.* Paris, France: Charpentier et Co, 1883.

Shahvar, Soli. The Forgotten Schools: The Baha'is and Modern Education in Iran, 1899-1934. New York: IB Tauris and Co Ltd, 2009.

Sheil, Lady Mary. *Glimpses of life and manners in Persia.* London: John Murray, Albemarle Street, 1856.

Singh, Nagendra Kr, and Abdul Mabud Khan, editors. *Encyclopaedia of the World Muslims: Tribes, Castes and Communities.* Delhi, India: Global Vision Publishing House, 2004.

"Sir Francis Younghusband (1863-1942)." *Baha'i Tributes.* Accessed June 25, 2013.
https://bahaitributes.wordpress.com/category/bab/.

Smith, Gail K. "The Sentimental Novel: The Example of Harriet Beecher Stowe." In *The Cambridge Companion to Nineteenth-Century American Women's Writing,* edited by Dale M. Bauer and Philip Gould. Cambridge, UK: Cambridge University Press, 2001, 221-243.

Smith, Timothy L.. *Revivalism and Social Reform.* New York: Harper and Row Publishers, 1957.

"Sr. Elizabeth Ann Seton." *The Archdiocese of Baltimore.* Accessed January 10, 2014.
http://www.archbalt.org/about-us/the-archdiocese/our-history/people/seton.cfm.

Stange, Mary Zeiss, Carol K. Oyster, and Jane E. Sloan editors. *Encyclopedia of Women in Today's World, Volume 1.* Los Angeles: Sage Pub., 2011.

Stanton, Elizabeth Cady. "Elizabeth Cady Stanton: Seneca Falls Keynote Address." *Great American Documents.* Accessed July 5, 2013.
http://www.greatamericandocuments.com/speeches/stanton-seneca-falls.html.

Taherzadeh, Adib. *The Revelation of Baha'u'llah, vol. 4, vol. 8.* Oxford: George Ronald, 1987.

Taylor, Babara. *Eve and the New Jerusalem: Socialism and Feminism.* Cambridge, MA: Harvard U. Press, 1993.

Tomaschewski, W. "The Last Chapter." *Stephen Collins Foster.* Accessed August 4, 2012.
http://www.stephen-foster-songs.de/end.htm.

"Travelers and Scholars on the Bábí/Baha'i Faiths." In the *Bahaikipedia.* Accessed September 10, 2013. https://bahaikipedia.org/.

"Troy Female Seminary." *Encyclopedia Britannica Online.* Accessed October 10, 2013. https://www.britannica.com/topic/Troy-Female-Seminary.

Trollope, Mrs. Frances. "from Chapter VIII of Domestic Manners of the Americans." *American Studies at the University of Virginia.* Accessed October 2, 2013. http://xroads.virginia.edu/~HYPER/DETOC/religion/trollrev.html.

Tunis, John. "Woman in the Ministry: An Appeal to Fact." *Unity*, Vol XV, No 6, (1885):92-94.

Turhan, Filiz. *The Other Empire: British Romantic Writings about the Ottoman Empire.* New York: Routledge, 2003.

Twain, Mark. Autobiography of Mark Twain, Volume 1: The Complete and Authoritative Edition. New York: Harper Collins, 1990.

"University of the Punjab." *University of the Punjab.* Accessed November 1, 2013. http://pu.edu.pk/page.

"US Territorial Acquisitions." *United States History.* Accessed 6, 2013. http://www.u-s-history.com/pages/h1049.html.

Van Zandt, Franklin K. "Expansion and growth of the United States." *USGS Publications Warehouse.* Accessed October 2, 2013. http://pubs.usgs.gov/pp/0909/report.pdf.

Vanzan, Anna. "Harem ii. in the Qajar period." In the *Encyclopaedia Iranica,* edited by Ehsan Yarshater. Accessed November 11, 2013. www.iranicaonline.org/articles/harem-ii.

Volo, Dorothy Denneed, and James M. Volo, and. *Family Life in Nineteenth-century America.* Greenwhich, CT: Greenwood Press, 2007.

Walbridge, John. "Chapter Four—The Baha'i Faith in Turkey." *Occasional Papers in Shaykhi, Babi and Baha'i Studies.* Accessed 21, 2013.
http://www.h-net.org/~bahai/bhpapers.htm.

Wallace, Carol. *All Dressed in White: The Irresistible Rise of the American Wedding.* New York: Penguin Books, 2004.

Watson, Elizabeth Lowe. *Song and Sermon.* San Fransisco: The Thicks Judd Company, 1905.

Watson, Robert Grant. *A History of Persia.* London: Smith, Elder and Co., 1866.

Weisberg, Barbara. Talking to the Dead, Kate and Maggie Fox and the Rise of SPiritualism. New York: Harper Collins, 2004.

Werner, Christoph, "POLAK, Jakob Eduard, (1818-1891)." In the *Encyclopaedia Iranica,* edited by Ehsan Yarshater. Accessed October 1, 2013.
http://www.iranicaonline.org/articles/polak-jakob-eduard.

"Wesleyan University: A Brief History." *Wesleyan University.* Accessed October 3, 2013.
http://www.wesleyan.edu/about/history.html.

White, Arthur L. "Ellen G. White: A Brief Biography." *The Ellen G. White Estate, Inc..* Accessed November 4, 2013.
http://www.whiteestate.org/about/egwbio.asp.

White, Ellen G.. "Proper Education." *The Health Reformer* v. 7, # 9 (1872): 284-6.

White, Richard. *Railroaded: The Transcontinentals and the Making of Modern America.* New York: W. W. Norton & Company, 2012.

Wickens, G. Michael. "Browne's Life and Academic Career." In the *Encyclopaedia Iranica,* edited by Ehsan Yarshater. Accessed November 24, 2013.
http://www.iranicaonline.org/articles/browne-edward-granville.

Wills, C. J. MD. *In the Land of the Lion and the Sun.* London: MacMillan and Co., 1883.

Wilson, Mary. "Story of the Bab." *The Library* v. 7 (Jan-April 1886): 137-148.

"Witness to American History." *Gettysburg College.* Accessed September 9, 2013.
http://www.gettysburg.edu/about/college_history/.

Yeomans, Donald K.. "Great Comets in History." *Jet Propulsion Laboratory/California Institute of Technology.* Accessed October 25, 2013. ssd.jpl.nasa.gov/?great_comets.

Younghusband, Sir Francis. *The Gleam.* London: John Murray, 1923.

Yuri, Suhl. *Ernestine L. Rose: Women's Rights Pioneer.* New York: Biblio Press, 1990.

Zarandi, Nabíl. *The Dawn-Breakers,* Translated by Shoghi Effendi. London: Bahá'í Publishing Trust, 1953.

INDEX OF NAMES

Made in the USA
Las Vegas, NV
07 November 2023

80414716R00187